M
A M

...ISA

THE HOLY CITY

MEMOIRS OF
A MOUNTAINEER
LHASA
THE HOLY CITY

F. SPENCER CHAPMAN

ALAN SUTTON
1984

Alan Sutton Publishing Limited
Brunswick Road · Gloucester

Copyright © 1938 F. Spencer Chapman
Reprinted by permission of
Chatto & Windus · The Hogarth Press

First published 1938
This edition published 1984

British Library Cataloguing in Publication Data

Chapman, F. Spencer
    Memoirs of a mountaineer.—(Sovereign)
    2: Lhasa; The holy city
    1. Tibet (China)—Description and travel
    I. Title
    915.1'50442   DS785

    ISBN 0-86299-145-5

Cover picture: Himalayan Monastery
Photograph: J. Elizabeth Pratt

Printed and bound in Great Britain

CHAPTER ONE

THE train left the sweltering heat of Calcutta at nine o'clock in the evening of July 27th, 1936, and reached Siliguri, the terminus of the full-gauge railway, at six-thirty the following morning.

When I woke up at six, we were still crossing the interminable plain of Bengal. But already, with a growing excitement, I could see ahead of us the misty blue line of the Himalayan foot-hills. In the early mornings and late evening the plain has a strange nebulous beauty which vanishes in the cruel heat of day. In the uncertain light of approaching dawn shadowy forms gradually reveal themselves: groves of graceful olive-green bamboos like bunches of Prince of Wales' feathers, big-leafed banana trees slashed and torn by the recent monsoon rains, a village of thatched mud huts, groups of clumsy water-buffaloes, and everywhere paddy-fields separated by low walls of mud. They say that so fine is the alluvial deposit brought down from the Himalaya to form this immense plain, that the whole way from Siliguri to Calcutta there is found no stone bigger than a child's fist.

At Siliguri there was an infectious holiday spirit abroad, and in the air a sweet tang of the hills. How good it was to see the smiling, oblique-eyed faces of the hillmen again after the impenetrable sly hostility of the Bengali Babu! I felt that one had so much in common with these virile, cheerful folk; they smile, and are obviously glad to see one. The narrow-gauge Darjeeling line starts at Siliguri, and most of the way to Teesta Bridge plays hide-and-seek with the road. There is something very romantic about these Lilliputian railways: possibly because of their resemblance to the clockwork trains of one's childhood.

After eggs and bacon at the station, I chose a spacious open car and, with all my luggage in the back, set off for Gangtok, a journey of about fifty miles in which we would have to climb 5000 feet. My driver was a lithe, yellow-skinned Nepali, wearing an embroidered black hat like a small fez. Unfortunately we had no common language.

The village of Siliguri, set about with mango trees and dingy fly-infested roadside shops, is depressingly squalid; but soon the road crosses an open stretch of country where the houses are raised on stilts—presumably because of floods—and where heavy-horned water-buffaloes plough the dark rich soil. Here a big roadside tree was clustered with vultures somnolently replete after some loathsome feast; exquisite azure-blue jays sat sunning themselves on telegraph wires and long-tailed emerald or white parrots flew screaming from tree to tree. For several miles the road crosses the level strip of jungle between the plains and the Himalayan foot-hills known as the Terai, a belt of swampy fever-haunted forest, the home of countless elephants, rhinos and tigers. Between the pale, straight tree-trunks I could see for a long way, but near the ground the undergrowth flourishes with such luxuriance that it would be almost impossible to force a way through, except along the occasional tracks.

Soon after this we entered the forbidding gorge of the Teesta River, appropriately called by the natives " the Cleft of the Winds ". The Teesta, a wide and turbulent river at this stage, is famous for marseer (the Indian hill salmon), but in its lower reaches has an evil reputation as a haunt for cerebral malaria. Rising from the glaciers of Kangchenjunga and the great mountains along the Tibetan border, the Teesta flows down the centre of Sikkim eventually to join the Brahmaputra just as that mysterious river takes its final southward bend five hundred miles north of Calcutta. The valley becomes deeper and deeper, and the road is forced to follow the tortuous gorge of the river, occasionally making long detours to cross by suspension bridges the steep-sided valleys that tributary streams have carved out of the rocky mountain-sides. The road is very narrow here, and seems to consist of an endless succession of blind corners and hairpin bends.

My Nepali drove well, but like most Indian drivers seemed to have a violent prejudice against changing gear, and an obsession for blowing his horn whenever he could see less than a hundred yards ahead.

Above the road the forest-clad mountain-sides rose steeply for thousands of feet; below they led, often in a series of precipices, to the turbid torrent below. The forest was tropical in its luxuriance: tree-trunks were shrouded in ferns and creepers; parasitic tree-orchids with sprays of white or magenta flowers sprouted from branches; palms, tree-ferns, and banana trees strained to reach the sunlight through the choking dim-day undergrowth. The trees themselves grew to a surprising height. Their straight ashen trunks looked as thick above, where, reaching the sunlight, they suddenly burst into exuberant foliage, as they were near the ground.

In one place a landslide had recently blocked the way, and as stones were still falling from the scarred cliff above the road, a protecting wooden shelter had been built. As we went beneath this, a shower of boulders and earth crashed on to the roof above us, and hurtled away beyond us to fall into the river below. A cone of debris containing uprooted trees and tons of earth spread steeply below the road down to the waterside. During the monsoon such disturbances are frequent and whole sections of the road may disappear into the river; on little-used roads cars may be held up indefinitely. Thirty-two miles from Siliguri we crossed the Teesta by a magnificent single-span concrete bridge. We were now about seven hundred feet above sea-level. Had we gone straight on past a ramshackle village of dilapidated tin-roofed huts, the road would eventually have climbed through prim tea-gardens and then coniferous and rhododendron forest to Darjeeling. Above the bridge was a string of multi-coloured bunting stretched from side to side of the river. A closer scrutiny showed that each was covered with fine Tibetan characters. They were Buddhist charms and prayer-flags, put here to ensure the safety of travellers crossing the river—a strange contrast to the ferro-concrete bridge!

Soon after this we passed a signpost pointing up to the right, which read "Kalimpong 9 miles". Ignoring this we continued to follow the Teesta, whose valley opened up sufficiently to allow a certain amount of crazy cultivation: here an alluvial fan of rich soil, deposited for centuries by a mountain stream which now wound peacefully through its handiwork, was lined with concentric steps of mud-walled paddy-fields; here a clearing in the forest showed a fine crop of maize with lush green stalks ten or twelve feet high; and further up were groves of trim dark-green orange trees like overgrown privet bushes. In some places the mountain-sides, too steep for trees, overhung the river; and sometimes a causeway, little wider than the breadth of the car, was precariously supported on wooden props a hundred feet above the water. It was at just such a corner that we met a bullock-cart plodding slowly down the middle of the road. The driver, a low-caste Hindoo, was fast asleep or drunk on top of his load, and no amount of horn-blowing would wake him. I wanted my driver, after passing the cart, to turn it round and leave the Hindoo, still asleep, progressing in the wrong direction; but the man, though quite deaf to our clamour, woke up the instant his cart stopped, and as the bullocks wisely refused to go backwards we were forced to reverse to a place where the road was wide enough for two-way traffic.

At Rangpo we passed from Bengal to the State of Sikkim; and my permit to enter the country, issued by the Deputy Commissioner at Darjeeling, was examined by two Nepali policemen. I also had to sign my name together with innumerable particulars in the police book.

One of the first things that struck me in Sikkim was the extraordinary profusion of large brilliant butterflies. Twenty or thirty scarlet, green and blue swallow-tails, settled or hovering above every patch of moisture in the road, would rise like a flock of iridescent humming-birds as the car approached.

The road continued to climb. The undergrowth became less exuberant. The air grew cool and fresh. Suddenly, above the high forested ridges, there was a glimpse of the far snows. We had reached Gangtok, the capital of Sikkim, a large village which straggles along a ridge running out from the centre of a great horseshoe of densely wooded hills. The sides of this ridge, wrinkled with steeply terraced paddy-fields, drop precipitously to the rushing torrents at the valley foot; while at the lower end lies the Maharajah's palace and his private temple. From here a wide concrete road, lit by electric light and bordered with carefully laid out trees and flower-beds, runs past the rest-house and up to the Residency, which is hidden in trees a mile from the main part of the village. The native bazaar—full of strange people and stranger smells—lies just below the ridge.

The Residency is a most attractive house, solidly built of stone, and roofed with red felting instead of the hideous corrugated iron so common in India, while the entrance hall and rooms are panelled with attractive local woods. The garden, with its well-kept lawns, rustic lily-pool, and flower-beds of Sweet Williams, asters and hollyhocks, forms a pleasantly trim oasis in the tangled undergrowth of the encroaching forest with its graceful tree ferns and orchid-festooned branches. The only Europeans in Gangtok besides the Political Officer, who is frequently away on tour as he is responsible for our diplomatic relations with Tibet and Bhutan, are a lady missionary, the schoolmaster and his wife, and the wife of the State doctor.

The population of Gangtok is about two thousand, and of the whole of Sikkim, eighty or ninety thousand. The ruling family is related to many of the leading Lhasa families. The people are Lepchas—the original inhabitants of the Sikkim forests—Nepalis and Tibetans. In recent years the aggressive and more enterprising Nepali has gradually driven back the easy-going improvident Lepcha, so that nowadays, except in the more remote valleys, the pure Lepcha is rarely seen. He is a guileless gnome-like person with a great knowledge of the trees and plants of the forest.

From Gangtok the mule-track starts for the Natu La, and from Kalimpong the longer and more difficult road leaves for the Jelep La. By these two passes the road from Lhasa crosses the main range of the Himalaya on its way to India, consequently Kalimpong and Gangtok are the great centres for the Tibetan trade, especially in wool. In each of these places many Tibetans reside, and there is accommodation for the muleteer and his animals.

The personnel of the 1936 Mission comprised seven; it was thus the largest Diplomatic Mission ever to visit Lhasa. Of these, all except two were assembled at the Residency on the last day of July, ready to set off for Lhasa. H. E. Richardson of the Indian Civil Service, British Trade Agent at Gyantse, and Captain W. S. Morgan of the Indian Medical Service, both recently appointed, were already at Gyantse, about half-way along the road to Lhasa, and we were to pick them up there on our way north. As well as the Political Officer, who was in charge of the Mission, Brigadier P. Neame, V.C., D.S.O., Royal Engineers, accompanied us, since he was going to give the Tibetans advice upon military matters. He was at that time Brigadier, General Staff, to General Sir Douglas Baird, at Eastern Command Headquarters, and could be spared only until October. The Brigadier, in addition to his distinguished military record, is a well-known big-game hunter and " trekker " and a keen photographer.

When making our plans for the journey we had absolutely no idea how long we would be away. We had been invited up to Lhasa to help the young Regent and his Cabinet to solve several exceptionally difficult problems which had arisen in the last few years. The chief of these was to persuade the Tashi Lama, who had fled to China in 1923 as a result of a quarrel with the late Dalai Lama and who refused to come back to his monastery at Tashi-lhünpo without an escort of 300 Chinese troops, to return to his native country. As the Dalai and Tashi Lamas are the two most revered pontiffs of the Buddhist church, the continued absence of the latter virtually paralysed the religious life of a country where religion is always the primary consideration. The peaceful and speedy return of His Serenity (the title by which the Tashi Lama is usually known) was especially imperative at this time, as the Dalai Lama had died in 1933 and his successor had not yet been found. We were therefore prepared when we left Gangtok to travel to the Chinese border, perhaps as far as Jyekundo, to meet His Serenity and to escort him back to the Holy City on his way to Tashi-lhünpo.

There is a telegraph line from Kalimpong to Lhasa. This was laid to Gyantse by the 1904 Expedition, and continued to Lhasa by British engineers in 1921. As far as Gyantse it belongs to us, but from there onwards it is under Tibetan control. There is also a wireless transmitting station at Lhasa, but this had been left, not entirely with the consent of the Tibetans, in charge of a Chinese operator, by General Huang Mu Sung, after the Chinese Mission of 1934. As it was necessary for Gould to keep in touch with the Government of India, he had asked the Royal Corps of Signals to lend him two young officers who would be able to do the necessary wireless work, and also enough equipment for us to be able to establish and maintain an independent transmitting station should we go far beyond Lhasa. Lieutenants E. Y. Nepean and S. G. Dagg were chosen for this work. I was attached to the Mission as Private Secretary to the Political Officer in order to help him with cipher and other work which could not be done by his staff of Sikkimese clerks. As I had been trained as a surveyor and had had experience of cinemaphotography, these would be useful; the former especially so if we were to cross the little-known upper reaches of the Salween and Mekong rivers on our way to Jyekundo. I was also to undertake natural history work, especially by collecting pressed plants and seeds, and by making notes on the birds seen.

Owing to the uncertain duration of the Mission, and the fact that the official invitation from Lhasa had come through only at the last moment, Gould had had the greatest difficulty in making preparations. We knew that mutton, eggs, potatoes and butter could be obtained at Lhasa and at the various rest-houses, but otherwise we should have to rely entirely on what we ourselves brought from India; and as we would have to do a great deal of entertaining this meant that our supplies of food and drink alone were enormous. After Gyantse—roughly half-way to Lhasa—there were no rest-houses, and we would have to rely on tents. Though most of us were used to travelling light and living simply, and would probably have preferred this, nevertheless a certain amount of display was necessary to impress the Tibetans, whose own officials travel in magnificent style with many mounted servants and an immense quantity of baggage. In a feudal country such as Tibet these outward forms are very important, especially on a Diplomatic Mission.

For a few days at the end of July, while preparations for our departure were in full swing, the yard at the back of the Residency was a scene of great disorder and activity. Nepean and Dagg were packing things that had arrived at the last moment, and trying to reduce charging motors, accumulators and wireless sets into loads suitable for mules. I struggled with theodolites, cinema cameras and flower presses, and tried to make up my mind what I would need on the journey and what could be sent ahead.

July 31st, the day chosen for our departure, dawned inauspiciously enough. At daybreak the clamour of the muleteers and their animals in the Residency yard made further sleep impossible. A thin rain was falling. The stately tree ferns at the foot of the Residency garden were silhouetted against a valley full of billowing white mist. On the opposite side of the valley, thickly wooded spurs, dank and forbidding in the early morning light, led steeply to an undulating crest which was half obscured in cloud. Beyond this should have been visible the far snows of Kangchenjunga and its satellite peaks, but on this drab morning they were totally hidden from view. The boom of a trumpet and a confused throbbing of gongs came up from the monastery below, but was almost lost in the clatter of mule-bells nearer at hand.

The tumult in the Residency yard increased tenfold. The mules were picketed in lines to yak-hair ropes held to the ground by staples. They were small animals, but strong and with that air of sleek well-being that mules seem to maintain under conditions that reduce donkeys and ponies to mere skin and bone. Some of them had terribly sore backs, and all showed the white scars of former galls. A crude wooden pack-saddle was put above several layers of felting, and to this the loads, usually a couple of boxes each of about eighty pounds weight, were attached with thongs of yak-hide. Most of the mules were gaily decorated. Several had strings of bells round their necks or a large single bell, of the type associated with Swiss cattle, hanging on their chests. Another favourite form of embellishment was tassels of yak-tails dyed a brilliant scarlet, and hung about the head and neck of the mule. All had on their foreheads a star-shaped piece of brightly-coloured carpet material, in the centre of which was occasionally a small circular mirror.

It surprised me to see how docile these animals were; even a stranger could thread his way through their close ranks with no fear of being bitten or kicked. The muleteers themselves were a ruggedly handsome crowd of vagabonds with scarred, sunburnt faces, who clearly did not believe in too much washing. They had long pigtails usually finished with a scarlet thread or tassel. Often the plait was brought round over the front brim of their dilapidated felt hats, to prevent them blowing away. The better-dressed ones wore a large single ear-ring in the left ear and a plain piece of turquoise in the other. This ear-ring took the form of a fluted gold ring about two inches in diameter, with a turquoise mounted in the front. As this ring is very heavy, it is supported by a loop of red cotton over the top of the ear. Covering a very dirty shirt, a homespun robe was worn hitched up at the waist to leave the knees free. Very often only one sleeve was used, the other hanging loose and leaving one shoulder bare. Homespun trousers were tucked into cloth knee-boots with thick yak-hide or rope soles. All had a wooden whip-handle with a short lash thrust into the belt. Many of them also carried swords.

Even more striking than the muleteers were the orderlies of the Sikkim Residency who were helping to arrange the loads, and many of whom would accompany us as servants. These men, in common with the servants of the Maharajah, wear the uniform of the old Sikkimese militia. A robe of brightly striped woven material comes almost down to the knees. Over this is a very short jacket of bright scarlet with black facings. Puttees are worn, but the knees and feet are bare. The hat is of cortical wickerwork, like an upturned waste-paper basket, on the summit of which is a bunch of peacock feathers. From the back of this hat protrudes the inevitable pigtail. A broad Sikkimese sword in an open bamboo scabbard is usually worn.

Most of the mules set off in advance of us, one driver being in charge of eight or nine animals. Occasionally their loads became entangled, or a mule took the wrong turning, but beyond ruining the appearance of a part of the lawn which seemed to attract them, they were persuaded without undue difficulty to take the steep zigzag track that led from the garden to the roadway above.

CHAPTER TWO

TO PHARI

THE main Lhasa–India trade route, together with the telegraph line, goes to Kalimpong in the extreme north of Bengal. This route crosses the southern ridge of the Himalaya by the Jelep La, a pass slightly higher and much more difficult than the Natu La, which descends directly to Gangtok. Kalimpong is connected by a ropeway to the Darjeeling Railway, whereas any merchandise arriving at Gangtok has to be carried by car or bullock-cart beyond Teesta Bridge before it can be brought to the railway. Thus it is that the bulk of the Tibetan trade, more especially the wool traffic, goes to Kalimpong, leaving the shorter Natu La track comparatively free.

Taking a steep short-cut straight up from the Residency garden we passed the Sikkim State gaol with its cheerful-looking prisoners and met the Tibet road on the further side of the spur on which Gangtok is built. For the first few miles the road is possible for motor traffic, though I have never seen a car there. The track zigzags steeply for a thousand feet, then, having gained the requisite height, contours precariously around the steep wooded curve of an immense horse-shoe valley carved during centuries by the upper waters of the Rongni Chu.

It came on to rain soon after we started, and became oppres-

sively hot. The atmosphere of the forest on the lower stretches
of the road seemed to be a combination of the Tropical House at
Kew and the Parrot House at Regent's Park. Every leaf and
twig scintillated with drops of moisture; the brooding silence
was punctuated by the monotonous dripping of sodden foliage;
a heavy fragrance hung everywhere—the fetid smell of decaying
vegetation mingled with a hot-house perfume of orchids and
other sub-tropical blooms. At intervals birds would start to
shriek, continually repeating some haunting clarion call; and
if they showed themselves one saw the vivid colours associated
with tropical forest and jungle—the lapis lazuli blue of a verditer
fly-catcher, the peacock iridescence of a king-crow, the gold and
scarlet of elegant minivets.

The scenery was magnificent; but, to me, depressing in its
dank luxuriance, especially so in the silent drizzle. The track
occasionally led across level clearings where hump-backed cattle,
reminiscent of the plains, wandered knee-deep in the lush grass.
Here would be frail huts walled and roofed with strips of woven
bamboo, and occasionally a more substantial house of wood.
Their occupants, heavy-featured Nepalis or effete sallow-faced
Lepchas, watched us with expressionless faces as if they had long
since been overcome by the leaden spirit of the forest.

The track was about nine feet wide and very well constructed,
with large cobbles neatly aligned at the edge. This surface
provided a good footing for the pack-animals, and successfully
withstood the monsoon rains without becoming a quagmire.
On the left there was a steep grassy bank of a few feet, on which
flourished all sorts of flowering plants; but immediately above
this the impenetrable forest started, and sloped steeply upward
to be lost in lowering clouds a thousand feet above the track.
On the right the wooded mountain-side dropped thousands of
feet to the river in the valley bottom, invisible among the tree-
tops and shreds of cloud. From the other bank of the stream a
similar mountain-side, with never a patch of grass or earth showing
through the trees, ran straight up to disappear far above in the
same sullen clouds.

As we climbed, the character of the forest changed. At first
there were semi-tropical trees with straight pale trunks and large
leaves, while the undergrowth consisted of flamboyant bamboos
and tree ferns. Gradually the big trees became fewer, partly

owing to the increasing height, but also because the hillside inclines ever more steeply, leaving insufficient subsoil for the nourishment of any but the most hardy trees. It seemed incredible that vegetation could cleave to such vertiginous hillsides; indeed in many places the very earth had peeled away, leaving long scars of naked rock like the ribs of an ancient wreck half choked in moss and seaweed.

We soon noticed rhododendrons, not the stunted bushes of the tree-line border-land, but great trees with scaly red bark and leathery emerald-green foliage. One variety had leaves a foot in length hanging in the form of a spearhead at the summit of each gnarled twig. Their flowering season was long over but there were still a few belated and bedraggled clusters of pink or scarlet blossom.

The ponies were in excellent condition, and we reached the rest-house of Karponang, nine miles from Gangtok, at one o'clock. These rest-houses have been put up every ten or fifteen miles along the way from Gangtok to Gyantse. They were originally built soon after the Younghusband expedition of 1904, but most of them have been enlarged or rebuilt since. They are intended for the use of Government officials, but are also at the disposal of tourists, a limited number of whom are each year allowed up the trade route as far as Gyantse.

Karponang is the dog-Tibetan name given to the place by a British subaltern who was attached to the escort at Gyantse. It is a literal translation of the words White House; but in the first place the two words would be the other way round in the Tibetan language, and in any case they are not the right words. The bungalow is built on a steep ridge overlooking the track. It is made of wood, and has half a dozen rooms furnished with beds, wooden arm-chairs, tables and large open fire-places. Visitors provide their own bedding and food, but, from the watchman, paraffin for the lamps can be bought, and an unlimited quantity of firewood. At one time an enterprising Political Officer ornamented the walls with menus of sumptuous dinners from most of the best-known eating-houses of London and Paris. But one of his successors, thinking these too tantalizing for an exile living on eggs and tinned food, had them removed. In each bungalow there is a collection of literature, including, inevitably, venerable bound volumes of *Punch*, *Blackwood's Magazine*, *Vogue*—for lady travellers—and a mixed collection of cheap thrillers, Victorian novelettes and obsolete text-books on the most abstruse subjects under the sun. Karponang bungalow was exceptionally large and imposing. A glass-fronted veranda enclosed one side of the building from which doors opened to the rooms. As the cook and his mate had gone on ahead, a hot lunch was ready for us on our arrival.

When the pack-mules came in I collected all my gear and sorted it, leaving out the boiling-point thermometer so that I could estimate the exact altitude of the bungalow. Some difficulty was experienced in carrying my cameras so that they would be available at a moment's notice, especially as some of them were so bulky. No saddle-bags were available at Gangtok and I had not had time to have any made. In the end I packed most of the cameras in a large rucksack which was carried, not without some complaint, by one of the grooms (the word groom is rather flattering: most of the *syces*, as they are called in India, know little about the care of horses, relying on their masters for instruction).

After lunch I went out to collect plants. The forest flora is fairly well known, as botanists since the time of Sir Joseph Hooker have collected in Sikkim. I did not really intend to collect and press specimens until we reached the highlands of Tibet, but there were many plants entirely new to me, and I could not resist making a collection of these. So engrossed was I in blue campanulas, new primulas and other exciting flowers that I forgot all about the leeches, those insidious pests of the forest that for me, at any rate, take all the pleasure from forest travel at this time of the year. Suddenly, as I stooped to pick a flower, I saw two of these slimy slug-like creatures moving over my hand trying to secure themselves in their favourite place for blood-sucking—the soft flesh between the fingers. They were impossible to shake off, and plucking at them merely transferred them from one hand to the other. Desperately wringing my hands to get rid of them, I saw another, an enormous one, looping its hideous way from my stocking to my bare knee; several were disappearing over the tops of my shoes; another, anchored firmly to my shorts, blindly waved its body as it searched for my flesh. All around me through the wet grass I could see them undulating their way towards me relentlessly, their eyeless senses telling them that here, at last, was the smell of living blood, the meal of a lifetime—for how many of all the millions of leeches can ever get the chance of a good drink of warm red blood? Leeches always fill me with an inordinate fear, and I was paralysed with terror. Was it better to stay there desperately plucking off the creatures while more and more surrounded me and crawled on to my shoes, or should I allow many of them to get a hold while I bolted for the open path where I could keep pace with their attacks? The latter course prevailed, and I charged precipitantly through the clinging undergrowth and half ran, half slithered to the track a hundred yards below. I pulled off those that had not already attached themselves, and then ran back to the bungalow where I could get salt, which instantly makes them release their hold. I knew that there were a good many already sucking, and to be without salt (or a cigarette-end, which is equally effective) and to watch these loathsome creatures gradually bloating themselves, and knowing that if you pull them off not only will it hurt, but the wound will go on bleeding for hours, is a horrible predicament. Even when the replete leech lets go of his own accord the small puncture will bleed for several hours and will itch terribly for days, because the insect injects some chemical which prevents the blood from coagulating. Leeches have a way of lying in wait on the extremities of twigs, so that as the victims brushes past they can attach themselves. Some say they drop from trees. But most of them come from the ground, clinging to your shoes as you pass. This can be prevented if you wear two pairs of socks or stockings, and smear them well with a solution of areca nut. The natives sometimes go about with a small bag of damp salt on the end of a stick and one touch with this makes the leech drop off. The above may sound rather exaggerated seeing that these forest leeches are a mere couple of inches in length at the most; but it is an understatement of the paralytic terror that seizes me when I find myself among them.

After dinner we sat round a roaring log fire, and for the first time I could really believe we had started. Though I had gone to Dehra Dun to take a " refresher " course in survey, and though for some time I had been practising cipher work and trying to learn the Tibetan language, it had not been certain until only a week or two previously that we would actually go to Lhasa; and since the official invitation came through I had been so busy making last-minute preparations and not thinking beyond the matter in hand that I had scarcely had time to realize that I was about to satisfy a life's ambition—to visit the Holy City of Lhasa; that once more I was embarking on an expedition—leaving civilization (as we smugly call it) with a few chosen companions in order to undertake a difficult enterprise.

There is always a feeling of overwhelming liberation in setting off on some carefully planned expedition that has occupied your mind, possibly for years; but there was something essentially dramatic in the beginning of this journey to Lhasa. One day we did not know if we would even start: a day later—as it seemed— we were on the road.

That night, after spending some time pressing plants and writing up my various logs, I went out to look at the weather. I could hear the laughter of the muleteers as they sat—probably gambling —round the fire in the hut a hundred feet below, through the frail walls of which the lamplight feebly glowed. The mist had rolled away. The clouds had vanished. It was a clear starlit night. Far, far above me I could make out the broken line where the summit trees were silhouetted against the sky. And the Great Bear, who usually rides so freely in the heavens, appeared to be shut in and almost surrounded by the encroaching sides of a bay in this high horizon.

Next day, the 1st of August, we left soon after five o'clock. It was cloudy, but the hills were clear. Their wooded slopes cut by deep gorges rose right up above us; and coasting across them, disappearing only to follow the contours round the edges of hidden ravines, could be seen our track until it disappeared among pine trees over the Lagyap La, a pass just over 10,000 feet, the lowest exit from the great amphitheatre formed by the head of the valley. The track here was in a few places really steep, but was far more spectacular than the day before. In some places, supported only by crazy scaffolding, it cut across precipices. On many stretches an iron railing was necessary to protect the animals from a vertical drop of hundreds of feet on to the tree-tops below. There were still a few large rhododendron trees beside the track, but higher up the steep slopes were covered with scrubby bushes of an exquisite blue-green colour, a contrast to the yellower green of the dwarf hill bamboos.

The flowers increased in number as we approached the pass, and

I grew weary of getting on and off my pony to collect them. In one place, turning a sharp corner, we came upon a waterfall pouring down on to the track. There was just room to splash across a narrow platform, where the water ran level, before plunging over the edge and falling in a series of cascades to be lost in the tree-tops below. The ponies were imperturbable, having been bred to forest tracks and passes. Just as we reached the Lagyap La, looking back, we had our last view of Gangtok: 4000 feet below us on the end of a wooded spur we could see the Maharajah's palace, and the golden roof of the temple shining in the sunlight. Above the ridge, hill behind hill paled into distance.

Beyond the head of the pass we seemed once again to be in a different world. Here were only coniferous trees; and the track at first followed a clear mountain stream, occasionally crossing it by wooden bridges. The fir-clad hills sloped steeply to bare hill-tops over which the clouds hung low. The aromatic fragrance of pines, the clear cold air blowing off the hills in front of us, the bright primulas growing out of the moss beside pellucid springs, the sound of yak bells falling sweetly from the upland pastures, and the houses roofed like chalets with ash-grey wooden tiles weighted down with stones, all carried an atmosphere of Switzerland.

We passed a wayside monastery where a surly monk stood at the entrance gate and watched us with expressionless face. The track zigzagged steeply for several miles through the lichen-covered fir trees, then suddenly, in company with a fair-sized cascade which tumbled down the rocks, it emerged above the final wooded ridge and entered a cup-shaped valley filled with a still grey lake. The trees stopped abruptly. On the right of the lake a steep slope clothed in birch and rhododendron scrub ran down to the water's edge. On the left a bare rocky hill-side just left us sufficient room along the margin. A mile ahead of us the lonely bungalow of Changu overlooked the lake, and beyond it the track led over a low ridge covered with dwarf rhododendron and azalea bushes. The scenery reminded me of the north of Sutherland, especially as the clouds had descended again and low mist swept across the hills.

Changu has a bad reputation. Hardened travellers feel ill here and blame the water, which they say is poisoned by the rhododendrons. But the explanation is simple: being at an altitude of just over 12,000 feet, it is high enough to bring on a temporary attack of mountain sickness, especially in those who come up from Gangtok, more than 6000 feet lower down, in a single day. We had lunch at the bungalow, and a much-needed rest. Though none of us felt ill we were all rather weary. Through the window of the bungalow we looked out on to a border of tall *Primula Sikkimensis* and wild blue iris. Below us lay the lake, sombre and grey. At the far end, just at the outflow of the water, the mountains fell back on either side so that the sky appeared to meet the lake in which it was reflected. Beyond there seemed to be a great void.

After lunch we climbed the low hill behind the bungalow and contoured round the head of a deep but narrow valley to the foot of the Natu La. On this stage of the journey there were open meadows covered with gay flowers like an Alpine pasture. Just at the foot of the pass lay a shallow lake, and near this a track came in from the right, and there was actually a signpost. Had we turned to the right we should have reached, after seven or eight miles, the village and bungalow of Kopup on the main Lhasa–Kalimpong trade route, just south of the Jelep La.

Our own track climbed the rock-strewn grassy slopes to the summit of the Natu La (14,300 feet) in a series of carefully graded zigzags. Unfortunately there was thick mist on the top, and we were deprived of a magnificent view across to the highlands of Tibet. From here we should have seen the distant peak of Chomolhari (pronounced Cho-mo-lha-ri) rising in majestic isolation to a height of 24,000 feet. Near the summit of the pass we met a herd of yaks picking their way carefully down the stony pathway. Grotesque, with their matted coats hanging like plus-fours to their knees, they are, in spite of their formidable horns, as docile as domestic cattle. At the very top of the pass were several large heaps of stone surmounted with bunches of many-coloured prayer-flags tied to sticks. These were not only used to afford spiritual protection to travellers, but to mark the frontier between Sikkim and Tibet. Some of the muleteers threw additional stones on to the cairns, and one of the more pious attached a scarlet flag covered with black writing. I could hear the querulous note of choughs coming through the mist, and once the deep croak of a raven. On the far side we soon got clear of the mist, and here the whole hill-side was carpeted with rhododendron bushes three feet or so in height. It was indeed a pity they were not in bloom. Once more we descended from the upland meadows to the belt of birches and flowering shrubs, then to the woods of deodar, silver fir and pine. When we stopped by the roadside for a picnic lunch we were intrigued by a great number of spikes, four to six feet in height, standing like candles on the bare hill-sides above us. At that distance they seemed too straight and regular to be any kind of flowering plant, but on investigation we discovered that they were giant wild rhubarb.

The road was no longer paved with stones, and henceforward it deteriorated into a treacherous muddy track with puddles up to the horses' knees. At four o'clock we reached the bungalow of Champithang (13,350 feet), having covered a double stage of about twenty-five miles. This bungalow has three rooms—a small dining-room and two bedrooms—but that night I think we would have slept anywhere.

I now make more direct use of my diary:

August 2nd, Sunday.—Stayed up till midnight pressing flowers and drying their paper before the fire; in this damp country it has to be changed almost daily. Called at five. Feel dull and heavy owing to the height, but not really ill. Porridge, tinned herrings, scrambled eggs, bacon and potatoes: the height doesn't affect our appetites! Arranged my camera gear into a coolie load and two saddle-bags. The big tripod is awkward to carry on horseback. Away soon after seven. Raining intermittently and lowering clouds. The track is vile here: alternate ridges of clayey mud and water, as if the foundation were railway sleepers. Tree-trunks were put down in the worst places to lead across the mud. Neame, who had a headache last night, rode; Gould and I walked all the way to the monastery. I collected flowers. Two new primulas today: a deep violet variety with grape-like bloom on it, and a cowslip-coloured one with the flowers in several whorls. The periwinkle gentian is common and a new blue one. Very few birds. Saw two blood pheasants and a monal. The path ran gently downhill among pine trees for several miles, then quite suddenly came out at the top of an open bank sloping steeply down to Kargyu monastery.

This south-facing slope was a veritable flower-garden. There was a wild red rose in flower, and two varieties of the single waxy azalea, deep cherry-coloured and cream. Several kinds of orchid grow here, including a vivid pink one I haven't seen before. Away down below we can see the winding river of the Chumbi valley set among a chequer-work of fields, green and gold and brown. Villages of grey-roofed chalets cluster at the foot of the heavily wooded hill-sides; and up above, intermittently visible through a hanging curtain of mist, are clearings of open pasture where yaks graze.

Took some cinema shots of our baggage mules descending the hill. Met a few travellers: women dressed in brightly striped homespun, carrying immense loads of grass and bamboo shoots for fodder; vagabond men with square turquoise ear-rings, untidy pigtails tied round their heads, and unkempt straggly beards; itinerant monks, with shaven heads and deep-set unfriendly eyes, wearing dirty mulberry-coloured robes; and always trains of mules and donkeys carrying wool. The muleteers and yak-herds are often accompanied by large black mastiffs with heavy red woollen collars, worn as protection against wolves. Often they are kept on chains. They are very independent and aloof, but not aggressive.

The monastery of Kargyü, on the spur of a hill commanding the Chumbi valley, looks lovely from above with its ash-grey shingled roof and brightly painted walls. The monks of the monastery belong to a special sect of Buddhism called Kargyü, which is prominent in Bhutan but rare in Tibet. On the hill-side above, and just beside the monastery, are a number of *chortens* (curiously shaped monuments of stone usually erected over the ashes or relics of a holy man; similar to the Indian *stupa*). As we approached we heard the deep resonant boom of the long trumpets, like a buffalo in pain. Just outside the monastery entrance was a *mane*, or prayer-wall, overgrown with moss and ferns. Religious custom demands that the traveller leave these on his right-hand side. Just here we were met by a lama [1] band of drums and cymbals, which preceded us to the monastery. As in Sikkim, one man carries the drum on his back while another walks after him and beats it. The musicians were cheerful grubby youths with deep terra-cotta robes and close-cropped hair.

[1] The word lama means " superior one " and is correctly applicable only to monks who are the incarnations of certain Buddhist saints, or to those who, by their devotion and learning, have raised themselves to that status. It has now come to include any Buddhist monk.

We followed them through a most attractive wooden gateway into a large cobbled courtyard where a crowd of monks welcomed us. Behind carved pillars there was an ambulatory right round the yard with ancient-looking frescoes on the walls, depicting fierce gods embracing, meditating Buddhas, multi-headed Buddhas, Buddhas with blue, green or red skins—hundreds of Buddhas, and all different; also the wheel of life depicting man's vicissitudes through endless cycles of existence. A fine pony was tied to a pole in the centre of the court; many dogs prowled round.

We climbed a rickety wooden stair, up and up till we reached the Abbot's room. Here we were presented with blue, instead of the customary white silk scarves of greeting, which were collected again before we left. The Abbot (he has held that position for twenty-seven years) is an aged man with a benign yet lively face; unlike the other monks we had met, he wore a grey robe, and had a great mass of hair tied in a bundle on top of his head. We were told that never during his life had he cut his hair. He wore flat discs of spiral-curled ivory in his ears and rings on his fingers—surely unusual for a monk. He also wore steel-rimmed glasses. A very striking figure, but that of a man of the world rather than of an ascetic. When we asked him if it were going to be fine, he replied that it was bound to rain for three days as the Holy Pig had just risen from Mansorawar Lake (near Mount Kailas) and that three days of rain were necessary to consecrate it.

He was extremely affable and gave us tea, cakes made with maize-meal, and russet apples grown in the valley below. The room was painted everywhere with vivid colours, and on the two walls were richly coloured religious paintings hanging in frames of silk brocade. One side of the room was filled with holy books and innumerable images of Buddha in gaily coloured pigeon-holes. (A Tibetan book consists of rectangular unbound pages of manuscript held between two carved wooden boards; the whole is usually wrapped in a cloth to preserve it.) The tumult of bright colours was bizarre but effective. Before going outside again we followed the Abbot into a long musty-smelling room where we walked between rows of huge gilded figures. We then wandered round the outside of the monastery, and returned to the yard, where we took photos of the monks. They enjoyed this thoroughly. Some of them looked intelligent, others

G

degenerate and criminal. They were all very dirty. Gould gave them the customary present of 50 rupees (nearly £4)—an expensive tea! Escorted by our child band, we followed the track downhill. Here we were met by Captain Salomons, of the 2/7 Rajputs, who is in charge of the escorts stationed at Gyantse and Yatung. A cheerful Scot who is very fond of Tibet, both people and country.

Below the monastery the track dropped steeply through fir woods to the village of Pipitang. The Tibetan Trade Agent, usually a fairly senior Lhasa official, lives here. It looked like some Tyrolean village with its wide-eaved roofs almost meeting over narrow streets. There were some fine houses, built of stone up to the foot of the gables, with beautifully carved wooden window-frames and huge frescoes on the walls. In the middle of an open space is a building encircled by a row of wooden cylinders containing prayers written on tightly rolled paper. These are carefully fixed on axles so that the pious can set them revolving, and thus be so many million prayers to the good. Some of those who turned the big wheels were spinning their own little prayer-wheels with the other hand to make doubly sure.

The Jelep La track comes in here, and from now onwards we should have the company of the telegraph line We crossed a bridge and passed a number of chortens surrounded by fluttering prayer-flags on enormous poles; on the flags were charms and invocations to various divinities. As there was a good wide track by the river we rode again, rejoicing in the contrast to the steep forest. I saw several bronze-winged turtle-doves in a field of pink buckwheat. A pair of hoopoes crossed the river, and a white wagtail. Many crows too, and orange-billed choughs. The river is twelve or fifteen yards wide and very green and swift. It should be a wonderful wet-fly stream, but I don't think there are any trout here. Passed several small water-mills, then a shed containing an enormous water-driven prayer-wheel eight or ten feet high, and nearly twenty feet in circumference, a prodigious cylinder of prayers painted brightly, and with gold lettering on the outside. Passed more chortens and prayer-flags; then rounded a corner and saw Yatung, a prosperous village of stone houses with grey shingled roofs nestling at the foot of a narrow valley. Steep fir-clad hill-sides rise all round to open grassy meadows.

Gould and Neame inspected a platoon of Indian troops stationed here for the benefit of the British Trade Agent; fine-looking men and well turned out. Then we inspected a group of tiny school-boys, each with a Union Jack. After that we walked up to the Agency, which overlooks the village—a lovely long low red-roofed bungalow with a glass veranda in front. It possesses a most heavenly garden: the drive bordered by riotous masses of nasturtiums, green lawns, a pergola of rambling roses in full bloom, a paved garden with huge pansies, lupins, antirrhinums, esch-scholtzias and petunias—all you could wish for. I should have liked to live there. There are *burrhal* (wild sheep) in the hills, and many bears, which come down from the woods and raid the crops. The rest-house is very comfortable and lies on the other side of the river. On this side are the village, the barracks, the Agency, and Post Office. Yatung is almost 10,000 feet above sea-level, but being so shut in by mountains it cannot get much sun in winter, though in the summer it is delectable.

The Chumbi valley, wedged in between Sikkim and Bhutan on the southern slope of the Himalaya and therefore geographically outside Tibet, has played an important part in our relations with the Tibetans, as it holds the shortest and most practicable route from Lhasa to India. The prosperous natives, who make the most of their position on the trade route, have frequently been disturbed by reminders of the outside world. After the return of the 1904 Mission the British occupied the Chumbi valley until the indemnity had been paid. In 1910, when large numbers of Chinese soldiers suddenly appeared in Lhasa, the Dalai Lama fled from the Holy City. Closely pursued by Chinese officials he made his way down the Chumbi valley and reached the sanctuary of the Agency at Yatung. Next morning, at earliest dawn, he took the Jelep La route to Kalimpong, where he stayed for a few days before proceeding to Darjeeling, where His Holiness was to spend three years as a guest of the British Government. Eight years later the tables were turned: owing to internal strife con-nected with the overthrow of the Monarchy and the establishment of the Chinese Republic, the soldiers at Lhasa found themselves without pay and without orders. It was through the Chumbi valley again that these disarmed Chinese soldiers fled on their way to seek temporary asylum in India.

The valley holds many monuments of the decay of Chinese

power in Tibet. Where Yatung lies, the valley is comparatively open; but a mile or two above the village the rocky walls close in, and in one place almost block the valley. Just here we noticed the crumbled remains of a wall built by the Chinese in the eighties of the last century to strangle any trade between Tibet and India. A little to the north of this lie the ruins of Chinese barracks and official residences.

August 4th, Tuesday : to Gautsa (12,400 *feet*) : 15 *miles.*—Left Yatung and followed an eastern tributary of the Amo Chu between mountains 15,000 feet high. The river became a rushing mountain stream overhung with thickets of wild rose, daphne and jasmine. The stony track, driven to the bottom of the valley, was forced to follow the stream, and rose with extraordinary steepness. Up among the bare crags on our left were a number of desolate hermitages connected with the monastery of Tungkar, which overlooks the plain of Lingmatang. As we rose higher, snowy mountains appeared above the fir-clad slopes.

This level tract of country set among the surrounding hills forms one of the most striking changes of scenery I have ever encountered. The whole valley has been blocked by some ancient landslide, and the resulting lake has gradually silted up and dried. The track, shut in by steep hill-sides, comes suddenly to the crest of the heaped-up landslide débris, and as if by magic the mountains fall back, leaving a dead level expanse, several miles in length, of lush green grass starred with flowers. The river, reminiscent of the Usk in its peaceful meanderings, wanders through the verdant pasture which in most parts is carpeted with the cowslip-like blooms of *Primula Sikkimensis* and other flowers. We lunched beside this pleasant stream which in places forms deep pools. Gould put his rod together and tried for a fish, but though we saw some fry nothing bigger showed itself. Many yaks grazed on these meadows, and several of the dark yak-hair tents of the herdsmen were pitched upon a ring of bales of wool. They seem to travel in the early morning and let their animals graze for the rest of the day.

From Lingmatang to the bungalow of Gautsa the scenery became increasingly wild. The road climbed steeply at the foot of the bare mountain-sides broken with desolate crags and huge detached rocks. At each turn the valley was so shut in that it seemed impossible that there could be any escape for the boulder-strewn track; yet always another gorge appeared with beetling walls or naked tumbled screes—the wildest and most formidably beautiful valley I have ever seen. Crossing a primitive cantilever bridge, we reached the bungalow of Gautsa in a tiny village of wooden houses roofed with shingles. There was a big shed here for the mules and accommodation for the muleteers, who were heard making merry far into the night.

August 5th, Wednesday : to Phari (14,600 *feet) : 23 miles.*—An amazing day. Filmed the laden mules with a rushing torrent in the foreground and a savage rock-strewn mountain-side behind. A vile track as yesterday. Uneven boulders sticking out of mud, and more mud on each side. Awkward for the ponies. Wonderful flowers. The lavender-coloured campanula still here, and the periwinkle gentian; also several varieties of pedicularis, including the deep magenta one. Much ragwort too. In one place the track ran just beside the stream along the foot of the gorge. Here were prayer-flags on sticks, and a great heap of stones to which every mule-driver added as he passed.

Met three begging monks. The chief one, a gaunt old man with a lovely copper prayer-wheel bound with silver, had a large religious painting which he explained to us in a queer chanting voice. Filmed him. Many travellers on the road today; and always wool, load after load of it. We left the bottom of the gorge with its hard-bitten trees, and climbed up and up past scrubby slopes, seeing new plants all the time, so that I got left far behind trying to collect them. Found a wonderful sky-blue poppy with yellow sepals and prickly stem (*Mecanopsis horridula*); fields of pale mauve cranesbill, smiling blue gentians, and tiny china-pink primulas with yellow centres.

Gradually the country became transformed, and we entered the real Tibet of my imagination. The gorge opened out until we were among rounded hills, grassy low down and marked with scars of scree and ancient landslides, but quite bare and stony on top. There was now not a tree or bush in sight; only a great waterfall dropped from a cleft among some rugged hills on the right. Hundreds of yaks grazed on the fertile valley bottoms or up in the hills, while the blue smoke rising from their dung fires showed where the herdsmen had pitched their tents. Often we would pass a cheerful group of them in the open, naked to the waist, sitting round a fire and eating tea and *tsamba* (roasted barley meal), scooping it out of their polished wooden cups and cramming it into their mouths. They all turned to stare at our cavalcade, but not unkindly. The track passed another great heap of stones surmounted with fluttering prayer-flags, and entered a wide grassy valley which gradually opened up to form a rolling plain about ten miles in length bounded at the sides by rounded hills and sloping gently uphill to the summit of the Tang La. Turning a corner we saw Phari Dzong (fort) away in the distance, and the track going straight across the plain towards it.

CHAPTER THREE

TO GYANTSE

August 5th (continued).—We have entered another world. A world of immense distances: the dun plateau slopes up to meet the rounded sienna-scarred hills, and behind them the far snows are dominated by the ethereal spire of Chomolhari rising alone into the clouds. In the distance the flat-roofed village of Phari looks like an excrescence on the barren plain. Around it there seems to be a lake of blue water several miles in extent, though we know that this is not so. As we approach we find to our amazement that certain parts of the plain are thickly carpeted with blue forget-me-not and darker aconite. One of the most beautiful things I have ever seen in my life—the sober olives and browns of the plain, then suddenly these exuberant splashes of cerulean blue running up to the massive keep of the Phari fort and the mud boundary-walls of the village.

The plateau, austere and lifeless at a casual glance, is actually full of life. Tiny blue gentians and a minute yellow flower like a celandine smile up at one. I saw several kinds of snow and mountain finches, and Elwes' horned lark with its black and white face like a ringed plover. Soaring above are many birds of prey—lammergeyers, Himalayan vultures, kites and a solitary harrier. Hundreds of mouse-hares, attractive little rodents of the shape and size of guinea-pigs, sit up and watch us, only scuttling into their burrows at the very last moment. At one time I could count over two hundred baggage animals—ponies, mules, donkeys, yaks and oxen straggled along the track between us and Phari, and away beyond where the track sloped gradually up to the summit of the Tang La. I was far behind the rest of the party, having often stopped to collect plants and watch birds, but I could see various officials riding out to present the traditional white silk scarves of greeting.

On the right, coming down from a pass between two rounded hills, can be seen the Tremo La, the main route between Bhutan and Tibet. There are a good many Bhutanese traders here, including the representatives permanently stationed at Phari. They are bigger, wilder-looking men than the Tibetans; they wear their hair short, and their kilt-like robes, usually of a characteristic striped weave, come only as far as the knees. Nearly all of them carry straight swords in beautifully worked silver sheaths. The Bhutanese are inveterate raiders, and up till quite recently they would terrorize the less virile inhabitants of the Phari plain and the Chumbi valley by suddenly crossing the frontier hills and attacking mule-trains and even plundering private houses and monasteries.

The Phari bungalow is flat-roofed, as are all the buildings here, and faces onto a cobbled courtyard together with the Post Office and the rooms of the Postmaster, who is a Nepali, and the hut-keeper, who is rather a superior-looking Tibetan with a long plait, and a heavy gold ring in his left ear. The Post Office, at 15,000 feet, is supposed to be the highest in the world. Soon after our arrival the local headmen, four or five in number, came round to make arrangements for supplying transport for the next stage of the journey. To see them clustered round Gyaltsen, the clerk in charge of the department, was very entertaining. Tibet is a completely feudal country, and except from those in the highest positions there is a great show of obsequiousness. The headman, successful traders and middlemen, stood there with bowed heads nodding in unison as each order was given. In Tibet to obtrude the tongue is a mark of respect, so is a sharp suck-in of the breath so that it will not pollute the air that the honoured person is breathing. As the servant takes orders he continually says the word la-les, which means "yes, sir", in a high-pitched sobbing voice, sucking in his breath at the same time.

The effect is most ludicrous. The result of these negotiations was at any rate successful, for later in the day there were about 200 yaks and *dzos* (cross-bred yaks and cattle) picketed outside the bungalow wall.

The *Dzongpön* (fort commander) of Phari came in for tea. Even fairly minor officials seem to have perfect natural manners. This man wore a long silk robe of a very lovely violet colour with a pattern woven into the material. It was held in at the waist with an orange sash. A white silk shirt was folded down over his collar and cuffs. From his left ear hung a turquoise and gold ear-ring with a single pearl in the middle. (This type of ear-ring is about five inches in length and is worn by Tibetan officials of any standing. The strict sumptuary laws of Lhasa insist that the large tear-shaped stone at the end of the ear-ring shall be of blue porcelain and not turquoise.) His black hair was parted in the middle and arranged in two plaits which were brought up to the crown of his head, where they were held in place by scarlet ribbon tied into a double knot. Thus it has been said that in Tibet the officials even have their hair tied up with red tape. He wore a conical hat of white parchment covered with red tassels which hung down over it like a lamp-shade.

Most writers agree that Phari is a bleak and filthy place with no redeeming feature except its superb surroundings. In the afternoon I went to look at the fort. The roads are deep in mud and dung and no one seems to trouble to remove dead and decaying dogs and mules. There are great piles of dung on all sides. Lean curs wander disconsolately round corners. The streets themselves are so choked with the accumulated garbage of centuries that they are many feet higher than formerly and in most cases actually obscure the ground-floor windows; when leaving the road to enter the courtyards round which most of the houses are built one steps down a considerable distance.

The people are dressed in very dirty robes of dark homespun. The women look cheerful but disfigure their faces by smearing blood onto their cheeks and noses as protection against the sun and wind. Some wear the high hooped head-dress of the Tsang or Gyantse province, while others favour the triangular Lhasa style. Most of them wear turquoise charm boxes. Just east of the fort there is a street of bazaar stalls containing a surprising variety of merchandise: mirrors, ribbons, cheap jewellery, cooking vessels, bricks of Chinese tea, iron and copper goods, spices, china, and wooden tea-cups—all sorts of things. Here innumerable beggars sit cross-legged beside the road spinning prayer-wheels and importuning passers-by for charity. They stretch out and shake their arms with fists clenched and thumbs in the air, at the same time protruding their tongues and whining. Several are maimed and deformed, but many seem young and capable of work.

The walls of the fort are solidly built and in good repair, but no one seems to live there. I went up some steps and through a massive gateway into a cobbled yard, on the far side of which, at the top of more stone steps, was a great double door beautifully carved and painted. Outside this door were stocks, pillories, wide wooden collars that lock round the neck, iron fetters, and several thong whips, all prominently displayed to remind the people to behave themselves. A rickety wooden stair led up three floors to a flat roof. All the doors that I passed were locked with heavy padlocks of local design and workmanship. The whole building seemed to be deserted, but from the roof a low droning complaint could be heard, accompanied by the intermittent beating of a deep-toned drum. I traced this to a dark cell-like room opening off one corner of the flat roof, where a solitary monk was praying. He took no notice of me whatsoever, looking straight through me as if I were not there.

There was a cold wind blowing, and Chomolhari was hidden in scudding storm-clouds. In winter Phari must be unutterably bleak and desolate, a target for all the winds that blow. The roofs are flat and surrounded by parapets, from the corners of which flutter white prayer-flags on branches of bamboo. I took some photos, then returned. That evening was spent sitting round a blazing wood fire. The wood, juniper and pine, is carried from Bhutan, for yak-dung is the usual fuel here. The wireless made queer noises, Gould composed telegrams, Neame made corrections to the military route book of Tibet, while I changed some films and wrote up my bird diary.

August 6th : to Tuna (10,000 *feet*) : 21 *miles*.—Slept well. Woke at four to see Chomolhari a forbidding black cone surrounded by a wreath of nebulous cloud. An incredible mountain—for impression of sheer height and grandeur it surpasses any I have ever seen, except the Matterhorn.

Across on the other side of the plain rises the great snowy mass of Pauhunri with no very striking peaks. Got back in time to photograph our yaks being loaded up. They don't like the smell of Europeans, but are most placid with their own drivers. Their horns and shaggy coats resemble those of Highland cattle, but they are much larger and have long thin faces. Went down to film the forget-me-nots in colour. Rai Sahib Tondup, the Sikkimese doctor from Yatung, is staying with me to interpret to my camera men. I practise my Tibetan on him as we ride along. He is going up to Gyantse to take charge while Morgan and Rai Sahib Bo Tsering, the other Sikkimese doctor, go up with us to Lhasa.

A vast crowd of beggars and other people lined the road as we cut through a corner of the town. Crossed several streams, then got into the open plain again. It is very dusty and reddish coloured. Long stretches are covered with stones. On the south and west of Phari there is considerable cultivation, but I gather the barley never ripens up here, but is cut for fodder. The local officials escorted us for a considerable distance along the track, then before returning they presented Gould with more white silk scarves. This scarf technique is complicated. A senior official accepts .a scarf from a junior but does not give one in return; sometimes he places the one he has received over the donor's shoulders like a stole. With officials of equal rank scarves are simply exchanged, and the art is, as you hold out your hands with the scarf, to receive yours underneath. The scarves one receives can be passed on again so that one does not accumulate them.

I am getting very sore from all this riding. Gould's pony, like all the best Tibetan ponies, is an ambler; that is to say it moves like a camel, using the two legs on each side together. He progresses at a slow amble of about six miles per hour, a tireless pace for man and animal. My pony only trots. Going fast is comfortable, but a slow trot throws me up and down intolerably.

We passed fairly near a red-walled monastery and then through the cheerless hamlet of Chu-gya, which means " frozen stream ". It is at a height of 15,000 feet. Just a few houses with mud walls and a square chorten from which a couple of old ravens cursed us. A great many nettles growing here.

Our party of about fifty horsemen looks most impressive. The track gradually rises to the summit of the Tang La. It means "level pass", and certainly presents no difficulty to horse or man. Were it not for the line of cairns it would be difficult to locate the summit. We are at our nearest to Chomolhari here, but though the rocky foot-hills were visible, the snows are hidden in cloud. It is most amazing the way the peak rises suddenly from the level grassy plain. Saw two red foxes skulking along near the top of the pass. Hoped to see some *kiang* (wild asses) but there are none, only great herds of sheep and yaks.

From the top of the Tang La the plain falls only a little to Tuna, our next halt. The country is very barren and stony; only a few scrubby vetches and the sere plateau grass survive. In front of us is a range of low pinkish hills with the village of Tuna at their foot. To the left, the plain continues towards Kampa Dzong, one of the routes taken by Everest expeditions. Our way lies to the right beside a great lake which is hidden in stormy clouds. Lunch was ready for us when we got in just before a heavy rain-storm.

Later I walked up the cindery red hills behind the bungalow, and found a surprising number of flowers, including a magnificent blue poppy. The barrenness of its surroundings emphasized the beauty of its transparent blue petals and yellow sepals so that one literally gasped to see it. There was also a blue allium, arenaria, several androsacae, a pink saussurea, and some mauve asters. For the rest it was very wild and lonely, the more obvious vegetation consisting of nettles and thistles. On the far side I could see for miles and miles; there the wide level bay of the plain rose to another range of scarified red hills paling to amethyst in the distance. I have never seen such colouring. The salmon pink of the Tuna hills; the rich shades of bracken and russet where the sun lights up the grassy foothills; the deep violet of the cloud-shadows chasing each other across the plateau; the clear blue of Dochen Lake, and the white snow-clad peaks beyond.

I saw six burrhal in the distance, and a grey animal which might have been a wolf or a snow leopard. I tried to stalk it but lost sight of it. There is plenty of water at Tuna, and the squares of green barley-field look dark against the olive-coloured plateau. From up here the track can be seen plainly all the way back to the top of the Tang La, twelve miles to the south.

I ran down the scree slope to the bungalow, much to the amazement of the muleteers, who had probably never seen anybody
run before. I had a long talk with one of them, but I don't
think either of us understood very much. He was telling me
about the Gods on Chomolhari. He had tied his pigtail right
over the top of his battered felt hat to stop it blowing away.
What magnificent teeth many of these men have!

Some monk beggars appeared at dusk. One had a black
beard and a curious frilled eye-shade of stiff black hair. The
chief one had a drum made from two human skulls, and a *dorje*
(symbolical thunderbolt) bell. They chanted a mournful
prayer.

Nepean and Dagg fixed up a couple of amplifiers and persuaded
some of the muleteers to sing Tibetan songs. A great crowd
collected. Their singing is curiously harsh and broken.

August 7th : to Dochen (14,950 feet) : 13 miles.—Got up at five
and ran up the hill behind the bungalow. I seem to be fairly
well acclimatized, as I climbed a thousand feet in forty minutes
and took seven to get down again. The pyramid of Chomolhari
is clear but does not stand out, for from here it is no longer isolated but forms the western peak of a magnificent line of mountains.
Dochen Lake, the Hram Tso or Otter Lake, can be seen running
up to the foot of them. All the photographers were at work
taking the Chomolhari range and our yaks moving off. We
had changed transport at Yatung and again at Phari, but we keep
this lot as far as Gyantse; these stages are carefully regulated, as
different types of country require different animals.

The track led round the corner of the Tuna hills and away
across a wide level plain. There were tufts of vetch, occasional
thistles and a sedum-like plant, otherwise it was barren and stony.
Still no wild asses, only Tibetan gazelle seen dimly in the far heat
haze. There are solidly built square milestones along the track,
but many have been razed, and the mileage is only written in
Tibetan.

I like to walk and then canter, but we go along at a slow trot
which causes a stitch and a sore backside and makes me bad
tempered. Met some craggy red hills on the left and soon reached
the hot springs of Guru, where General Macdonald had to fight
the Tibetans in 1904. There are still traces of the wall which
the Tibetans built between the hills and the marsh. A great

many birds in the warm water—mallard, redshank and some new wagtails. Very wild, broken country away to the left.

Soon we met David Macdonald returning from Gyantse. We had hoped he would accompany us to Lhasa to teach us Tibetan, but he has not been well. He is an old man now, an interesting character. His father was a Scot, his mother Sikkimese, and his wife a Nepali; and as he was for twenty years British Trade Agent at Gyantse and Yatung, and was at Lhasa with the 1904 Mission, he has a wider knowledge of the Tibetans than any other English-speaking man. A little later we met a woman and two children with their faces completely muffled up, but for the eyes. Their importance was shown by the number of their retinue. This was the wife of Tsa Serkang, one of the high Tibetan officials with the Tashi Lama. She was coming down to Calcutta to collect her husband's baggage, which had come from China by sea. She had a frank conversation with the Political Officer, and told him that the Tashi Lama had already left China for Lhasa; but one has heard that story for many years and he has not arrived yet.

Soon we reached the lake. Between it and the bare reddish conical hills is a mile of fertile grass where gaze innumerable sheep, goats, donkeys, mules, ponies and yaks. Passed a village of flat-roofed houses built of low mud walls striped vertically with brown paint, and reached Dochen bungalow, which is built round a cobbled courtyard. No trees grow up here, but the grazing seems good and the black tents of nomads are dotted about the pasture-land.

After lunch I walked for several miles back along the lake, then returned over the hills as it got dark. It was a fascinating walk. I watched a pair of red foxes playing like puppies. The lake is very wide, about eight miles across; on the far side the mountains rise steeply to be lost in the clouds. I saw Pallas' fish-eagle soaring above the lake; first I've ever seen. Hundreds of redshank here. There are many flowers in the hills, which at first sight look completely barren. Watched some bright-coloured redstarts and rose-finches. On the way home I suddenly saw two kiang walking past and keeping a careful eye on the people in the fields down below. There was no cover, but I lay flat and they came within thirty yards before they saw me and cantered away. They are most beautiful creatures, not like donkeys at all, but more like zebras. They have cream-coloured legs, belly and chest, and rich chocolate-brown back and flanks with curious diagonal markings on the shoulders. A black line runs from the mane down the back and tail. After cantering away they turned several times to look at me, and each time advanced a few paces as if overcome by curiosity.

Behind the village are many fields of barley and potatoes. As I walked round from the back of the rest-house a big mastiff, which was chained in a niche on the corner, shot out with fierce growls and very nearly got me. Luckily he was firmly chained, but my heart almost stopped beating.

Pressed flowers; had a Tibetan lesson; listened to a German concert on the wireless. Neame developing photographs; Gould studying mysterious files. I am sleeping in a tent now, as the bungalows are small. A vast tent designed to impress the natives of Bengal, but the coldest, draughtiest marquee of a tent I have ever lain awake in.

The evening sunlight illuminates the blue smoke of our yak-herds' fires as it drifts through the black roofs of their hair tents. There are prayer-flags fluttering over each; these too are trans-figured by the setting sun.

August 8th: to Kala (14,850 *feet*) : 12 *miles*.—Fearful noise of dogs and muleteers from three o'clock onwards, so got up and wandered down to the lake. Some large calandra larks here with an unusual melodious whistle; innumerable terns, gulls and ducks. Clouds down over the mountains but sunny and warm. Neame, Nepean and Dagg went over the hills to Kala to see if they could stalk an *Ovis ammon* (big-horned wild sheep) or gazelle.

We rode along the shores of the lake in blazing sunshine. Several black-necked cranes standing far out: so it must be shallow. They were perfectly reflected in the still water. Hundreds of yaks and dzos coming south, mostly loaded with wool: yaks go at a steady three miles per hour, mules a mile faster. Many of the men carry antiquated flint-lock guns with two projecting prongs of antelope horn to use as a rest when firing. Others carry swords, often with silver scabbards set with coral and turquoise. They are grand-looking men, swarthy and independent as Bedouins. They are very cruel to their animals; I watched donkeys being beaten along with huge loads dragging on the ground. Often when the donkeys stop they lie down and have to be hauled up again by their tails, ears and loads. The foals of many of the animals run alongside while their mothers work.

All along on the left are bare rounded hills of reddish earth. We reached a corner of the lake where a river overflowed into a narrow valley. Crossed the river by a causeway gay with flowers, and followed the valley down to Kala. There is a ribbon of luxuriant cultivation along the foot of the valley, then barren rocky hillsides go up to meet the sky. Excellent crops of barley and mustard with wonderful wild flowers—red and yellow pedicularis, forget-me-not, wild asters and primulas. Passed a bare fort and the small mud-walled village of Chalu. Very biblical scenery: parched white sand, rocky track, ochrous boulder-strewn hill-sides, flat-topped houses with grain and straw stored on the roof, and a blazing sun. Reached the wide Kala valley and saw the lake over to the left; and to the right an immense grassy plain running up to rounded foot-hills and higher mountains to the north.

The low flat-roofed rest-house is surrounded by fields of wonderfully rich barley. Walked down to the lake and watched a man ploughing with two yaks. Followed a winding stream to the lake, and put up a pair of goosanders. There are thousands of animals grazing on the pasture-land here. The lake is very shallow and muddy with sandbanks running far out. Some large fish rippling the surface. Many different kinds of waders and ducks here. Returned by the village. It has turned cold now and is overcast. My face is very sore from the sun. The others returned in the afternoon having seen only one gazelle in the distance.

August 9th : to Samada (14,100 *feet*) : *14 miles.*—Up at five, and down to the lake before breakfast. It is cool and peaceful in the early morning, but too hot later on. The Tibetans are all out at dawn. Set off at eight o'clock. Passed a village where all the inhabitants came out and begged. The women wear a strange hooped head-dress with tousled pigtails hanging from the horizontal base of the hoop; they are all very dirty and ragged, but I dare say they have everything they want of life. The plain is eight miles wide here, and in many places is only sand, parched and cracked. There are flocks of hundreds of piebald goats and sheep tended by ragged boys. Lammergeyers and kites soar above us. Saw a good many kiang and gazelle. Nepean and I tried to photograph them, but they were as wild as could be. I hid behind a sandbank, and Nepean and two grooms drove five gazelle and some kiang quite close; I was so overcome by the grace and beauty of the kiang's movements I almost forgot to use the camera.

Soon we left the plain and met the Nyang Chu, which flows to the north and takes us all the way to Gyantse. It eventually flows into the Tsang-po (the Tibetan name for the Brahmaputra) at Shigatse; so we are really getting on. To the south-east across another plain I saw a remarkable range of snowy mountains which run from Chomolhari north-east to the peaks beside the Karo La; I don't suppose anyone has ever even tried to climb them, except perhaps some lama hermit plodding to his desolate cave. All along the sides of the stream there is lush marshy ground abounding in flowers, while tall yellow senecios and blue delphiniums grow on steep banks carved ages ago by the river. While we rested, the six coolies carrying the charging motor walked past chanting the most weird and haunting dirge to keep in step: four double notes repeated over and over again with variations. Then came a coolie carrying on his back a basket containing three black-and-white cocker spaniel puppies which are going up to Lhasa as a personal present from the Viceroy of India to the Regent of Tibet.

Innumerable ruins here of ancient Tibetan forts and houses. Some say the earlier inhabitants were wiped out by smallpox, others say Bhutanese and Tartar invaders. Certainly the population and cultivation have decreased, for along the lower slopes of the hills are the scars of aqueducts and terraced cultivation which are no longer kept up. Reached Samada, at the junction of two valleys, just before a heavy hailstorm and thunder. Across the river are beautiful rounded hills; on this side there are dry ridges of parched red rock. Near the camp is a massive chorten.

Beside the bungalow is a field of dark-blue aconite, in others yellow mustard grows. The barley is beginning to ripen. Turnips, potatoes and peas are also grown up here. Skylarks are singing, and there are hoopoes and yellow wagtails. A few willow groves here, the first trees since Chumbi.

There is a monastery up the side valley with walls painted

red and ochre. I wish I could like these hostile inscrutable monks, but I cannot see what good they do either to themselves or anybody else. The word charity means nothing to them: they do not heal or minister to the people. They have secured the material detachment advocated by Buddha, but they use it to aggravate and exploit the superstitions of the layman.

August 10th : to Kangma (13,900 *feet*) : 14 *miles.*—From 3 A.M. onwards a fearful noise of donkey-bells and shouting people. The rains have worn great gorges down the hill-sides, leaving vertical walls fifteen or twenty feet deep. Soon after starting we passed a very fine monastery on the roadside. There were cylindrical banners and brass ornaments on the roof. A few monks stared insolently as we rode past.

In some places there are low broad walls built right down the middle of the road. Along the sides of these are flat stones carved with Buddhas and with the mystic formula *OM MANE PADME HUM* ("Hail to the Jewel in the Lotus!"); referring to the Buddha, who is often depicted sitting cross-legged upon a lotus bloom). We have always to keep to the left of these.

Followed the river downhill all day to Kangma (red house). Dried-up hill-sides covered with emerald-coloured artemisia scrub and empty watercourses. Except near the rivers the country is intensely parched and desert-like. Many ruins again today.

Some fine villages with gaunt fortress-like houses, whose walls are painted in horizontal stripes of red, brown and white. There are rows of thorns along the parapets surrounding the flat roofs, and prayer-flags built up at the corners. The river falls steeply, and on each side aqueducts lead from it along the sides of the valley to water the barley-fields. The Tibetans are most skilful irrigators. Many blue delphiniums by the side of the track, also a big white gentian and a trailing clematis.

Two miles short of Kangma we met Norbhu, who had come down from Lhasa to meet us. Resplendent he was, in orange silk robe, purple sleeveless jacket, pink, white and blue striped boots, and a hat with a multicoloured braid crown almost hidden by a high brim of black velvet, and with a scarlet tassel hanging down behind. He rode a dun horse with a black tail and flowing mane, gorgeously caparisoned, and with two scarlet tassels hanging from its chest. As soon as we came in sight Norbhu dismounted and presented a scarf to the Political Officer.

[Rai Bahardur Norbhu Tondup is the confidential adviser to the Political Officer of Sikkim. He holds the very high title of Dzasa in Tibet, which is next to that of Cabinet Minister. He has had a most interesting career. By birth he is a Sikkimese Tibetan. When he was sixteen he was at school at Darjeeling when Captain—now Sir Frederick—O'Connor came to choose four boys to accompany the 1904 Mission to Tibet as interpreters. Norbhu, who passed out at the top of the list, was made personal interpreter to Colonel Waddell, who was not only the senior Mission Doctor but a serious student of Tibetan customs and religion. Norbhu witnessed the battles at Guru, Kangma, Red Idol Gorge and the storming of Gyantse fort.

He stayed at Gyantse with Waddell, then went to Phari on a temporary clerkship, and later looked after the 200 Indian drivers of the mule and yak carts there. When the Mission left Tibet, Norbhu, who was engaged to a Tibetan girl, refused to leave and was treated as a deserter. A year later, when the Tashi Lama visited India, Captain O'Connor took Norbhu as interpreter, and afterwards sent him to the office at Gyantse for training. In 1906–7 Norbhu was doing survey work in the Punjab. After this he became Trade Registration Clerk at Pipitang (Yatung) and then Tibet Clerk at Gyantse. He was there in 1912 when the Chinese were driven out of Tibet. In 1913–14, when Gould, as British Trade Agent, Gyantse, was acting Political Officer, Norbhu went to Gangtok as his Confidential Clerk.

In 1913, as the Tashi Lama returned from his visit to India, the Dalai Lama was on his way home after his exile in Darjeeling. They determined to meet and settle their differences. Gould and Norbhu met the Dalai Lama at Phari and escorted him to Gyantse. From 1915 to 1919 Norbhu was Confidential Clerk to the British Trade Agent, Gyantse, and to the Political Officer, Sikkim. In 1920 he accompanied Sir Charles Bell to Lhasa. In 1923 he became Rai Bahardur and that year visited Lhasa with Lieut.-Col. Bailey, having previously gone there alone with a present of ponies for the Dalai Lama. In 1927 the Dalai made Norbhu a Depön (military rank equivalent to a general).

In 1928 Norbhu went up to arrange Lieut.-Col. Weir's visit to Lhasa, and later accompanied it. Both visits were repeated in 1930, when the Dalai Lama conferred the rank of Dzasa on

Norbhu. In 1934 he went alone to Lhasa to counteract the Chinese Mission of General Huang Mu Sung and remained there in considerable danger for eight months. In the following year he accompanied Mr. Williamson to Lhasa and, after the tragic death of the latter, went to Gangtok to be Confidential Clerk to Gould. In May 1936 he went up to Lhasa to make the necessary arrangements for our Mission. He has recently been appointed British Trade Agent, Yatung, a post that for many years has been combined with British Trade Agent, Gyantse. At the end of the Mission he received the O.B.E. For the last thirty years, therefore, Norbhu has been in very close touch with Tibetan affairs and people; he has a wife at Kalimpong and another at Lhasa. From a former wife he has a son of sixteen who is at school at Darjeeling.]

In the afternoon heavy rain came on and there was a thunderstorm. Had champagne for dinner in honour of Norbhu. Lhasa seems much nearer now that he has joined us.

August 11th : to Saugang (13,000 *feet*) : 15 *miles*.—To begin with we followed the river along the foot of a deep grassy valley where there was little cultivation. The chief object of interest was some hot springs on the right of the track. Suddenly the mountains steepened and closed in. We had reached Red Idol Gorge, the scene of a battle in 1904 and certainly the most marvellous place for an ambush. The river falls more steeply here, and for several miles is forced from side to side by immense rocky spurs running out from the all but perpendicular sides of the gorge, which tower a thousand feet above the track. The slopes are a chaos of enormous reddish boulders, many of which almost block the way through. The track is paved with slabs of granite, and is continually forced aside by boulders. White quartz crystals have been heaped together by the pious, and there are Buddhas carved on the rocks and often protected from the weather by side walls and an overhanging lintel. The sacred prayer is also cut in the rocks and there are splashes of dull red paint and innumerable prayer-flags. An awesome and forbidding place, wilder than Glencoe or Killiecrankie.

At the foot of the gorge is a huge carved and painted Buddha about twenty feet high. In front of it is a pile of stones collected as an act of piety. At the end of the gorge a valley came in from the north and we looked down on to fields of barley, mustard and peas. Here were several fine houses surrounded by groves of willow trees. Soon afterwards we crossed the river by a cantilever bridge resting on an enormous central pier, and reached the rest-house of Saugang.

This is a delightful place: groves of willows and a few poplars surround the bungalow; magpies, sand-martins, rose-finches, willow-warblers and partridges abound nearby, and I found a new deep-purple primula. A wonderfully fertile valley carefully irrigated and tended. Was much pestered by beggars. Just above the village and bungalow on the far side of the river many Buddhas have been carved and painted on the vertical walls of rock.

After dinner worked at Tibetan. The man in charge of the rest-house produced a 1½-lb. fish which he had caught in the river; it looks like a kind of char.

August 12th: to Gyantse (13,120 feet) : 14 *miles.*—Rai Sahib Tondup and I went on an hour ahead to photograph the officials who will come out to receive us. He wears lovely silk robes but spoils the effect with a Homburg hat. A parching hot day; clear blue sky above and heavy cumulus clouds over the hills. More and more trees. One poplar growing in a village was as big as I've seen anywhere. Passed donkeys carrying loads of rice sewn up in skins. Magnificent scenery here: a great pyramid of rock with a fort on the summit; hills running up for thousands of feet on either side, and in one place overhanging the track in huge vertical rust-coloured cliffs.

Soon the valley opened out and I saw tall delphiniums and aconites as well as wonderful crops of barley and potatoes. Up in the hills on the left was a tiny monastery approached by a precarious track. Suddenly, by a chorten, we saw a group of horsemen, and I dismounted to be introduced to a dark-complexioned man wearing a conical hat with a jewelled ornament, and heavily flowered silk robes. This was Rajah Tering, the half-brother of the Sikkim Maharajah, who had some trouble with the British Government many years ago and now lives on his estates near Gyantse. We exchanged compliments in Tibetan, and I photographed him. The Sikkimese doctor and servants bowed down to the ground three times to him, as he is of their royal family. Soon afterwards we met a platoon of Mounted Infantry, drawn up with Captain Salomons in charge.

Richardson, the British Trade Agent, Gyantse, Morgan the doctor, and Guthrie, from whom he is taking over, were also there. I filmed Gould arriving and inspecting the escort. The clerks were all there in brightly coloured silk robes and the Agency orderlies in short scarlet coats—all mounted, of course.

Soon afterwards we met the Eastern and Western Dzongpöns of Gyantse, who had come out to present scarves to the Political Officer. Then a little further on we were stopped again by the Tibetan Trade Agent and the Abbot of Gyantse monastery. All these were fantastically clad in gorgeous silks and jewels. The last two are very high officials; for the more senior a Tibetan is, the less distance he rides out to meet a superior.

All these gaily-dressed officials and their servants fell in at the back of our procession, so that by the time we crossed Gyantse bridge and clattered up to the bungalow we resembled some brilliant scene of Elizabethan pageantry.

CHAPTER FOUR

TO LHASA

August 12*th* (*continued*).—Gyantse at last! The third biggest town of Tibet, it owes its importance to the trade routes from India, Bhutan, Nepal, Ladakh and Shigatse meeting here on their way to Lhasa.

Immediately after crossing the massive pier bridge yesterday we saw Changlo, the 1904 Mission headquarters, where they were attacked by night and besieged. Half a mile nearer the town, in a grove of willows and poplars, is the rest-house. The dzong is at this end of the town, on the summit of a volcano-like rock 600–700 feet high : a magnificent situation. At the other end of the town, on the southern slopes of a rocky amphitheatre, are the various buildings of the Parkor Choide monastery surrounded by a twenty-foot wall which runs along the top of the rocky spur. The dzong and the monastery, from the summits of the only two eminences of the plain, completely dominate the low white-walled houses of the town, which lie on either side of a rocky saddle connecting them.

These spurs are offshoots of a ridge forming part of a 17,500-foot mountain, the highest in the district, which shelters Gyantse on the north-west. Each hanging valley of this mountain has a white monastery or nunnery secluded in its clump of willows. The plain is wide and of great length, full of fields of barley, wheat, oats, peas, beans and potatoes. Dotted about are little farms and villas, each in its grove of willows. There is much flood-water at this time of year. Mountains rise on every side, but only on the north are they near at hand. We have put up our tents on a beautiful lawn surrounded by willows and poplars. We expect many guests tomorrow, so leave the bungalow free for entertainment. Spent the evening doing cyphers.

August 13th: at Gyantse.—Left bungalow at 4 A.M. to climb the high mountain to the north-west. I cut along the edge of barley-fields, through the end of the town, by a vilely muddy street full of barking dogs, and across an open stretch of plain covered with vetch, artemisia and thistles. The foot-hills are seared by great gorges as from torrential rain. Lovely white buildings in the hollows of the hills with trees and shrubs round about, and the inevitable chorten in front. On a spur of the hill some people were chanting and beating drums, and the white smoke of incense drifted up. I presume they were cutting up a dead body because, one after another, twenty-eight vultures whizzed from the hills above me and settled in a circle round the group. I was too far away to see much, and it was only just growing light.

Wonderful flowers here. I found white roses in bloom at 15,500 feet, blue and yellow poppies, several new vetches and a scabious. As I came over the col on to the final ridge I saw twenty burrhal in the mist on the far side. There is quite a good track up to the summit, on which there is an immense square cairn and bundles of prayer-flags of all colours. A line of smaller cairns goes off to the north.

I reached the top, 17,500 feet, at 6.30 A.M., that is 4000 feet in two and a half hours, including taking photographs and collecting plants. Pulse 104 to the minute. Stayed half an hour on top. I saw a hundred laden yaks and a man on a pass to the north-east. A party of eight large burrhal stags just below me took no notice of the man's shouts. It grew cold as clouds scudded across the summit. The country has a marvellous relief-map appearance: the ridge far below me with the dzong and monastery; the wide chessboard plain with its winding waterways and clumps of dark willows; and then the parched ochrous mountain ranges, ridge behind ridge visible for an unbelievable distance. Some snow peaks still visible to the south-west, probably the range that runs from Chomolhari to the Karo La.

Ran down a vile way over rough screes and dry watercourses. Saw several blue hares and a weasel. From one of the villages half a dozen huge black and yellowish mastiffs came at me; after keeping them at bay for some time with stones, they pressed me so hard that I had to climb up a chorten for sanctuary. A most terrifying experience. They would have finished me in no time if they could have got me. After a time a man came out and rescued me. He was very friendly and thought it the hell of a good joke. Got back at eight-thirty.

Spent morning pressing flowers and changing drying-papers. The Brigadier went outside to inspect the barracks and lines. Wireless officers tried in vain to start the charging motor; a bad show if it won't run at this height, even though it doesn't at the moment look as if we shall go beyond Lhasa. But it limits our entertainment programme. Gould received visitors all day. The first was the Tibetan Trade Agent, who is a very important lay official; he is a wizened little man with a pock-marked face. The last Trade Agent was a monk official. He was a great friend of the late Dalai Lama and used to supply him regularly with news. But he was degraded because he forgot the words of a prayer while he was officiating at some important ceremony. At least that is what we are told. The present man lives in a building which used to be the English school run by Frank Ludlow. It lasted from 1923 to 1925, but was closed down, as the Tibetans did not really support it.

The Eastern and Western Dzongpöns also called. One is tall and has very aristocratic Mongolian features. The other, Ten-dong, who is coming up to Lhasa as our guide, speaks English, having been at Ludlow's school. He is a younger brother of one of the Cabinet Ministers; a shy and very attractive man. The titles Eastern and Western refer to the location of their houses, not to the districts which they control. They work together and watch each other's step.

After the Nepalese representative had called, a monk, Tering Rimpoche (*rimpoche* means " precious one "), came to see us.

He is a brother of the Maharajah of Sikkim, and was at one time in charge of all Sikkim monasteries. He has the wisest and most expressive eyes in all Asia. His brother Tering Rajah came too, with his son, another pupil of Ludlow's. All these officials have the distinguished bearing and perfect natural manners of an ancient and proud civilization.

In the evening we had a dinner-party. The guests were Richardson, Salomons, Morgan, Guthrie and Norbhu. After dinner each of us in turn had to sing a song or tell a story. I sang an Eskimo folk-song, and Norbhu said it was exactly like Tibetan music—a doubtful compliment, but interesting, seeing that the Eskimos and Tibetans are, ethnologically speaking, fairly closely related.

August 14th : at Gyantse.—All very busy. Charging motor still only spluttering. Nepean and I sorting big film for the entertainment of Lhasa audiences, with Norbhu as censor. We have Douglas Fairbank's round-the-world trip, a selection of news reels and my Greenland films. The first is a series of shots showing Douglas dancing with dazzlingly beautiful girls of innumerable different nationalities; it won't do for Lhasa. The news reels are too disjointed, and as the subjects are mostly unfamiliar to Tibetans, and the shots all very short, they will be incomprehensible. Probably we shall leave the big projector here and rely on the smaller one.

We rushed round returning calls and drinking Tibetan tea. This is made from Chinese brick-tea. Norbhu says they spread it in the road for several days to let it acquire the strength and flavour demanded by Tibetan palates; certainly we cannot grow it in India, which is a pity, because every year thousands of loads of tea come over the high passes several months' journey from China. Any good Tibetan drinks fifty or sixty cups of tea every day of his life. The leaves are boiled for several hours, then the infusion is poured into a section of hollow bamboo, where it is churned up with a plunger, together with a handful of salt, a pinch of soda and a good lump of butter—usually rancid. The result is a purplish liquid of unusual taste for tea, but as soup excellent. The great thing is to blow aside the floating scum of butter before you drink. The moment you put the cup down, even if you have only taken a sip, it is filled up by a servant who stands ready with a silver or earthenware teapot. Custom demands that one drinks at least twice, but however much one has, the cup is always left full. To eat, we were offered dried apricots, sweets and biscuits.

In the late morning we went to a local race meeting organized by the British Trade Agency. The " Fort " is a solidly built two-storied building surrounding an open square. The rooms seem very comfortable, which is probably necessary, since in winter Gyantse is a grim place, the most frightful dust-storms raging almost every afternoon for months on end and the temperature below zero at nights. In the old days there was considerable trouble here because it was never quite clear who was the senior, the British Trade Agent or the officer in charge of the escort. As the latter was often a major and the former a captain, the position was further complicated. Later it was pointed out that as it is the British Trade Agent's escort, the B.T.A. is obviously in charge. It must be a terrible place in winter for the men's nerves, in spite of the peacefulness of the hills and the people. No English women are ever stationed here. At present it is delightful, with a wonderful vegetable garden (at 13,500 feet) and lines of pollard willows all round to act as wind-breaks.

The polo-field near by had been arranged as a race-course with a smallish track, and tents for grandstands. A pony race came first, then a yak race. Actually they were all cattle or rather under-sized *dzos*. They were ridden bareback with a single rein running from the nose-ring. Most of them ran wide, but three finished. Then there was a pacing race, in which all but one broke into a canter and were disqualified. After this came tent-pegging by the Mounted Infantry of the 2/7 Rajputs, finally egg-and-spoon races and pillow fighting on a greasy pole. It was terribly hot. Clear pale sky above, the ring of dun and olive hills shimmering in the heat, and very heavy cotton-wool clouds like stage scenery. Several hundred of the inhabitants came. The better-class ones brought tents where they drank tea and *chang* (the local beer brewed from barley). The others were incredibly dirty but very cheerful. We then lunched in a big marquee behind the Fort. All the local worthies were there in resplendent silks and brocades. To drink we had chang, which I found to be excellent. It is flat and yeasty and of the colour of cloudy lemonade. Tibetans also have a remarkable liking for crème de menthe; perhaps the colour appeals to them. I sat next to Rai Sahib Bo Tsering, the sub-

assistant surgeon, who works under the Agency doctor. He is
coming to Lhasa with us. A red-faced genial Sikkimese in loud
checks, he is a famous horse-coper and is liked by everybody.
His pony won the open race today.

August 15th: at Gyantse.—Neame and I visited the dzong.
Passed through the bazaar on the way. It lies beside the road
leading to the monastery. The goods are on trellis tables or simply
on the ground under umbrellas. Queer roots and vegetables,
rice and grain, wool, dyes, carpets, dried and fresh fruit, cups,
jewellery, swords and all sorts of odds and ends. An open sewer
runs the whole length of the street, which is absolutely filthy.
Most of the women have red pigment smeared on their faces to
protect their complexions. Innumerable scrofulous and clamorous beggars. The walls and doors are covered with lucky signs—
swastikas, stars, crescents, and above the doors are intricate devices
of rams' horns and coloured wool in geometric patterns to divert
the visitations of evil spirits. Lean and hungry dogs everywhere.
To reach the dzong we rode up and up a rough roadway. Massive
wooden gates with crudely stuffed wild yaks and mastiffs hanging
in the rafters as emblems of ferocity.

Tendong showed us round. The dzong is full of small monasteries. Saw six huge Buddhas in one room and a gigantic seventh
in a room below. Drank Tibetan tea with the monk in charge.
The dzong, which is half ruined, is built tier upon tier to the
summit of the steep rock; not unlike Mont St. Michel. Went
right up to the top. There are no staircases, so we had to pull the
ladder up from roof to roof. In a tiny dark room at the very
top sat a monk, muffled up in a heavy red cape, beating a huge
gong and praying to the spirit of the dzong. He seemed to be in
a trance and appeared quite oblivious of our presence. I felt an
unaccountable terror, as if in the presence of something deeply
sinister. Superb view: green barley-fields, blue winding rivers,
russet and sienna hills. The big monastery of Tse-chen lies on
the southern side of a rocky hill a mile or two to the north-east.
The monasteries here are more like fortified cities than the abode
of peaceful monks. One wonders exactly what goes on inside
them.

Had tea with Tendong and watched his carpet-weavers working
on the balcony outside. Three of them work on one carpet.
They use wonderful vegetable dyes of local preparation and rather

a coarse weave, but their colours and designs are good. Gyantse is famous for its carpets.

Spent afternoon sorting entomological and survey gear. Tremendous discussion about the wireless. Nepean is to stay here and get things going while Dagg returns to Calcutta to obtain a hand charging machine. We wired to Kalimpong to see if we could get the Everest Expedition charging motor, but it has been sent back to England.

In the evening Dinka Depön, the Shigatse Dzongpön, appeared to call on Gould. He is an important official, being the most senior of all the dzongpöns. A very stout man, he had ridden over at great inconvenience to discuss important matters with Gould. It appears that the Shigatse Tibetans are increasingly anxious to get the Tashi Lama back. In their eyes he is more holy than the Dalai Lama, and without his presence at Tashi-lhünpo their religious life is crippled. A cheerful dinner-party at the Agency Fort. Wonderful how the ponies know the way home in the dark.

August 16th : to Gobshi (13,800 *feet*) : 17½ *miles*.—Couldn't get away early as we had to receive scarves and were lunching with Rajah Tering on the way. Dull and raining. Followed the Nyang Chu valley. Very dried-up this side, with queer barren hillocks sticking out of stone and sand deserts. The hills are parched and seared by dried-up watercourses. It's like a landscape on a dead planet. A few lammergeyers and kites circling high up over the hill-tops. Down on the right is a fertile strip of cultivation by the river, and then the same desolate hills beyond.

Tering has a beautiful country estate—which bears his name—about six miles from Gyantse. He is noted for his hospitality and the excellence of his chang. His wife, a large cheerful woman, is a wonderful hostess. We had seen women wearing the hooped head-dress, but hers was incredible. The hoop was about two feet in radius and was held together with wide bands consisting of strings of seed pearls. The horizontal part of the hoop was studded with large stones of turquoise and coral. From a necklace hung a diamond-shaped charm-box inlaid with turquoise and other gems. " Daisy ", the son's young wife, is very pretty, and has a beautiful complexion. She has her black hair brushed back and plaited, without adornments. The room was spoilt by European furniture and inferior Chinese hangings. We had a good Tibetan lunch: a dozen small dishes—eggs, curried beans, meat, etc., then five or six big bowls of such delicacies as mince and peas, boiled mutton and mushrooms. Finally, as many bowlsful as we could drink of vermicelli soup. Chopsticks are very difficult at first, but soon yield to practice. Chang was poured out by a beautifully dressed girl. The chang jug was of silver with embossed designs picked out in gold. A magnificent and cheerful party; got away at one o'clock.

Soon after Tering the road enters a stony valley and the river rushes down below in a gorge. Further along it becomes a muddy turgid river crossed by unfenced cantilever bridges. The water coming down the side valleys is led off in aqueducts to water the fields. Gobshi is a desolate half-ruinous village at the junction of several barren valleys. It is guarded by a derelict fort on the summit of a rocky pinnacle.

Just managed to get one of the tents up before deluges of rain came down. There are no more rest-houses now and we rely solely on our tents, of which we have one each. There are also two mess tents, one of which is sent ahead.

Now that we have left behind the thirty loads of wireless and projection gear, we have 200 pack animals—ponies, mules and donkeys. A third of them have gone ahead. The arrangement is for the majority of the gear to set off at daybreak (about four o'clock); our own tents are packed up at six o'clock and, with an hour's start, get in soon after us. Of the two mess tents, one goes on at earliest dawn and is ready when we arrive, and the other is left for breakfast and for us to use after our own tents are packed. The muleteers are very careless. Each is in charge of nine or ten animals, and they let them get too far ahead, when they are apt to knock their loads against the rocks. They continually encourage their charges with loud cries. Yaks seem to respond to whistling rather than shouting. The drivers also have a wild ululating cry which they use to signal to each other at a distance: for instance, when approaching a stretch of one-way track to see if anybody is already on it.

Many flowers here in spite of the apparent barrenness of the country. Tall delphiniums and monkshood by the track, and in the hills a small deep-violet delphinium and a large blue gentian growing from a rosette of leaves. Much edelweiss and deep-red rhubarb. Many choughs and magpies here and innumerable small birds, mostly larks, wagtails, redstarts and rosefinches. Did one cypher after dinner, then pressed plants till midnight.

August 17th : to Ralung (14,800 feet) : 155 miles.—We are called at five, breakfast at six, away at seven. We crossed the Nyang Chu gorge by a high and precarious cantilever bridge, and then struck up a side valley to Ralung. Soon the gorge opened out to a narrow fertile valley. Side streams continually come in, providing irrigation water for a cone of cultivated fields. Barley does well at 14,000 feet, but the upper limit for oats seems to be 12,000 feet, and for wheat 11,000 feet, though this depends upon the amount of shelter. Along the river are dark-green twisted willows exactly like those in willow-pattern china. Just as the road cut round a projecting spur of rock I saw a clump of white spiraea. Pale emerald of artemisia up in the hills, tall yellow senecio, marvellous blue delphiniums and, for the first time, masses of an orange poppy with glaucous leaves. On each side of the valley red and orange volcanic mountains scarred with scree slopes and crags run up for 3000 feet. The houses, with their mud walls and flat roofs with dung-cakes on top, are like Egyptian villages. The desert scenery and houses make the strangest contrast to the wonderful crops and flowers in the valley bottom.

Got in at 10.30 A.M.—a fantastic time to finish the day's march. Ralung is a squalid little village at the junction of two streams. There is a walled Chinese posting-house here, still in a good state of preservation. Our camp is on a great level stretch of turf. In one place some stone paving has been put down with a square of white stones for the Dalai Lama's or Tashi Lama's tent and a pathway. They use this route when travelling to and from Lhasa.

The local headman came and presented a scarf, the dried year-old carcase of a sheep, and a box of eggs. Unfortunately practically all the latter were bad. Climbed a hill behind the camp. There is a magnificent view over to the peaks and glaciers by the Karo La, which we cross tomorrow. These mountains run up to 23,500 feet, and no one has ever tried to climb them though they do not look at all difficult. Many small tortoise-shell and blue butterflies here, and an astonishing variety of beetles and flies. The country ahead is exactly like the north of Sikkim. There is no cultivation, just wide rolling valleys with winding streams in the centre of them, and grassy foot-hills going up to 18,000 or 19,000 feet. The dark tents of nomads are conspicuous again, and immense herds of yaks, sheep and goats. The nomads have black mastiffs with them, but dogs are never used to round up the animals, only for protection against wolves. Over the other side of the hill I could see Ralung monastery where monks and nuns are housed together. This sect are permitted to marry and the children follow their parents' calling. Ralung means " the valley of the goat ".

Carefully following Nepean's directions I joined up innumerable different-coloured wires to aerials, batteries of all sizes, accumulators, earths, and a portable wireless set. As I have never touched a set before—except to turn knobs—we were all very surprised when it worked and we could get the news. An ibisbill and several redshanks are calling down by the stream.

August 18th : to Dzara (15,700 *feet) : 16 miles.*—Followed Ralung valley for a time, then crossed a wide level plain of wonderful pasture-land. Terribly hot sun. Saw a buzzard. Filmed a party of wild-looking herdsmen sitting round a yak-dung fire eating barley-meal and tea. Innumerable mouse-hares on the plain but no kiang or gazelle. Magnificent view of the glaciers and snows ahead. Soon we turned to the right and followed a narrow valley to the summit of the Karo La (16,800 feet). Met a big party of yaks coming down with wool. They prefer to walk on the rocky broken land by the stream rather than on the track, and are in fact, in spite of their efficiency, the most wayward and grotesque of animals. Saw a wall-creeper, my favourite bird; last one I saw was on the Grepon at Chamonix. The track follows a rocky river-bed with steep pudding-stone rocks on each side leading up to precipitous snow-clad mountains with hanging glaciers. Heard a snow-cock clucking up on the right. Extraordinary luxuriance of plants : even juniper, roses and jasmine grow here up to 15,000 feet, as well as the usual delphiniums and saxifrages. Near the summit are wide level valleys as if the gorge has at some time been dammed up by landslides. Crossed a river of glacier water by a bridge—not many bridges at 16,000 feet! On the summit are two cairns joined by festoons of prayer-flags. All the muleteers raise their hats and shout *Lha Gya-lo* (God be praised). A continuous stream of baggage animals over this pass. On the descent we noticed wide subsidiary valleys of rolling grassland up to 19,000 feet, without any snow.

Soon came to our camp on a stretch of level ground beside the altogether desolate village of Dzara, which has a Chinese posting-house as protection against the brigands for which this valley is famous. On the far side of the stream I saw several large marmots sitting up like kangaroos. They are brown and cream, and have faces like otters. The largest stand three feet high. They have a loud shrill whistle like a bird, and when disturbed run awkwardly along the ground and disappear down their burrows. They hibernate all the winter.

After lunch Richardson and I climbed a mountain behind the camp. The top thousand feet consisted of enormous granite boulders piled together. Among the rocks we found the skull and most of the skeleton of a Tibetan. A little farther up we found the pigtail, rotten but still plaited, caught between two rocks. Probably one of the casualties of the 1904 battle; for there are still the remains of walls here put up by the Tibetans to stop the British Mission. A heavy snowstorm is sweeping over the pass, which is spread below us like a map. There are two lakes here surrounded by glaciers and snowy peaks. Several parties of burrhal in the hills. Found a new striped blue gentian and a pale delphinium with sticky foliage and a nauseous smell of cheap scent and sweat; we are going to call it *Aconitum Barmaidiae.* Had tea in Richardson's tent and discussed books while a sleet-storm raged outside. Dzara in this weather is the bleakest and most unfriendly place in the world.

August 19th : to Nangartse (14,500 *feet*) : 14 *miles.*—Bitterly cold morning with new snow on the ground and a chilling wind. Sun not up yet, so we walked on ahead of the ponies to get warm. This side of the pass is unutterably wild and desolate with bare scree slopes leading up to overhanging rocks and snow-sprinkled stony summits. The gorge narrowed occasionally and there was only just room for the track between the stream and the rocky spurs. Soon we got out of the gorge into open pasture-land. There are several forts on conical hill-tops, long prayer-walls beside the track, and Buddhas and prayers carved and painted on the rocks. Many burrhal up in the hills and gazelle on the wide plain beside the lake, which we can see in front of us. The rounded mountains on the left run down to a massive fort on a spur above Nangartse village, which is separated from the lake by a mile or two of very green grass. Thousands of animals grazing on the level turf. The lake is intensely blue, and rounded green hills rise on the far side of the water. The fort is most impressive, with grim bare whitewashed walls, and a line of dark red along the summit.

On the far side of the plain is the famous monastery of Samding, which is the home of Dorje Phagmo, the "Thunderbolt Sow", the only female incarnation in Tibet. With the Dalai and Tashi Lamas (and in former days the Chinese Ambans) she shares the privilege of being allowed to ride in a palanquin.

Our camp lies at the foot of the dzong. After lunch and some cypher work Richardson and I walked down to the lake. A fresh wind now raising white and angry waves on the pale emerald waters of the reedy shallows. Out in the middle are deep-blue spray-flecked strips of water, and beyond, the purple hills are greyed by passing snowstorms—for all the world like a stormy Scottish loch.

This is the Yamdrok Tso, "the lake of the upper pastures". It is about fifty miles long and almost as wide. In the centre is a piece of land twenty miles across, which would be an island were it not joined by an isthmus near Samding. This peninsula itself contains a lake of considerable size. The water is very slightly brackish and has recently receded, judging by the wide plain which is only a foot or two higher than the lake. It is at a height of 14,500 feet above sea-level.

Small waxy pink primulas, yellow pedicularis and mauve asters flower profusely beside the lake, and there are hundreds of bar-headed geese, Brahminy ducks (the same as our ruddy shelduck) and other wildfowl. On the south-facing hill-side beside Samding is a gróve of large willows—surely one of the highest in the world; juniper, wild roses and clematis also flourish.

The two dzongpöns came to present scarves. One is a monk, the other a layman. They seem to work very well together; often one would start a sentence and the other would finish it. They brought the usual presents of dried sheep, eggs and peas.

At four o'clock there was a thunderstorm followed by heavy rain. We have about forty tents on the plain and resemble a small army. I hope the Tibetans are duly impressed!

August 20th; to Pede (14,500 feet) : 16½ miles.—Off early in spite of the rain. The dzongpöns rode out a mile or two to present scarves. There are many chortens and massive prayer-walls in the road, while rock frescoes increase in number as we approach Lhasa.

All day we rode along beside the lake. I kept a rough check of the pack-animals going south: about 1250 passed us today, of which nearly half were yaks. It is extraordinary how the yaks avoid the track and choose the roughest sort of country. Very often grassy flats lay between the track and the lake, and we could cut across. Saw a grebe's nest floating, and hundreds of sand-martins on the telegraph wire. Many goosanders on the lake and snow-finches and mountain-finches hopping about in the roadway. A pair of black-necked cranes strutted about in a marsh. When I went to photograph them I was attacked by hungry mosquitoes. The birds here are quite tame: I can get within forty yards of goosanders on the lake and even nearer to the cranes. An old fish-eagle sitting (most unsuitably) on a telegraph post allowed me to walk right up to the foot of the post. There is also a strange little bird called a ground-chough that allows me to get quite close; he seems to share burrows with the mouse-hares.

A causeway cuts off a mile of the road just where the Shigatse track branches away to the east. Here we saw innumerable fish, some up to 3 lb. weight. They looked like char. The wild flowers were surprisingly beautiful. On the upper side of the path was the most superb natural rock-garden, while the boulders themselves were carved with exquisitely coloured Buddhas. Deep-blue and violet delphiniums three feet high literally covered the rocks for hundreds of yards. It was just like one of Sutton's seed fields. There were also several kinds of gentian, yellow marigolds, a lavender-coloured mint and clumps of yellow asters. The grass beside the lake was carpeted with bright-yellow pedicularis.

Soon we saw Pede Dzöng on the end of a point running out into the lake. It is just like an old Scottish castle. Unlike Nangartse Dzöng, it is now ruined. The village lies behind. In the valley nearby barley and peas grow very well in spite of the height. We finished our ride in pouring rain and camped on a flooded field beyond the dzong. There are prayer-flags even here in the water, tied to bamboo poles which are stuck into the

H

bottom of the lake. Spent two hours doing Tibetan, and stayed up till eleven pressing flowers.

August 21st : to Singma Kang-chung (11,700 feet) : 11 miles.—Set off at dawn. Overcast. Crossed Nyapso La to Tsang-po (Brahmaputra) valley. Followed the lake for a few miles, then rode up a fertile valley to the left past some square buildings like blockhouses. I suppose these isolated farms and villages must be capable of withstanding the attacks of bandits.

A superb view over the arms of this fantastic lake. It looks more like a Scottish loch every day except that there is no heather on the hills. There are fertile valleys and villages on the far side, but many signs of a decreasing population. Today we must have passed dozens of ruins in small valleys where the terraces of former cultivation and aqueducts still show. The ancient buildings seem to have been taller and even more strongly built than the modern ones.

The top of the Nyapso La is 16,000 feet above sea-level. The ascent was fairly easy. Drifting cloud spread over the top. I left my pony with my groom and started to walk down. Suddenly the mist started to clear, and I found myself gazing through a hole in the clouds into the mysterious Brahmaputra valley, 4500 feet below me. Through this I saw a wide silvery river winding its way among the sandy waste caused by its annual floods. On the far side were areas of rich cultivation and groves of willows on the lower valleys of high mountain ranges. For years this great river flowing at 11,500 feet from east to west beyond the Himalaya was known, but it was not till the adventurous boat journey of Morshead and Bailey that this was proved to be the same as the Brahmaputra of Assam.

The track here descends in a series of steep zigzags. As we got lower the vegetation became more and more luxuriant, and I found many new flowers. A wine-coloured primula, a blue gentian two feet high, periwinkle, and the usual delphiniums and asters. This valley is riotously fertile. Saw a partridge near our camp, which is in a field beside a willow grove.

After lunch I went down to pay my respects to the river, and found a turbid brownish torrent surging past at great speed, never breaking into waves—nothing so undignified—but with fearful power in its writhing eddies. At this time of year, with the melting snow-water from the Himalaya augmented by the torrential monsoon rains, the Tsang-po is at least 400 feet wide even where it is constricted into a single channel. Up to the east are two pointed rock mountains covered in snow. They should just be climbable.

Found clumps of iris here; it has long since flowered, but I got some seeds. Found a new blue flower. Watched an ibisbill by the river. Blackbirds are fluting in the willow groves, and turtle-doves cooing. Again we are in a different world. The barley here is golden ripe and as fine a crop as I have seen anywhere. The women cut it with sickles, singing as they work. There are cherry trees here and apricots. Clouded over and came on to rain.

Morgan, as usual, receives patients and administers medicines. They are nearly all cases of venereal disease. Spent evening pressing flowers and doing a cypher. Millions of midges come in round our pressure-lamps.

August 22nd: to Chu-shur (11,600 *feet*): 16 *miles.*—A very thrilling day though dull and overcast—the two pinnacle peaks only occasionally showing through. Many butterflies here, painted ladies, tortoise-shell, dark clouded yellows and blues, also hundreds of big black beetles with red markings on their backs.

We cross the river here by coracle as it is too swollen for the Chaksam ferries to be used. Chaksam is twelve miles farther down. Rode for a mile over rough stony ground where extra banking has been built to hold in the river. The coracles are rectangular and made of yak-hide stretched over a framework of willow branches. Each boat is about 8 feet by 6 feet, and weighs 80 to 90 lb. During the crossing they get swept down nearly half a mile, so the boatmen lift the coracles on to their heads and walk up-stream again, afterwards propping the boats up on one oar to dry. They float very high out of the water and are abso-lutely unstreamlined. Although one boat is fairly steady, for greater safety we used them lashed together end to end in couples. The unfortunate ponies had to swim alongside while one of the boatmen held the head ropes. As the men would insist on taking three or four together, and the ponies plunged about and got very excited, the back ones were apt to get kicked by those in front. Several broke away before we could persuade them to take to the water, but they soon returned when they saw their companions had disappeared. Rai Sahib Bo's best pony, the one that won the race at Gyantse the other day, got kicked on the way across and, having reached the far shore, broke loose and swam back, but it got washed away downstream and was drowned. Two others that broke back succeeded in getting safely across.

The boatmen row furiously with oars like ping-pong bats on the ends of poles, but even then the coracles go ten yeards downstream for every yard across. We changed transport here, so only the loads had to be ferried across and this had been accomplished without loss early in the morning. Actually most of the baggage is going the whole way to Chu-shur by boat; we ourselves are not allowed to go by boat as it is considered too dangerous and undignified.

On the far bank a Tibetan appliqué-worked tent had been put up, and we were given chang and Tibetan tea by the local headmen. Then a procession of wild-looking yet obsequious ruffians appeared with the usual presents: dried carcases of sheep, eggs and grain. We had a grand gallop over the sandy plain, where there are many prayer-walls and chortens. Cinnamon sparrows nest in these. The banks of the river are too high here to allow of any irrigation, and only at the foot of streams coming from the hills are there villages, monasteries and cultivation. The valley is dead flat and the mountains rise straight out of the plain as from the sea. The river has reduced miles of land to sandy wastes with occasional islands of willow scrub. The sand-storms must be terrible in winter.

We can see the Kamba La zigzagging up the hills. This is the pass used when Chaksam ferry is running. We rode by some huge walnut trees, also peaches, apricots, cherries, alders, poplars and willows. The crops—barley, oats, a little wheat, beans, peas and potatoes—look very rich. We also passed a very beautiful monastery beside the track. The windows and doorways were exquisitely carved and coloured, the chortens pierced by archways under which we rode. There were window-boxes full of bright flowers, and very lovely trees.

Had lunch by the river. Saw a cormorant and watched a pair of Tibetan babax making loud fluting notes—the first we have seen or heard.

A very high percentage of the people here have goitres, sometimes of enormous size. Although the valley is so fertile the peasants seem very poor and ill-clad. There are many alternative tracks winding through the willow groves and fields; some are flooded, others are so rocky that the ponies can scarcely use them, and it is quite difficult to find the way.

It is curious that the sand carried down and left by the flooded river has been blown up into the hills by the winter storms so that valleys several thousand feet above the river are completely choked with sand which is formed into dappled drifts by the wind.

Just before Chu-shur a number of rocky spurs come right down to the river, which throws itself against the foot of the hills in a fearsome boiling torrent. The track was, in many places, under water, so dozens of ragged men and boys were waiting to lead our ponies for the last mile or two. Even then the water came up to our stirrups. One false step and horse and rider would have been swirled away for good.

There are two ruined dzongs perched high up on the pinnacles of the serrated spur which protects the village. Bhuddas, prayer-flags, piles of stones and carved prayers are scattered all along this part of the track, and little shrines protected by iron grilles. At the foot of Chu-shur village is a prayer-wall fifty yards long encircled by slates with attractive coloured deities carved thereon. Some prosperous farms here. Our camp is in a grove of stately pollard willows.

After lunch I climbed to the ruined dzong and had an impressive view of the Tsang-po in flood. The Kyi Chu (meaning either " river of happiness " or " middle river "), the stream on which Lhasa stands, joins the Tsang-po at Chu-shur, and it too is flooded. Each of these rivers has innumerable channels which join and part again, leaving scrub-covered island and sand-banks. The river-beds are therefore about two miles wide. In the other direction lay the rich cultivation of the Chu-shur valley, with yellow-gold fields of mustard, dark-green pea-fields and the varying shades of ripening oats and barley.

The sun was setting in tattered storm-clouds above the Tsang-po, and long shafts of light filled the valley with molten silver.

A busy evening packing up film to be sent to India for processing.

August 23rd : to Nethang (11,600 *feet*) : 23 *miles.*—It is most important to reach the Holy City on an auspicious date, so we are doing a double march today and getting to Lhasa early tomorrow

morning. All day we followed the Kyi Chu, sometimes crossing level arid plains, at other times splashing through water or
following precarious tracks over spurs which jutted out into the
flooded river-bed. Wherever there is any irrigation the land
abounds with rich crops and groves of trees, but in between these
oases the scenery is as desolate and barren as any we have passed.
The more shallow valleys and the hills themselves are completely
smothered in sand; for miles on end nothing grows except coarse
grass and weeds. At the heads of the valleys are red and white
monasteries and small villages. More traffic than ever today,
mostly wool. Many monks on the road; they are usually bare-
footed, but often carry their boots to save wear. In one place
reddish granite cliffs rose for a thousand feet above the track,
which limped along beside the river. It was exactly like stage
scenery—the clear blue sky, hard cumulus clouds as if cut out of
cardboard, red rocks going straight up in magnificent cliffs and
overhangs, and farther up the valley the blue hills surrounding
Lhasa flecked with transient cloud shadows.

About half-way we were met by a monk official who is to be
one of our guides during our stay. He is a fifth-rank official in
Lhasa, but he counts as fourth rank away from the city. He is a
very polished and intelligent man. Oddly enough, his mulberry-
coloured robe, which is quite new, has small patches on it, not
because it is torn but, I suppose, to indicate conventional poverty.
He rides a fine pacing mule and wears a remarkable wide-brimmed
hat of papier-mâché, covered with gold lacquer. I gather he has
travelled in China and other places. Hence his cleanliness and
savoir-faire.

Nethang is a fair-sized village in the middle of the valley. The
tomb of Atisha is here, the originator of the yellow hat or reformed
church of Tibet. He came up from India just before the Norman
Conquest of England. We camped on a grassy field just beside
the river. Watched a pair of ibisbills and some ringed plover.
Many hoopoes here. Heavy rain in the evening. Some coracles
swished by, doing a good ten knots; one was laden with red
earthenware pots, another with skins of butter.

August 24th : to Lhasa (11,800 *feet*) : 16 *miles*.—Lhasa at last :
the Holy and Forbidden City. Had anyone told me a year ago
that I should be in Lhasa today, I would not even for a moment
have taken him seriously.

Country similar to yesterday's. Far ahead we can see a grey-green hill-side in the middle of which is a small hermitage some 3000 feet above the river. This, says Norbhu, is exactly above Drepung, the largest monastery in the world. In one place the flooded river forced us to climb a granite spur. The track became a rocky staircase with a sheer drop on the right-hand side into the deep clear pools below. From up there we saw the monastery of the State Oracle at Nechung just beside Drepung. I could see a golden roof in a grove of large trees. This temple is only four miles from Lhasa. A serrated spur coming down on the opposite side of the Kyi Chu shuts off any view of the Potala [1] Palace or of the city. After taking to the rocks again we passed a colossal Buddha carved in low relief on the rock. This figure is seated and faces the Holy City. In front of it is a huge pile of small stones collected as an offering.

Once more the flooded track forced us to take an alternative path over a spur, and this time, at a distance of ten miles, we had our first view of the Potala, the monastery palace of the Dalai Lamas. In the centre of the wide valley, which is thickly clustered with groves of trees, two cones of rock reach up some 700 feet above the plain. The one on the right is the Iron Hill, on which the Medical College stands; on the other is the Potala, seen from here as a white building surmounted by the glittering roof pavilions which cover the mortal remains of former Dalai Lamas. The city itself is completely hidden by these two hills.

The valley here is broad and fertile, though large parts of it are completely inundated or covered with rushes. The villages look more cheerful and prosperous. From the left another valley joins the Kyi Chu and we saw a large monastery in a bay of the hills. There are many country villas in groves of willows; and crops of barley, oats, peas, beans and potatoes.

This tributary river is fifty yards wide and is kept in check with long stone embankments. The old cantilever bridge called Trisum Sampa used to be washed away almost every summer, so now they are replacing it by a modern construction of girders. At present there are two wooden arches and one of steel. The Government refused to have an engineer up from India, so photographs were sent down in charge of a young official who had been at Ludlow's school and spoke a little English. All the girders

[1] Pronounced *Po-ta-la*, with each syllable equally accentuated.

had to be carried right across the Himalaya on the backs of coolies. They followed the instructions and, having assembled all the pieces, which were of course numbered, they put the bridge together. Rumour has it that there were some thirty girders unaccountably left over, but the bridge seems to hold and they are going to build another one with the surplus.

Avoiding more flooded land, we reached a village called Shingdonkar, where there is a disused Chinese fort. The road climbs steeply between the flat-roofed houses to cross yet another jagged granite spur, gay with prayer-flags and wall paintings. Most of the inhabitants came out to have a look at us. They are incredibly dirty and ill-clad, many are goitrous. The children are often stark naked. Everybody seems very cheerful and friendly. Anyone on horseback dismounts as a sign of respect. The whole valley here seems to be laid waste by the river, whose various channels fill the valley for a width of about two miles. The islands between are sandy and bare or else covered with thorn and willow scrub.

Just short of Drepung Monastery we were met by Möndö, a monk official who, by the most remarkable anomaly, is an Old Rugbeian. Many years ago the last Dalai Lama, a man of very advanced ideas, decided, on the advice of the Government of India, to send four boys to be educated in England. Gould took them home in 1913, and after some discussion they were sent to Rugby and were later trained respectively as a soldier, a surveyor, a mining and an electrical engineer. Möndö, who was already a monk when he went to England, is the mining engineer, but having tried unsuccessfully to overcome the prejudice of the monks to his activities, he has returned to more normal work and is here to welcome us on behalf of the Lhasa Government. Möndö is now a man of between thirty-five and forty. He is a large, genial man, with cropped hair and a moustache. He still speaks the most delightful English, fairly idiomatic and perfectly pronounced. We were also met and presented with scarves by our lay guide, a young official in splendid clothes. He wears a flowered-silk robe the colour of fallen beech-leaves, and over it a loose sleeveless gown of the brightest scarlet lined with pale blue. His flat-topped hat of yellow wool balances on top of his head like a porridge-bowl. The monk and the lay guides are to be attached to the Mission during our stay at Lhasa.

Just after this we passed below Drepung Monastery, which lies across the head of a sandy valley running up to the hills on our left. From here it is very much foreshortened, but even so it looks like a large and fortified city with a long white wall running across the front of it, and tier behind tier of buildings, some with golden roof pavilions, others with cylindrical ornaments or fluttering prayer-flags to relieve the monotony of their straight lines. Below the monastery, just beside the road, live a community of butchers who supply the monastery and city with meat, in spite of the Buddhist prohibitions against taking life.

From here to Lhasa, a distance of three miles, the road is built up on a causeway between reed-covered marshes where pink water-lilies bloom.

We were soon met by more officials, who escorted us to a small roadside tea-garden which, being half-way between the Potala and Drepung, was in former times used by the Dalai Lamas as a resting place. It is called the Garden of the Mystics. Here we rode into a walled enclosure where a tent had been put up for our reception. We were then presented with scarves on behalf of the Regent, Prime Minister and Cabinet. After which we sat on low mattress-like cushions in front of beautifully carved and lacquered tables on which Tibetan tea and biscuits were served. The servants wore dark homespun robes and wide flat-topped hats covered with scarlet tasselling exactly like lamp-shades. The officials are all most courteous and friendly, and full of solicitous enquiries about our health and the discomfort of the journey.

On the right of the track a high sand-bank marks the route of an aqueduct; on the left is a level grassy plain, on which was today drawn up a Guard of Honour, consisting of a company of soldiers and another of police, complete with flying colours and two military bands. They presented arms and so on, while Gould was introduced to the officers. The two young army generals were dressed in extremely smart uniforms, but the soldiers gave rather a comic-opera effect, being dressed in khaki uniforms and battered Wolseley topees, from the back of which their pigtails hung down somewhat incongruously. But they drilled and marched better than one would have expected. Perhaps because the Chief of Police is another Rugbeian called Kyipup. Half the population of Lhasa had come down to see us. They looked a cosmopolitan crowd: a few Chinese, several

H 2

turbaned Ladakis, blue-uniformed soldiers of the escort to the Nepalese representative, Mongolian traders, nomad yak-herds from the desolate high plateau of the Chang Tang, and always crowds of sullen monks with shaven heads and bare arms.

Riding along flooded roads between groves of willows we reached the Deyki Lingka (" garden of happiness "), a small house that has been lent to us by the Abbot of the near-by Gundeling monastery.

CHAPTER FIVE

THE LHASA OFFICIALS COME TO CALL

OUR first four days at Lhasa were taken up in entertaining an almost continuous stream of callers, varying in rank from the Prime Minister to the lowest Government secretaries. The arrival and departure of this kaleidoscopic procession of gorgeously clad monk and lay officials gave us a unique opportunity, at the very outset of our visit, to make the acquaintance of this privileged class of Tibetan society and to find out something of the peculiar government of the country. On the day before an official intended to call he would send a secretary or servant round to Norbhu to arrange a suitable hour for his arrival. No serious matters were discussed on these preliminary visits; they were simply occasions for presenting scarves of welcome and for exchanging conventional compliments. Gould, as Political Officer, supported by Neame and myself, received visitors in our upper room; while Richardson, as British Trade Agent, Gyantse, received them afterwards in a specially appointed tent at the end of the garden.

No sooner had we finished lunch on the day of our arrival than Yuto Depön, a young general of the army, came to deliver to the Mission scarves of greeting and presents from the Cabinet Ministers. He was dressed in the smartest of British-made military uniforms, but wore the single long turquoise ear-ring and had his hair tied with red ribbon into the usual double top-knot with a turquoise and gold charm-box in the centre. This

CROSSING THE YAMDROK LAKE IN FEBRUARY. NINGDZINGZONKA (23,000 ft.) IN BACKGROUND. NAN-GARTSE VILLAGE IS VISIBLE BEYOND THE WHITE PONY'S HEAD

THE OLD ABBOT OF SERA
MONASTERY

THE LORD CHAMBERLAIN
(CHIKYAK KHEM-PO)

LHASA : WE ENTERTAIN VISITORS, NORBHU, TRIMON, TSARONG

A NOMAD HEADMAN—BANDIT

A NOMAD WOMAN

A DISPOSER OF DEAD BODIES

A VILLAGE HEADMAN

AN OUTCAST'S TENT SURROUNDED BY A WALL OF BONES FROM ANIMALS HE HAS SLAUGHTERED

THE LATE DALAI LAMA
(FROM A PHOTOGRAPH SEEN IN LHASA)

THE PRIME MINISTER WITH
HIS WIFE AND DAUGHTER

A LHASA STREET WITH CEREMONIAL FIRE PREPARED

AN OFFICIAL'S LHASA HOUSE

CEREMONIAL TRUMPETS ON THE ROOF OF GUNDELING MONASTERY. THE TRUMPET STAND AND TURRET ARE COVERED IN GOLD LEAF

PAGODA COVERING THE LATE DALAI LAMA'S TOMB

IMAGES IN A TIBETAN MONASTERY

KAMPA DANCERS

A TINY INCARNATION LAMA IN THE REGENT'S PROCESSION

DANCE BY SOLDIERS WEARING ANCIENT ARMOUR

THE POTALA FROM THE EAST. NOMADS PERFORMING HOLY WALK

NORBHU LINGKA STABLES

A TIBETAN LEWIS-GUN SECTION, SHOWING OLD AND NEW UNIFORMS

LHASA UNITED FOOTBALL TEAM

RUGBEIANS ALL : MONDO, KYIPUP (CITY MAGISTRATE) AND RINGANG

TSARONG'S HOUSEHOLD DURING NEW YEAR CELEBRATIONS
TSARONG AND HIS WIFE

DELE RABDEN'S WIFE, MARY TERING, DAISY TERING

MONASTERY TO THE NORTH OF LHASA

ornament is worn by all Lhasa officials of fifth or higher rank, and by the sons of a few of the noble families who are in Government service.   Yuto, as well as being a Depön, comes from a very important Lhasa family: one of his ancestors was a Cabinet Minister at the time of the 1904 Mission.   Neame congratulated him on the turn-out and drill of the Guard of Honour, but Yuto disclaimed all credit, saying that owing to lack of practice he had forgotten all he had learnt in India, and was afraid that the Brigadier would laugh at the uniforms and drill of the soldiers.

The presents consisted of boxes of eggs, goat-skins of butter, striped woven bags of peas for our horses, and dried carcases of sheep.   The latter, still having the black hair on their heads and being dried in a life-like attitude, looked strangely pathetic stacked in line against the wall of our courtyard.   The butter was unfortunately rancid, and in any case goat-skins are not ideal containers.   When we came to test the eggs, only one in ten would sink; the others were not actually bad, but having been kept for so long in the dry Tibetan climate most of the contents had evaporated so that they floated right on top of the water like bubbles.

Our next visitors were the three lay members of the Cabinet, the Shap-pes, who came in their magnificence to pay a cere-monial call.   Although Norbhu had sent round a watch as requested, so that they would know our time, they arrived an hour late.   As we had discovered on the journey up, time means very little in Tibet.   The first sign of their approach was the arrival of a mounted servant, who came at a rapid amble to see that everything was prepared.   He was followed by a group of secretaries and servants on horseback, about two dozen in all, who came splashing through the flood-water of our drive.   The secretaries wore long broadcloth robes of an indigo colour held in at the waist with red and yellow sashes, from the back of which hung a small holder with chop-sticks and a jade-handled knife, pockets and other knick-knacks.   Pen-cases, often beauti-fully worked in brass, were pushed into their sashes.   Curious flat-topped hats of yellow wool were balanced like basins on top of their heads.   These looked most precarious but were actually clipped securely over the top-knot of hair.   The servants, who were surprisingly dirty, wore dark homespun robes and wide flat-topped hats tasselled with scarlet.   In the middle of their long plaits turquoise and gold charm-boxes were worn. Some were armed with whips with which to control the crowd.

The Shap-pes themselves rode slowly in order of seniority, one on a mule and the others on fine ponies. A row of wooden stools covered with carpet had been put out beside the path, and here they dismounted, the senior official using the highest step. Two servants held the horse, another steadied the stirrup, while two more took the Shap-pe's hands and carefully helped him down the step.

The Shap-pes were splendidly dressed in robes of saffron-yellow silk, with an interwoven dragon pattern which junior officials may not use. The robe, held in at the waist by a scarlet sash, comes right up to the neck, where a white silk shirt folds down over the collar. Like all Tibetan robes, it folds across the chest and is fastened by small gilt buttons under the right arm and down the right side: thus, with the belt, forming a large breast-pocket. The sleeves are cut very long indeed, while the cuffs of the inner shirt, unless folded back, come almost to the ground. The inevitable long ear-ring is worn and a wide-brimmed gold brocade hat, with coral and turquoise insignia on the top. From this ornament red tasselling hangs down as far as the brim, while from this two further strips of braid, united in a jewelled clasp, hang over the shoulders.

Norbhu, being a Dzasa, was similarly dressed. He came out to the courtyard to meet them and, putting his hands together before him, bowed to each in turn. The Shap-pes walked slowly, with a curiously self-conscious rocking gait, as though they were not accustomed to such exercise, as indeed is probably the case. Once upstairs, each bowed deeply to the Political Officer and presented him with a silk scarf, which he produced from the fold of his robe; after Gould had returned a similar scarf, they shook hands. When we had all exchanged scarves they sat down on the divans, strictly in order of precedence, while Gould had to take the highest seat of honour, beneath the canopy, as he is accorded the honorary title of Lon-chen (chief minister) and is therefore equal in rank to the Prime Minister and only inferior to God on Earth, at present incarnate in the person of the Regent. The Shap-pes sat cross-legged with their red, blue and white striped boots hidden in the skirts of their long robes. They did not remove their hats, as this was a ceremonial visit.

Langchungna, the senior Shap-pe by virtue of his having served longest, is not a striking personality. He rarely says anything, except to agree with the others, and habitually wears an expression of good-natured complacency. When he smiles his eyes disappear. His skin is completely covered with pock marks. Unlike most Tibetans, his hair is falling out and, in company with his straggly beard, is quite grey. He is very conservative, continually saying that Lhasa is not what it was when he was a boy, especially with regard to the weather, the deterioration of which, he declares, coincided with the installation of electric light. He says that wireless and electric light have made the winters stuffy. Nobody quite knows why he was made a Shap-pe, as he is neither of noble family nor of conspicuous brilliance. The story goes that when there was a vacancy in the Council several names were submitted to the Dalai Lama for choice. His Holiness, for some reason imagining that his Ministers were trying to coerce him to select a certain popular official, asked for more and more names of possible candidates, and at last chose a certain Langchungna, whom nobody had considered and who was at that time commander of Gartok in western Tibet.

Bhondong Shap-pe is a much younger man. He has a fat face, with a ready grin, and a moustache drooping over the corners of his mouth like a Mandarin. As he was for many years Secretary to the Cabinet, and successfully won his way to his present position, he has a great knowledge of the Lhasa methods of government. Being in possession of several estates formerly belonging to the Tashi Lama, he is popularly supposed to be opposing the return of that unfortunate Prelate. But withal he is a genuine fellow and is undoubtedly efficient.

Tendong Shap-pe was Depön in Kham for many years and has the reputation of being a great fighter. He is a large-featured and rather ugly man, of great natural charm and distinction. His skin is deeply pitted with smallpox scars.

To me the whole interview had an extraordinary air of unreality, as if I were watching a play or dreaming. On one side Gould, with carefully trimmed moustache and immaculate Saville Row suiting, smilingly made polite conversation that seemed additionally unreal in that none of the Tibetans could understand a word of it. Then Norbhu, interpreting, swallowing

his words with excitement, and the four Shap-pes bowing in
unison and smiling deferentially at each remark. The word
" lha-les " was continually used by both our guests and by
Norbhu, whispered with a swift sucking-in of the breath and a
quick bow. It may be interpreted " Yes, your Honour ". The
conversation followed traditional lines. I wondered how many
times old Langchungna had heard it before.

   Shap-pe (with Norbhu interpreting) : Is your noble self in good
      health?
   P.O. : Yes, thank your honour : and you?
   Shap-pe : Very well, thank you. Have you had a pleasant
      journey? No trouble of any sort on the way?
   P.O. : Thanks to your excellent arrangements no trouble at
      all, thank you.
   Shap-pe : I hope you did not feel the cold.
   P.O. : No, thank you; it was, in fact, pleasantly warm.
   Shap-pe : I hope you will find your house comfortable.
   And so it went on.

The Shap-pes also recalled the fact that the Political Officer
had a twenty-five-year acquaintanceship with Tibet, having
been British Trade Agent, Gyantse, in 1912, when he met the
Dalai Lama, and then in the following year having taken the
four Tibetan boys to England.

Tea was served meanwhile, with biscuits and cake, followed
by liqueurs. Crème de menthe was the most popular and after
that Benedictine. It seemed to be the custom to refuse everything the first time and then to accept under pressure. After a
time the Shap-pes whispered that the Political Officer must be
very busy and that they would now go, but that they would
meet again soon. They also declared their gratitude that the
Government of India had sent so senior an officer to advise them,
and they were sure that subsequent deliberations would be
auspicious.

The moment they got up there was a scurrying outside, as
servants rushed about getting the ponies ready for their departure. The trappings of the animals were most resplendent.
The saddle was padded with scarlet brocade and above this was
a piece of brightly coloured carpet material to keep off the dust.
The heavy stirrups of finely worked brass were padded with
cloth so that they would not damage the rider's boots. Over

the horse's forehead was a diamond-shaped piece of gaily woven cloth and from its neck and chest hung two scarlet tassels, which can only be carried by officials of fifth or higher rank.

As each Shap-pe climbed his wooden stool and mounted, servants smoothed the saddle-cloth and carefully straightened out his robes. With much bowing and smiling the Cabinet rode away. It was an unforgettable sight: the rich saffron of the Shap-pes' robes, the wide scarlet hats of the servants, the quick green of the pollard willows, the soft olives and duns of the far mountains against the pale turquoise sky.

In the afternoon the fourth member of the Cabinet came to pay his respects, apologizing that he had been unable to leave his duties in the morning so as to accompany his colleagues. This was the Kalön Lama, the ecclesiastical Cabinet Minister. He wore his terra-cotta monk's robe over the top of his yellow Shap-pe's silk and a square embroidered water-bottle cover hanging from his girdle. He also wore the stiff wide-brimmed monk official's hat of papier-mâché covered with gold lacquer. His boots were of the " Union Jack " pattern, but very much turned up at the toes, in the manner of the usual monk official's footwear. He seemed to be a mild and courteous old man of no special distinction. He said that the political situation was indeed serious, but that he didn't know what to do about it. After all, he said, he was a peaceful monk and what was he to know about Chinese escorts and machine guns? Actually I think he knows more than one would guess.

On the second day we received a call from the Dzasa of Reting Monastery, the chief official attached to the household of the Regent, on whose behalf he came to arrange our formal visit to the Potala to present ourselves to the Regent and Prime Minister. The former being at present the highest person in the land does not call on visitors, and the latter can only do so after they have first called on him.

Dzasa is a title conferred on monks or laymen who have rendered particularly meritorious service to the state. As a rule it is a non-hereditary title, but there are one or two noble houses that always have a Dzasa in the family. At this time there were six. Four were living inside the country, and two—Norbhu and Layden La, the Darjeeling-Tibetan Deputy Commissioner of Police who had come up to organize the new police force some years ago and died while we were in Lhasa—were living outside. The two Commissioners of Kham have also of recent years held this title.

Another Dzasa who came to pay his respects was the owner of our house, the head of the neighbouring Gundeling Monastery; though the incarnate lama, who is the spiritual head of the monastery, resides at Sera. Dzasa Gundeling is a leading power in the National Assembly, a body which will be described later. He is a most impressive man, very tall for a Tibetan and vigorous in spite of his advanced age, and with a deeply lined face full of character and determination. Though he has a charming gentle manner, he is obviously one of the most forceful personalities in Lhasa.

We also received a visit from the Lord Chamberlain (*chikyap kempo*), a very aged Lama who is the supreme head of the ecclesiastical organization of Tibet. He is also the chief official of the Dalai Lama's household, is responsible for the upkeep of the Potala, and is in charge of all the Lhasa parks. He is a frail and courteous old man who suffers from rheumatism and over-work. Soon after him came the Grand Secretaries for Clerical Affairs (*trung-yik chempo*), four monk officials who compose what is virtually the Lama Cabinet. One of these is Commander-in-Chief of the army, which seems a curious position for a monk to hold.

The sooner a call is returned the more respect does it reflect upon the caller, and no sooner had we returned from our visit to the Regent and Prime Minister at the Potala (this will be described in the next chapter), than the latter called on us. Usually the Prime Minister is a wise and experienced official from one of the ancient noble families, but the late Dalai went doubly against tradition by appointing a young man of no experience whatsoever and one who was his eldest brother's son. He is of a friendly nature and, being one of the people, is very popular with the townsfolk.

Another very distinguished visitor was the Duke (*yapshi phunkhang kung*), a title given to the father or brother of the reigning Dalai Lama. As the title is hereditary, there are usually several Kungs living at the same time, theoretically one for each Dalai Lama. As the Dalai Lama's family is normally a poor one and therefore without patrimony, the title of Kung carries with it considerable estates. The Kung used to be the first lay-

man of the land, but the late Dalai made the office of Prime
Minister even more exalted.

The Duke, who was dressed in the same way as the Shap-pes,
is a tall lean man with such bad sight that he has to hold everything up to his eyes before he can see it. He gives the impression of being completely absent-minded and unpractical
in a very aristocratic and charming way. After him came the
State Oracle, whose familiar spirit inhabits an ancient tree just
below Drepung Monastery. The Oracle himself lives in the
neighbouring Nechung Temple. This was the first time the
official Sage of Lhasa had deigned to call on a Political Officer.
He is a Ta Lama, one of the highest monk officials, and although
his profession is to work himself up into a trance, he seemed very
much a man of the world and invited us to come and visit his
Temple.

The most interesting visitor of all was Tsarong Dzasa, who
came on a friendly call with his wife. He holds no official
position now but is the leading figure in the National Assembly
and, at a time when a general air of indecision and uncertainty
prevails, assumes the position of the Strong Man of Lhasa.
He represents an extremely rare phenomenon in the feudal
oligarchy of Tibet, that of a man of humble birth who has won
his way to high position. A monk official can, by his natural
genius and hard work, rise to be an Abbot of his monastery with
a seat in the Assembly, but for a layman to do this is almost
unprecedented.

Tsarong, or Tsensar Namgyal, to give him his own name, was
the son of an archer in the Dalai Lama's bodyguard. A Tibetan
told me that he first came to His Holiness' notice in the following
way. In 1904, when the British Mission reached Lhasa, the
Dalai Lama fled northwards towards Mongolia. He took
Tsensar's father with him, but the boy, being young, was left
behind. A few days later, very early in the morning, the Dalai
was walking along, sunk in meditation, when he saw a boy
approaching on foot from Lhasa. This was the young Tsensar,
who, resenting being left behind, had walked all night to catch
up with the party. The Dalai Lama spoke to him and was so
impressed by the child that he took him into his own service,
where he rapidly gained promotion. Tsensar accompanied his
master during his four-year exile, and his mind was broadened

by visiting Urga, Peking and even Japan. When the Dalai fled southwards to India in 1910 Tsensar was in command of the escort that was left on the Lhasa side of the Tsang-po to deal with the pursuing Chinese force. Having sent all the coracles to the south side, Tsensar, who was exceedingly brave, waited for the enemy and utterly defeated them. Following his master, he ran the gauntlet of the Chinese in the Chumbi Valley and reached Yatung disguised as a coolie. By this time the Chinese realized he had slipped through their hands, and put a watch on every road, but Tsensar, this time disguised as a post runner, managed to elude them. A few months later he returned again by Kampa Dzong to Shigatse to rally the Tibetan troops against the Chinese.

Tsensar then spent two years in Darjeeling and other parts of India where the Dalai Lama was a guest of the British Government. When His Holiness returned to Lhasa in 1912 Tsensar was made a Shap-pe, and was chosen by the Lama as the husband to the heiress of the great estates of Tsarong, both her brother and father (the Tsarong Shap-pe who dealt with the British Mission in 1904) having been put to death, as they had backed the wrong side in the recent disturbances. Then it was that Tsensar Namgyal took the title of Tsarong. He sold the old Tsarong mansion which had brought bad luck to the family, and built a magnificent new house away from the dust and dirt of the city. He was then made lay Commander-in-Chief of the army, and put in charge of the Mint.

For ten years Tsarong held these important posts, until in 1923 there was a clash between the army and the newly organized and unpopular police force: they had started to fire at each other and things looked serious. Tsarong dealt firmly with the ringleader, cutting off the man's leg (a customary Tibetan punishment) so that he died. Other offenders had their ears removed.

The Dalai Lama, possibly jealous of the increasing power of his late favourite, thereupon considered that he had been guilty of unnecessary cruelty and degraded him from his high position. In the presence of all the other officials he had to remove his Shap-pe's robes. Since that time he has taken no high office, although he was invited to rejoin the Cabinet a few years ago. At present, together with Langchungna Shap-pe, he controls the Trap-je, the Government barracks, arsenal and mint, and is the moving force of the National Assembly. Tsarong also married a widow, the heiress of the Hor-kang family, who lives in a large house in the middle of the city. He is now fairly old by Tibetan standards (that is, getting on for fifty), a short thick-set jovial man getting rather short of teeth and hair.

The Tsarongs called formally on the Political Officer in our upstairs room and then, as another visitor arrived, went into the garden to present their compliments to Richardson. We all of us soon foregathered here and spent a very happy hour laughing and joking and discussing every sort of subject, as if we had known each other for years. This was a pleasant change after the more formal interviews of the morning. Neither of the Tsarongs know more than a few words of English, but, like all intelligent Tibetans, they are very anxious to learn.

Tsarong's wife is not exactly beautiful, bearing on her face the ravages of smallpox, but she is perfectly self-assured and charming and, as we found later, a perfect hostess. She wore a long sleeveless robe of purple silk held in at the waist, embroidered with gold devices, and a green silk blouse which showed at the sleeves and neck. A heavy gold charm-box, ornamented with turquoise, rubies and diamonds, hung from a necklace of large coral and agate beads, so that it was half tucked into the fold of the dress. An apron, striped horizontally with red, green, yellow and white, the top corners of heavily flowered gold braid, was tied round her waist. Her hair, neatly parted in the middle, was brought Madonna-like over the sides of her forehead to form two long plaits, which were looped up at the waist. It is not customary in Tibet to discuss any serious subject until the preliminary calls and luncheon parties are finished, but we gathered from Tsarong that the Tibetans were extremely worried and prepared to discuss things frankly with the Political Officer and to ask his advice. Whether they will take it or not is a different matter.

Another interesting caller was Kusho Chango Pa, better known as Ringang, the youngest of the four boys who went to Rugby in 1913. He apologized for not having come earlier, but he has to be careful not to appear too obviously pro-British, especially since the death of the late Dalai Lama, in whose favour he stood very high. As Ringang was the youngest of the Rugbeians, and as he spent considerably longer than the others in this country, he has profited most from that curious experiment. He still speaks the most perfect idiomatic English, although he gets little practice except when a British Mission is in Lhasa. Being at present only a sixth-rank official, he is not allowed to wear silk—except in the privacy of his own house—or the charm-box which higher officials wear on the tops of their heads, though his hair is bound in the same way with red ribbon. Instead of silk, a robe of dark purple broadcloth is worn, held in at the waist with a red, green, or yellow sash. In his official dress as a city magistrate he wears a scarlet gown with a sky-blue lining and the sponge hat. To look at, Ringang is a short thick-set man, inclined to fatness. Like most of the Tibetans, he grows no hair on his face.

His status as an official reflects many of the weaknesses of the administration of Lhasa. When Ringang returned from his additional course of engineering in England he was given the task of installing electric light in the city and in the Dalai Lama's summer palace. This involved a tremendous amount of work. A hydro-electric power-station had to be built at the foot of a mountain stream some six miles to the north of Lhasa, and the machinery for this had to be laboriously brought up from Calcutta and put into position. A power-line had to be laid to the city and accumulators brought from India and stored in the basement of Ringang's house. After several months' work the Dalai became impatient and could not understand why there was still no light. Yet Ringang had had to do most of it himself, as the Tibetans were not used to this sort of work. Now the power-station is in the charge of a Tibetan whom Ringang has trained and, except for a few months in winter when the stream is frozen, it works perfectly. At the present time, therefore, the Potala, the streets, and many of the private houses are lit by electric light.

Ringang is also official interpreter to the Cabinet, having to give them items of news from the Indian papers and to be present on the rare occasions when any Europeans visit Lhasa. He is, furthermore, a municipal officer of Lhasa and magistrate, or dzongpön, of a district called Purang in southern Tibet. For this plurality of offices he is paid very little in actual cash: that is not the Lhasa system. In Tibet the State owns practically all the land, and farms it out to the noble families on condition that they supply one or more officials, depending on the value of the estate, for Government employment.   Bribery is of course rife and is so ingrained in the system that it has become an indispensable part of it.   A young official pays a senior one to put in a good word for him.   Huge presents are received by those who have in their power the selection of candidates for a vacant post.   Bribes are even paid to spread bad reports of rivals, so there is little feeling of security for a Lhasa official.   But this system is tacitly accepted by the Government, who find it convenient not to have to pay salaries.

Ringang has never visited the district of which he is in charge, but his wife, an attractive capable woman, went there one winter to see that everything was all right.   The work is done by a deputy, who administers justice, manages the farms, and collects the revenues, usually in kind, through the local headmen.   Ringang is· supplied with practically all necessities from his estate at no cost to himself.   His servants and retainers are the children of his tenants; horses, mules, grain, butter, vegetables, and chang come from the farms; metal-work, carpets and clothes are made on the estate.   So at present Ringang is a very busy man and has every hope of one day being a Shap-pe; but he has the harassed air of one who is not quite high enough up in the scale of officialdom to feel secure from the calumnious attacks of his rivals.

The career of Ringang's elder brother, who also came to present a scarf, throws another sidelight onto the methods of the Lhasa Government.   Some years ago, when the Tibetan troops were driven out of an important district in the eastern part of the country, the four depöns in charge of the army were all removed from office, and Ringang, who was then in charge of the Government granaries, was one of the new generals appointed.   He neither knew the country nor had he any experience of military organization or fighting whatever.   Being very intelligent and feeling strongly on the subject, he was, nevertheless, able to give us much valuable information of conditions in Kham and of the complete inadequacy of the Tibetan army.   He held this position for several years and is now the Government expert on agriculture.   Once seen, the elder Ringang is not easily forgotten, being the very embodiment of Falstaff.   He is of enormous size, and is perpetually out of breath and perspiring.   His face is continually wreathed in smiles, and he is the champion drinker of chang in all Tibet, having the rare and enviable accomplishment of being able to pour a glass of beer straight down his throat without swallowing.

Of the many officials who came to see us, two more must be described, and these are the other two Rugbeians, Möndö and Kyipup. Of the four sent to England, Ghonkar, the soldier, who was perhaps the most promising of them all and who was most needed by his country, died soon after he returned to Tibet. His training at Woolwich should have fitted him for an administrative post at Lhasa, but it is typical of the Tibetan Government that he was sent to the Sino-Tibetan frontier as a subaltern. It is said that he fell in love with an English girl, but that the Dalai Lama would not allow him to marry her, and that he died from a broken heart.

Möndö was already a monk when he left Tibet in 1913. At Rugby he never seemed to learn anything, but his behaviour was always that of the perfect gentleman. He was also a very keen cricketer. After leaving Rugby he was trained as a mining engineer. When he returned to his native country he immediately set about looking for gold and other precious substances; but as soon as he started to dig or to disturb the soil in any way, the abbot of the nearest monastery would complain that all the local spirits were being disturbed, and would implore him to replace every stone he had dug up and to move on to the next district before the crops failed and the people were smitten with epidemics. After this had happened several times Möndö became discouraged and retired for a time to meditate. He then became an important monk-official. Now Möndö had brought a motor-cycle from India and he used to ride this in the streets of Lhasa, much to the consternation of both man and beast. One day a high official was thrown from his mule owing to the sudden appearance round a corner of this terrifying machine, and as a consequence Möndö was degraded and put in charge of a small district in remote western Tibet, where he spent several years. Now he is a fifth-rank official, sharing with Ramba, our lay guide, the charge of Sho, the village at the foot of the Potala. He also has an office in the Potala and is partly responsible for the park-lands of Lhasa. Möndö is a large genial man with a loud ringing laugh and the extraordinary consideration and politeness that is so strong a characteristic of all the official class. He must have considerable wealth, for he is at present building a large and very beautiful mansion behind Muru monastery in the extreme north-eastern corner of the city.

Kyipup was not a great success at Rugby, as he was not the least amused by either work or games. After two years there, he studied surveying with conspicuous lack of success. When he returned to Lhasa he was put in charge of developing the telegraph system, but as he knew little about this, and was given no encouragement by the Government, he retired to his family estates. He is a nervous little man with an apologetic air and a straggly moustache. At present he is a City Magistrate (*mi-pön*), a sixth-rank official, and in charge of the City Police. Having seen numbers of this force sitting dejectedly in their sentry-boxes sewing boot soles or engaged in similar occupations, I asked him one day what would happen if a smash-and-grab raid were carried out in a Lhasa shop. He replied that the policeman would blow his whistle, on which signal others would appear and, having restored order with their truncheons, the malefactors would be handcuffed and taken to prison. Upon enquiry I discovered that the police carry neither whistles nor truncheons, nor have they any handcuffs. Kyipup is married to a very beautiful daughter of the hospitable Tering Rajah with whom we lunched near Gyantse. They live in a small house near the Lhasa Cathedral.

A son of Rajah Tering also came to see us, a young depön, Jigme Tering. He has married a younger sister of Tsarong's wife and lives in a small house beside the Tsarong mansion. Jigme was at school at St. Paul's, Darjeeling, and speaks absolutely flawless English. We saw a great deal of him during our visit and he is as delightful a person as one could meet anywhere. Jigme, like Yuto, was dressed in the very smartest uniform and his whole turn-out would have done him credit in any European army.

Another English-speaking visitor was Surkang-se, whose father is High Commissioner in Kham (south-eastern Tibet). He comes of a very ancient family, so is allowed to wear the charm-box, although he has only a small job under Tsarong at the Mint. He it was who was sent down to Calcutta to arrange for the transport of the girders for Trisum bridge. Having been at Ludlow's school, he speaks good English, though he was only there for a year before, much to his regret, it closed down. Unfortunately he is rather nervous and has a bad lisp, so is not easy to understand.

The Lhasa Postmaster also spoke English, as he was trained in telegraphy at Kalimpong. The postal and telegraph system is most efficient. The line was laid from Kalimpong over the Jelep La as far as Gyantse during the 1904 Mission. After Sir Charles Bell's visit to Lhasa in 1920 it was continued to the city. It is maintained by Nepalese line-men with occasional visits—usually no farther than Gyantse—from British engineers. The muleteers sometimes take the posts for firewood and amuse themselves by throwing stones at the insulators, but during our visit we were always able to telegraph messages to India. The Potala is connected by telephone with the Post Office. Stamps, in five values and colours (green, yellow, blue and two shades of red), are printed at the Lhasa Mint; they are current only within Tibet. Post-runners carry the mails to Gangtok (our letters were re-stamped at Gyantse). Running from dawn to dusk in relays of about eight miles they covered the 330 miles from Lhasa to Gangtok in from eight to ten days. Our record time for getting an answer from Calcutta was seventeen days.

Trimon, an ex-Shap-pe, came to call. He is grey-haired and looks old and worried. He has just married a new and attractive wife, in whose Lhasa house he now lives; but soon he returns to Gyantse to occupy some estates he has gained possession of after a long and expensive lawsuit. They say that when he wanted to retire from his duties as a Cabinet Minister his resignation was refused by the Dalai Lama, so he took off all his clothes and, feigning madness, ran naked through the streets of Lhasa. He is anything but insane now, though he seems saturnine and dis-illusioned. He spoke very sensibly of the gravity of the Tashi Lama situation. So also did Ngagchen Rimpoche, who is the Tashi Lama's chief agent in Lhasa. He is a Ta Lama (a very high monk official) and a famous preacher. Prayers conducted by him are supposed to be more effective than any others. He told us that the real trouble is caused by the Tibetan officials in the Tashi Lama's entourage. Many of these are in Chinese pay, have Chinese wives, and do not want to return to their country, where they may be degraded, tortured, or even put to death. Tashi himself is a very old man by Tibetan standards. A true

Tibetan at heart and a man of most saintly character, he must yearn to spend his last few years in Shigatse, where his own people revere him as the holiest person in Tibet. But he has for so long accepted the hospitality and pay of China that he is virtually a prisoner there, and probably the Chinese escort is being forced upon him against his will. Ngagchen also deplored the vacillating attitude of the Tibetan Government, who have already conceded more than they should. Ngagchen is a small man of great intelligence with a high forehead and bald head. He has a goatee beard and wise twinkling eyes. He has travelled a great deal in India and China, but is now of advanced age. He complains that he has worms in his teeth.

The young and very aristocratic-looking Ra-ka-sha came in one day. A brother of the Maharani of Sikkim, I had made his acquaintance at Gangtok when he was visiting her. He is a member of one of the two Lhasa families who trace their ancestry to the " Religious Kings " who ruled Tibet in the eighth and ninth centuries. In memory of their ancestors the heads of these families are greeted by their tenants with the obeisances otherwise only accorded to high lamas. His wife is another of Tering Rajah's daughters.

Having endeavoured to describe the personalities and positions of various Lhasa officials it will be interesting to see how they are graded; also to see how the machinery of government worked under the dictatorship of the last Dalai Lama and how it is adapting itself to present contingencies.

Alone in the first rank of Tibetan officials are the Dalai and Tashi Lamas. The Regent, or King according to his Tibetan title, is between the first and second, for it is difficult to classify incarnate lamas. In the second rank is the Prime Minister (*silön* or *lönchen*) alone. The third is headed by the Royal Dukes (*yapshi kung*), and the four Shap-pes are of this rank, so also is the Lord Chamberlain (*chi-kyap kempo*), the head of the ecclesiastical party. Finally there are the Dzasas and *tejis*. The Tejis, of whom some are hereditary, are usually members of noble families who give their services to the Government without receiving payment in cash or estates.

In the fourth rank are several grades of officials: the four Financial Secretaries (*tsi-pön*) and the officials in charge of the

Dalai Lama's private treasury in the Potala and of the Government treasury beside the Cathedral. The monk and the lay Commanders-in-Chief of the army are of this grade, so are the Depöns, or "Lords of the Arrow" (the literal meaning of the title). These correspond to generals in the army, or to military commanders of important districts. The four members of the Lama Cabinet (trun-yik chempo), which is presided over by the Lord Chamberlain, are of this rank, so also is the Shigatse dzongpön and the Governor of Gartok.

In the fifth rank are several dzongpöns of important districts, City Magistrates (mi-pön), and various storekeepers, judges and receivers of fines. The sixth rank consists of the magistrates of smaller districts, and innumerable junior treasurers and secretaries.

These classifications are by no means rigid, and there was considerable disagreement among my Tibetan informers as to the class to which certain officials belonged. If a position that is normally fourth-class is held by a very important official he will rank as third; a post in the Dalai Lama's household that is responsible during His Holiness' life may be much less so during a Regency. One hundred and seventy-five lay officials are usually appointed, and a similar number of ecclesiastics. Very often certain positions are duplicated, a monk and a lay official being jointly in charge. For instance, the small hamlet at the foot of the Potala is in charge of Möndö (the monk Rugbeian) and Ramba (the acting lay guide to the Mission). The dzongpöns similarly work in pairs, so also do the Commanders-in-Chief of the army.

When there is a Dalai Lama he appoints a Prime Minister, a layman, who is in charge of criminal cases, and who is also the medium between the Shap-pes and the Dalai Lama, for it would be unfitting for the Dalai himself to deal with such matters.

The Cabinet, called Kashak (both vowels pronounced long and the last k not sounded) after the building in which it meets, was founded about two hundred years ago; the four members, three laymen and one monk, are directly appointed by His Holiness. After discussing any matter under consideration they draw up a report, which is forwarded to the Prime Minister, who appends his own opinion and submits it to the Dalai or, in his absence, to the Regent. If the Dalai wishes, he can ignore the recommendations of his Ministers, and in fact frequently did so.

There is yet another governing body which is summoned on occasions of national emergency; this is the National Assembly (*tsondu*). The full Assembly, which rarely meets, as it is somewhat cumbersome, comprises four hundred members, including all lay and monk officials above a certain rank, the Abbots of important monasteries, and various others. The inner Assembly, a variable body, consists of the Abbots of Drepung, Sera and Ganden, the Dzases and Tejis, and one or two other officials who happen to be especially powerful at the time. It is through the Assembly that the opinion of the great monasteries can make itself felt. The Prime Minister and Cabinet are allowed to attend the meetings of the Assembly but they may take no part in the discussion. Before the late Dalai took the government into his own hands, the Assembly used to deal with foreign affairs while the other Ministers confined themselves to internal administration. When the Dalai was alive, backed by the adoration of his subjects and by a small but highly trained bodyguard, he ruled absolutely. There was little precedent, as he came to power after a hundred years of Regency, and for the greater part of his long reign the Chinese had no power in Lhasa. The Assembly could only meet when summoned by him, and then only those whose names appeared on the list that he sent round. Questions of foreign policy he settled himself, even the Prime Minister and Cabinet could only advise. And now that he has gone, the officials, so accustomed to being told what to do, have lost the power of initiative. The Regent, a young incarnation lama, knows little of the art of government. The Prime Minister, though popular with the people, knows still less.

When the Dalai Lama died, in 1933, there was something of a crisis at Lhasa. In the first place, his favourites, who held no official status, were in danger. Kumpa-la especially, for he had enjoyed great power and was regarded with bitter jealousy. Some said he should be beheaded, others wanted to imprison him; in the end the monks had their way and he was banished to south-east Tibet. The Prime Minister was at that time a youth; the Cabinet Ministers, Trimon, Langchungna, Tendong, and the Kalön Lama (the last three being still in office), had little power and submitted questions of importance to the National Assembly, who had assumed control of affairs. The first thing they did was to enquire into the death of the Dalai Lama, for there was some suspicion that he had been poisoned. Shortly before his death he had been given some medicine by the State Oracle at Netchung (the predecessor of the present Oracle). It appeared that His Holiness had been ill for some time, although the people did not know it, and Kumpa-la was sent for, and asked why he had not reported the Dalai Lama's illness before. Lungsha, an ambitious fourth-rank official who was suspected of pro-Chinese tendencies and who had accompanied the Rugby boys to England in 1913, was the chief power in the National Assembly. He wanted to become a Shap-pe; he desired lucrative positions for his friends and also wanted to bring about certain reforms, to which end he prepared a petition signed by a hundred influential people. He suggested that for every post there should be a monk and a lay official; that these should be appointed by the National Assembly instead of by the Cabinet; and that the system of one official holding several jobs and enormous estates, while others had neither, should be stopped. He further plotted to ambush and kill Trimon Shap-pe and the Prime Minister as they walked round the Park Circle (a prescribed holy walk) in the early morning.

One of the enemies in the way of Lungsha's ambitions was a fourth-rank official called Kapshupa, who had had an administrative job in the Hor States in Kham, but who, owing to his financial intrigues, had become so unpopular that complaints of his conduct had been made to the National Assembly. As Kapshupa was known to be a great friend of the banished favourite Kumpa-la, Lungsha was doubly anxious to imprison him. Lungsha therefore accused Kapshupa before the National Assembly.

The Cabinet immediately summoned the two enemies to the Potala, where they were questioned. Suddenly fearing that too much was known of his intrigues, Lungsha endeavoured to flee, but was grasped by one of the gigantic monk door-keepers. In the struggle Lungsha's arm was broken and a loaded pistol fell from the pocket of his robe. At the same time one of his boots came off and, from the inside of the boot, two small pieces of paper fell on to the floor. Lungsha seized these and, putting

them into his mouth, tried to swallow them; but a monk
throttled him and recovered one piece on which was written the
name of Trimon Shap-pe. Presumably Kapshupa's name was
on the other. It appeared that Lungsha had been endeavouring
to kill his enemies by witchcraft in the same way that the Regent
of Tengye-ling Monastery had attempted to bring about the
death of the young Dalai Lama, as will be described later.

Lungsha was put in prison. His son, who was depön of the
Norbhu Lingka bodyguard, and others, tried to force his release;
but they were unsuccessful. The unfortunate Lungsha had his
eyes put out and was removed to the Government jail at the
foot of the Potala, where he still languishes. Kapshupa was
tried and imprisoned; soon afterwards he secured a reprieve,
though he was still dismissed from Government service. However, a year later he managed to get back again and is now the
chief financial secretary (tse-pön) and is building himself a magnificent new mansion near the Cathedral.

On the whole, the administration of Lhasa, though corrupt,
is efficient. The people are used to a certain amount of extortion,
but if the traditional limit is exceeded their natural independence
asserts itself and there is trouble; higher authority is appealed to,
and the over-rapacious official is punished. Tibet is in the position
of European countries in the Middle Ages—in many ways a position
which we are bound, nowadays, to envy. The country is run by
the monasteries and by the noble families. If the son of a merchant
or farmer is ambitious he enters a monastery, for only there can he
hope to rise to that position of importance to which he feels he is
entitled. But there is no unemployment, no underlying feeling
of insecurity, and—except for those who choose begging as a
profession—no real poverty.

One important caller who is neither a monk nor a lay official
was the trader Pangda Tsang, a short-haired phlegmatic young
Tibetan, who arrived on a magnificent ambler. He lives in a
large house next to the Surkang mansion. There is a romantic
story attached to him. A few years ago his younger brother,
a rupön (corresponding to a captain), rebelled against his general
in eastern Tibet. As Pangda Tsang was suspected of complicity,
the Government ordered his house to be surrounded by the
Tibetan army. The trader, strong in his innocence, armed himself and a dozen servants with rifles and swords, and declared

that the first soldier to cross his threshold would be a dead man. The army laid siege. After a few days one of the defenders fell asleep and accidentally let off his gun. The Tibetan army fled, and never returned. But Pangda Tsang did not have it all his own way; rumour has it that it cost him a lac and a half of rupees (£11,250) to make his peace with the Cabinet.

Apart from the Tibetans in Lhasa, there are various communities of foreigners who add their contribution to the character of the place. In 1885 the warlike Gurkhas from Nepal invaded Tibet for the second time and, by the resulting treaty, were allowed to establish an Agency in Lhasa and to have extra-territorial rights and free trading facilities. In Lhasa today there are six or seven hundred Nepalese and, as they are of Newar and not Gurkha stock, many of them are Buddhists and have Tibetan wives. Although the most artistic of the Nepalese tribes, they are not popular in Lhasa. Possibly the Tibetans resent their high-handed attitude, and perhaps also they consider that the Nepalese have not kept their side of the 1856 treaty, by which they undertook to come to the assistance of Tibet if any invader appeared. But there is another reason. As Lhasa is the Holy City of Buddhism, a religion that sets itself very strongly against the taking of any sort of life, the birds and animals there are unmolested by Tibetans and therefore very tame. Within a hundred yards of our house there lived flocks of bar-headed geese, Brahminy duck and mallard, and it would have been easy to have walked up to these and shot them. In the rivers too there are char and barbel up to eight and ten pounds in weight, just asking to be caught; but as we were members of a Diplomatic Mission, we took no advantage—in spite of great temptation—of these opportunities, out of respect to our hosts. The Nepalese, however, both shoot the birds and catch the fish. If there is any trouble, they are tried by their own courts and invariably acquitted. They are also to be seen smoking their hookahs in the streets of Lhasa, thereby infringing another Tibetan prohibition. We saw a great many of them in Lhasa, where they are shopkeepers, traders and metal-workers. We were possibly rather unfavourably impressed, because some of them, usually members of the Nepalese escort, were among the doctor's most repulsive patients. Riddled with venereal disease, they would be seen hobbling up to his surgery to receive their injections.

The Nepalese representative, Major Hamal, was one of the first to call on the Political Officer. He rode up to the Deyki Lingka in magnificent style. He wore a suit of dazzling cloth of gold, and a turban of the same material with a large white aigrette springing from a golden ornament. Over his head was carried an enormous canopied State umbrella. With him came an escort of two officers and twenty men clad in bright blue uniforms. The Major speaks good though slow English; he is somewhat portly, has a black moustache, and wears pince-nez. He dislikes Lhasa, finding the climate exceedingly trying. He has little use for the Tibetans and a genius for drinking innumerable liqueurs in the shortest possible time. Being very short-sighted he walks with difficulty, usually supported by the arms of his two officers. He was always very friendly and genial whenever we met him.

Another early caller was the Agent of Bhutan. The relationship between the Bhutanese and the Tibetans is close. They are of the same stock and religion, for the Bhutanese are followers of the Kagyü sect of Tibetan Buddhism. Bhutan, at one time or another in her obscure and mysterious past, has been under the suzerainty of Cooch Behar, Tibet and China. The inhabitants number a few hundred thousand only, and the country is little more than two and a half times as large as Wales, but it marches with the Indian frontier for 250 miles, overlooking the rich tea gardens of Assam. At the beginning of this century, when our relations with Tibet became strained, Bhutan was virtually an independent State inhabited by people of Tibetan stock, who acknowledged the spiritual authority of the Dalai Lama as head of their faith, and, until Bhutan came under British protection in 1910, the Bhutanese sent annual remittances to Lhasa, though they were careful to point out that these were only religious gifts to the Dalai Lama.

Only one or two commercial agents actually live in Lhasa, though parties of Bhutanese traders often visited the city and we occasionally saw these swarthy short-haired men, distinguished easily enough by their striped robes, which only reach to the knee. They seem less Mongolian-featured than the Tibetans and appear to have larger heads. Rice and birch teacups are the chief exports of Bhutan to Tibet.

Gulam Maidin Mahommad and Asatulla Mahommad, who had ridden out a day's journey to meet us on our arrival, came soon afterwards to pay their respects to the Political Officer. These men, together with their two or three hundred compatriots in Lhasa, are Mohammedans from Ladakh, the north-eastern province of Kashmir. Some of them are descendants of the Dogra force that unsuccessfully attacked western Tibet a hundred years ago. They are practically all traders and live in the south-eastern corner of the city, where they have a small mosque. They wear Tibetan dress, with the addition of a turban, and are clever and successful merchants. They approached the Political Officer to ask for extra-territorial rights similar to those enjoyed by the Nepalese, on the grounds that they come from Ladakh, which is part of British India; but as they have all the advantages and amenities of Lhasa and are not in any way oppressed, the request seemed unreasonable.

CHAPTER SIX

WE RETURN THEIR CALLS

ON 27th August, two days after our arrival at Lhasa, we rode in solemn procession to pay a ceremonial call on the Regent and Prime Minister at the Potala. The Political Officer wore his black diplomatic uniform complete with cocked-hat and decorations. Brigadier Neame and Captain Morgan were also in uniform; Richardson wore a morning-coat and white topee, while I, having no uniform, wore a dark-blue suit and, to show that the occasion was a very special one, a watch-chain.

As we rode between the willow trees and flooded meadows towards the Potala we were a brilliantly coloured procession: Norbhu in his scarlet and yellow Dzasa's dress; our two guides, the monk in his plum-coloured robes and gold hat, the layman wearing his scarlet magistrate's gown over a violet silk robe, and with his curious " basin " hat perched on top of his head; Rai Sahib Bo and the seven Sikkimese clerks in robes of gay-coloured brocade and short sleeveless jackets of another bright colour; ten scarlet-coated orderlies, those from Gangtok wearing basket-work hats ornamented with peacock feathers; and six grooms in gold-banded Tibetan hats and spotted coats edged with leopard skin. We rode up to the long flight of steps leading to the northern gateway of the Potala and, leaving our ponies, threaded our way along dark passages to an ante-room where the Reting Dzasa and other officials took charge of us.

The ceremonial is strict and carefully laid down. First we met the Prime Minister in an outer room, later we were received in the Regent's Throne Room. It was a small room with frescoes on the walls and a row of religious banners (*thankas*) hanging above the throne, which was a gaudily cushioned seat about two feet from the ground. The Prime Minister, who came in with us, took his place on a lower seat. We presented scarves and then sat on low cushions, while tea, biscuits and dried fruits were handed round by two colossal monks, who are the Regent's personal attendants. The larger was more than 6 feet 8 inches in height and had his shoulders padded to make him appear even bigger.

Meanwhile Norbhu and the Sikkimese clerks were presented. Each in turn kow-towed three times in Chinese fashion, touching the floor with his forehead, then advanced, bowing low, to present scarves, which were taken by an attendant. The Regent blessed each of them with both hands or only one, according to rank, and put over their necks a fillet of scarlet silk. Gould and the Regent had a formal conversation in which the former delivered a message of greeting from the Viceroy of India, and the usual compliments were exchanged. When we went the Regent got up and shook hands in the most cordial way with each of us in turn. The interview was impressive, although the Regent himself has little presence. He is a frail, undersized, almost emaciated-looking monk of about twenty-three years of age, with very prominent ears. He has a receding chin and peculiar creases above the bridge of his nose which when he frowns assume the shape of rudimentary horns. He wore ordinary monk's clothes, with a braided undercoat, stiff pinkish turned-up boots and red habit, leaving his thin arms bare. No hat was worn over his closely-cropped hair.

On the following day we called privately on the Regent at his newly built summer place, which lies about three-quarters of a mile east-north-east from the Potala, on the outskirts of the city. It is situated behind the Shiday monastery, which is

I

affiliated to his own monastery of Reting.   To reach this palace
we had to ride through flooded streets and narrow muddy alleys
smelling strongly of sewage.   The windows meanwhile were
crowded with inquisitive but friendly faces.

The palace is very small, containing only storerooms on
the ground floor and a single sitting-room above; but it is an
attractive building and beautifully decorated.   There are golden
turrets on the roof, and along the top of the wall the usual golden
emblems on a matt background of willow-twig walling.   The
woodwork round the windows is cleverly carved and painted
in bright colours.   Boxes of gay flowers stand on every window-
sill, protected from the sun by awnings of white cloth.   Moreover, the palace lies in a walled garden with well-kept lawns,
and beds full of English flowers in luxuriant bloom.   The
Regent is extremely fond of pets.   He has several cages full of
birds, including a talking " mina " and a laughing-thrush that
makes the most fantastic noises in the middle of the most serious
conversations.   He has a monkey, a fox cub, a leopard, a cage of
ornamental pheasants and several different kinds of dogs.

We reached the upper storey by a flight of stone steps outside
the palace and found a most attractive room full of light and
gay colours.   The walls were covered with frescoes of lay and
religious subjects, and there were glass cases crammed with
pieces of porcelain and cloisonné.   The only unbeautiful things
were the European table and chairs put ready for us.   The
young Regent was much more natural and talkative than on
the day before, and only the friendly Reting Dzasa, a monk-
secretary, and one or two other monks were in attendance.
His favourite was also present: a very good-looking monk of
about sixteen who is one of the Duke's sons.

As soon as we had presented scarves and drunk tea—both
the Tibetan and European drink was served—our presents were
brought in and given to the Regent.   These consisted of a fine
silver tea-service and tray, and such things as rifles, revolvers,
a gramophone and a thermos flask.   They also included the
" Kharitz " (letter of salutation) and a signed photograph from
the Viceroy of India, and three young spaniels that we had
brought up to Lhasa as a personal gift from His Excellency to
the Regent.   It is not the custom to show any pleasure at the
receipt of presents, but the young Regent could hardly conceal

his delight with the dogs, which, I regret to say, did not behave very well on this their first experience of the inside of a house. The visit did not last long. Just before we left the Regent asked Gould to talk freely to all officials because the Tibetans particularly wanted our help in a time of unusual perplexity. They were accustomed to leading a peaceful religious life, he said, and were unused to facing problems such as now confronted them.

When we all went into the garden the Regent had no objection to being photographed, and it was all I could do to persuade his huge orderly (whom we nicknamed Simple Simon) to move about when I wanted to take some cinema films; he struck what he thought was an imposing attitude and resolutely refused to move. Before we went the Regent obligingly blessed each of our servants in turn, placing with his own hands a small white scarf around their necks. It is moving to see with what deep reverence all Buddhists regard their spiritual ruler.

As soon as we had left the Regent's Palace we rode right across the western edge of the city to call on the Prime Minister, who lives fairly near the Kyi Chu (Lhasa river). On our journey between the dwellings of the two highest people in the land we had to splash through stinking puddles and past heaps of dung where ravens vied with mangy dogs in searching for the foulest imaginable carrion and garbage. The Prime Minister lives in a large and rather depressing mansion with a pleasant view over the tree-tops of his park to the mountain slopes across the river.

We rode through a solidly built gateway into a large cobbled courtyard which is overlooked on the southern side by his four-storied mansion. Two-storied outbuildings enclose the rest of the yard. Above the door was a room with an open veranda full of flowers. In the corner of the courtyard a group of labourers were grinding up peas with an ingenious stone handmill. On each side of the doorway were two granite mounting-blocks carved with the Swastika emblem.

We followed dark passages up to the top floor, where we found the Prime Minister waiting for us. He was not very easy to get on with, and remained very much the official, seated on a ceremonial divan at a higher level than one he had prepared for Gould. We did not meet his wife as it is not the custom for womenfolk to appear on ceremonial occasions. In his sitting-room, as is so often the case, the natural beauty of the Tibetan style of decoration was spoilt by a few traces of European influence. There was a map with the names in Russian on one wall, there were several framed photographs, a cheap alarm-clock and some tinsel and glass ornaments. After handing over the presents from the Government of India we took our leave, attributing the Prime Minister's stiffness to his youth and inexperience, rather than to any feeling of unfriendliness.

On the following day we called on the three lay Shap-pes, who live in large houses tucked away in obscure corners of the city. They were all extremely friendly and discussed matters freely. The Shap-pes, unlike the Prime Minister, sat with us in European chairs round a table, and gave us Indian tea as well as Tibetan.

For several days we were kept busy returning calls and delivering the presents from the Government of India. We went to call on the charming old Lord Chamberlain in his rooms at the Potala, and on the Yapshi Kung at his Lhasa house. In every case we were most hospitably entertained and were continually delighted by the dignified courtesy and urbanity of each official we met. Each house gave evidence of the highly developed artistic skill of the Tibetans, for though originally all their culture was derived from Mongolia or China, they have developed a characteristic national style both in architecture and interior decoration. Their carving, metal-work and painting is the work of highly skilled craftsmen; exquisite examples are to be seen in every house, for most of the noble families maintain their own silversmith, woodcarver, lacquer worker and fresco painter.

The private chapel or altar-room is usually the best in the house; here are golden images set with turquoise and other precious stones, priceless specimens of porcelain and cloisonné, inlaid chang jugs, and beautifully embossed silver and gold prayer-wheels. In Tibet religion comes first, and it is in the expression of their faith that the finest artistic work is produced.

Richly coloured thankas and lively frescoes ornament the walls. (The word thanka is pronounced more or less to rhyme with " bunker ".) They became familiar to us in Lhasa as perhaps the most remarkable, if not the finest, example of Tibetan art. They are usually in sets of four, eight or sixteen, and are hung in lines, often overlapping each other, in the monasteries or in the altar-rooms of private houses. The actual painting is usually about two feet wide and three feet long. The pigments used are made from various crushed minerals, the majority of which are imported from India. These are mixed with hot thin glue. Flame-red and green are used most, and several peculiarly rich dull blues. Yellows are rare, gold being frequently used instead. The colours, though garish at first, soon tone down in the smoke and gloom of a monastery temple. The canvas, which is of very fine texture, is stiffened with a chalky preparation. All thankas are not painted: some are of fine embroidery, others of appliqué work. One variety is drawn or embroidered in white on a black background; this is usually of a subject so hideous or obscene that, unlike other thankas, it is normally veiled. The paintings are framed with inch-wide strips of scarlet and gold—the former as a rule being on the inside—and then mounted on the finest silk, usually dark blue, so that the complete thanka is about three feet wide and five feet long—though they are sometimes several times as large as this—and has a wooden roller at top and bottom. The projecting ends of the rollers are occasionally of silver most beautifully embossed. A strip of specially valuable brocade is sewn on to the mount below the picture. Fine silk covers, usually three in number, hang over and protect the painting, together with two narrow strips of silk which are left hanging even when the covers are rolled up. Particularly valuable thankas have on their backs the impression of the entire left hand of the Dalai or Tashi Lama.

The subject-matter of the painting varies greatly. As a rule there is a large image in the centre, either of mild aspect and seated upon a lotus-flower, the symbol of divine birth, or fierce, consumed by flames, and terrible with elaborate hideousness. Every corner of the canvas is filled, either by other scenes and images or by trees, flowers and clouds in conventional Chinese style. Very often there is a small likeness of the artist in an attitude of adoration. Always they show a high standard of drawing and rare magnificence of colouring.

We could not be asked out to lunch until we had been officially entertained by the Cabinet, and this was delayed owing to Gould's rather severe indisposition; but one day we were invited to have tea with Tsarong.

The Tsarong mansion lies just beyond that of the Prime

Minister, between the City and the Kyi Chu. Turning out of a flooded stretch of waste-land we entered the usual type of terraced gateway, clattered across a small cobbled yard to another gateway, and then found ourselves looking at the most remarkable house in Lhasa. The Tsarong mansion, like all Tibetan houses, faces south, but it looks onto a skilfully laid out garden instead of onto the traditional courtyard surrounded by lower buildings. The style is a pleasant combination of Tibetan mansion and English country house. The roof is flat, and there are incense-burners and prayer-flags on it, but the windows are of the casement type and are fitted throughout with glass. The door is ornamented in the best Tibetan style, but in front of it are a dozen granite steps covered with pots of flowering plants.

Inside, the combination of styles is still more attractive. A spacious stone hall hung with Landseer and Farquharson prints in heavy oak frames leads by means of a staircase (practically the only one in Lhasa) to the first floor, on which are all the living-rooms.

We had tea in the private chapel, which is the largest and finest room of the house. Hinged casement windows, with a long window-seat below, take up one wall. Opposite are several half-life-sized golden images in ornate glass cases. The images wear golden diadems studded with precious gems, and round their necks are amber necklaces with stones as large as tangerines. On an altar in front are displayed holy-water vessels, cloisonné lions, a pair of priceless porcelain vases in a glass case, several silver teapots and jugs, and a gold reliquary. At the end of the altar is an ormolu clock and a large terrestrial globe. Another wall displays a line of magnificent thankas framed in purple and gold brocade. Beneath a gay canopy is the throne of the master of the house padded with silken cushions heavily embroidered with dragons and flowers. At the top of two of the pillars supporting the roof are large diamond-shaped scarlet boards bearing Chinese characters in black; these are decorations conferred on Tsarong by the Chinese. Another honourable Chinese order consists of two circular pieces of jade joined by a curving piece of dark lacquered wood. It is about eighteen inches long and is kept in a glass case. I have seen a similar emblem in the Chinese Pavilion of the King of Siam's Palace by the banks of Menong river.

The floor of the room is of sand and small pebbles beaten down and polished to the consistency of marble. On it are several carpets of Tibetan and Indian manufacture. The walls are brightly painted in scarlet, green, blue and ochre; round the top of the walls is painted a fluted scroll-work frieze shaded to resemble a pleated valance. Square wooden pillars support the roof beams, which are all painted red and ornamented with brightly coloured designs of dragons, flowers and clouds.

Another room of the house is furnished in English style with a heavy wooden dining-table, sideboard and chairs. On the walls are family photographs in heavy frames. But the majority of the rooms are Tibetan and are furnished with low divans and carved and lacquered tables. In one room is a huge painting in Chinese style of a well-known picture, showing the seven generations of one family all living at the same time. This was actually painted by the Dalai Lama when a young man and shows considerable talent. Tsarong also possesses a well-appointed bathroom with running water.

It was time for tea when we had looked round the house, and we sat round a low table while Mrs. Tsarong poured out the best Darjeeling tea from a silver teapot. We also had bread and butter, cakes, rock buns, and beautifully iced " penny buns "—one of Tsarong's cooks having been trained in India to make European cakes and dishes. The Tsarongs, unfortunately, cannot speak English, but the Jigmes, who live next door, were there and able to act as interpreters as well as Norbhu.

Jigme's wife Mary is a younger sister of Mrs. Tsarong and, having been at St. Joseph's School, Darjeeling, she speaks perfect English. Jigme and Mary Tering are as charming a young couple as it would be possible to find. Certainly we owe the Tsarongs and Terings a great debt of gratitude for their extraordinary hospitality and helpfulness to us in every way. In most Tibetan houses, except perhaps Ringang's, we had to be on our best behaviour, but Tsarong's parties were always completely riotous, especially when his three children came home from school. The Tsarongs are the most perfect natural host and hostess. Tsarong always drank (or pretended to have drunk) a little more chang than his guests; Mrs. Tsarong made us feel completely at home and, having studied what dishes we liked, she was careful to produce them the next time we came. After tea the Dele

Rabdens came in. He is an official in the service of the Tashi Lama. Here in Lhasa he has his hair done in a plait and does not wear silk; though when living at Shigatse he wears his hair in a top-knot. His wife is very distinguished-looking and has a quiet shy manner.

All three women were dressed in the complicated and resplendent finery of the Lhasa lady of fashion. The glossy black hair is parted in the middle and brushed down at the side to cover the ears. At the back it is neatly tied in two long plaits. The parting divides on the crown of the head so as to run each side of a small patch of hair as big as a penny, then unites again. The hair from this isolated portion is made into a small plait which covers the parting down the back of the head. Two heavy gold ear-rings set with large pieces of turquoise are hung from the hair above the ears, effectively framing the oval face. On the back of the head is worn a concave triangular crown closely covered with strings of seed pearls and further ornamented with a row of corals the size and colour of cherries. False hair is suspended from each side of the crown; it hangs loose to begin with and is then plaited with a red tassel so that it almost reaches the ground. The women are continually putting their hands up to the points of the crown to see that it is straight, which, as a matter of fact, it seldom is. Sometimes strings of beads and pieces of jade are tied across the sides of the triangle to meet in a pendent ornament hanging down the back. Cosmetics are used, but so skilfully, in most cases, as to pass unnoticed. When the Tibetan boys who came to England first saw fashionable English women, they said, " Ah, I see the women over here chew betel-nut !"

The charm-box is perhaps the most beautiful of all the ladies' adornments. In shape it is a square set across a diamond; it is made of dark Tibetan gold and is set in a geometric petal pattern with turquoise and other precious stones, including rubies, garnets, sapphires and diamonds. The charm-box is held by a short necklace of large stones, usually alternate corals and agate or black glass beads with wavy white bands. Strings of seed pearls form a flat band which hangs from the left shoulder down to the waist. In the centre of this is a circular ornament some three inches in diameter made of various precious stones. Other necklaces of large stones hang round the neck and are looped to the bottom of the pearl band. From the shoulder also hangs a bejewelled chatelaine holding a toothpick, tweezers, wax remover and other contrivances.

The dress, which can be with or without sleeves, is usually of rich purple silk with a pattern of dragons and lucky signs in purple and gold. It is held in at the waist with a bright-coloured sash. An apron with corner pieces of flowered gold braid hangs almost to the foot of the dress. This is woven in horizontal strips of red, blue, green, yellow and white, and is made in sections so that the strips do not continue right across. A silk blouse shows at the neck and sleeves. Thick flat-soled boots are worn of scarlet and green embroidered cloth. Although the head-dress might be considered somewhat grotesque, the whole costume is most effective. The jewellery worn by a Tibetan lady of fashion may be worth thousands of pounds.

It was at Tsarong's house that we first met Tibetan children, whom we found most delightful—quite unspoiled, and full of life and intelligence. Although learning is considered in Tibet to be the highest moral quality, education itself is somewhat primitive. The Tibetan child is taught to read and write, to recite prayers and long passages of the Buddhist scriptures, and the elements of arithmetic, which are taught with such elementary paraphernalia as the rosary and small pebbles or fruit stones. Of history, except in so far as it affects his religion, and of the very elements of geography, he has no knowledge whatsoever. In the case of the noble families, a private tutor is kept who is usually a monk. So excellent a mixture of feudalism and democracy is Tibet that the sons of the tenants and servants also attend the classes.

In Lhasa itself there are only two Government schools, and both are for budding officials. There is the college at the Potala for training young monk officials, and a similar one beside the Cathedral for laymen. The latter is reserved for sons of noble families. In the school for lay officials they are taught to keep accounts and to write letters. In a country where specific and high-flown honorific titles are used and extravagant compliments paid this is no easy task. Besides these there are many private schools, and as parents are nowadays very keen that their sons should learn English, such men as the Nepali dentist, the Tibetan postmaster and certain traders having an altogether inadequate knowledge of the languge, are teaching the boys to speak pidgin English. This is the greatest pity, as Tibetan boys

I 2

when properly taught speak the purest and most delightful English.

On several occasions I visited the school kept by the monk telegraphist. One day the children were all reading aloud, but no two seemed to be reading the same thing. Sometimes they repeated prayers. Usually they were sitting cross-legged on the floor writing from memory passages of the scriptures. The more advanced pupils wrote on parchment, the less skilful on blocks of polished wood; in the latter case, as soon as a child had finished, he would bring it up to the teacher, who would look at it, then rub it out. The child would then start again.

Tea was served at frequent intervals. When the postmaster had to attend to his other work the class was left in charge of the senior boy, who by his long ear-ring seemed to be of good family, for other children do not generally wear jewellery.

The last Dalai Lama was anxious that a school run on Western lines, with an English headmaster, should be established at Gyantse or Lhasa. The experiment in 1914 of sending four boys to be educated in England, though successful, had its disadvantages. It was expensive; the boys were separated from their parents for a very long time, and when they returned they were considered by the Tibetans to be uneducated, in that they had almost forgotten how to read and write their native language, and so were not given sufficiently responsible jobs. Tibetans in general are strongly opposed to parting with their children for any length of time and, though one or two are sent to Darjeeling, they have an innate mistrust of the Indian climate.

In 1923, as a result of Bell's advice, an English school was established at Gyantse in the charge of Mr. Frank Ludlow, who had had considerable experience of teaching in India. Although the Tibetans encouraged this school in theory, they did little to support it. Lhasa parents were reluctant to part with their sons and often sent them back several weeks late; and the Abbot of the Gyantse Monastery, saying that their religious education was being neglected, insisted on teaching them Tibetan for several hours each day. Ludlow found the parents and officials exasperating to deal with, though the children themselves were most intelligent and had the charming natural manners of their race. The Tibetans were most delighted with our system of arithmetic, finding multiplication and division far superior to their method of adding and subtracting with stones and beads. Owing to lack of support the school was abandoned in 1926, much to Ludlow's disappointment. We met several old boys of the Gyantse School and found that they spoke English extremely well, had perfect manners, and a fair knowledge of the game of football.

On 13th September the Shap-pes came to the Deyki Lingka for their first diplomatic talk. They arrived an hour late because the Potala clock, on which all Lhasa relies, seemed to have lost an hour.

In view of Neame's impending departure, military matters were first discussed. For three hours the Brigadier gave them his considered advice on the reforms needed in the Tibetan army. The Shap-pes, who wrote down every word, expressed their complete agreement, but added that they would have to refer all suggestions to the Regent and Prime Minister, nor did they know where the necessary money was coming from. It was part of Bell's policy that the British Government should supply arms and munitions to the Tibetan Government and should train a certain number of officers in India. The Cabinet are anxious that we should continue this policy, otherwise they may have to turn elsewhere for help—to Russia, China or Japan. We do not want to encourage the Tibetans to become once more a warlike nation; but in these days a country must be able to defend itself, and it has always been our policy to assist Tibet to maintain her position as an independent autonomous State under the nominal suzerainty of China.

On 14th September we were all invited to Tsarong's for a farewell dinner in honour of Neame; and the following day he set off for India, as the Eastern Command could spare him no longer. The Brigadier, with his extremely quiet manner—I have seldom known a man of his position throw his weight about less—and his uncanny knack of immediately seeing the essentials of a matter, impressed the Tibetans tremendously.

By 18th September Gould felt strong enough to cope with a Tibetan luncheon, so on this day the Shap-pes invited us to lunch in our garden at the Deyki Lingka. Nobody, not even the Regent or the Prime Minister, could invite us to a party until the Cabinet had given us this luncheon. As usual the Shap-pes' time and ours did not agree, and on this occasion they arrived an hour too early. From the first moment the party went with a swing, possibly because Tsarong and Ringang had also been invited together with our monk and lay guides. Music was provided before, during and after the meal by an orchestra of three curiously fashioned stringed instruments, and a flute played by a bearded Ladaki with a red fez. The band was led by a blind man who is in such high favour that he enjoys the rare privilege of being permitted to smoke even in front of the Cabinet. One of the instruments was remarkable in that the bow passed between the strings. In time with the music, which was to my ear Chinese in character, danced three " girls ", one about fifty, the other two somewhat younger. The dancing consisted in stamping on a plank in time with the music, and occasionally swinging one foot forward. After dancing in silence for some time they would burst into song, a shrill, harsh cacophony, swinging their arms from side to side. It was not very exciting for us and certainly did not appear to give them much pleasure. Their silk sleeves were worn right down over the hands out of respect; for the same reason they dared not look openly at such high officials as the Political Officer and the Shap-pes.

The menu started with the usual innumerable snacks, including sea slugs, sharks' fins and fish stomachs, and ended up with bowls of rice into which one put a selection from the various dishes. Most of these succulent delicacies seemed to be especially designed to elude the unpractised chop-sticks, but if one of the Shap-pes saw us struggling with a particularly slippery slug or an intractable slice of stomach he would deftly catch the morsel with his own chop-sticks and convey it to our plates.

The food was excellent and most skilfully prepared; our only criticism was that, as usual, there was too much of it. One of the many remarkable features of this party were the activities of three of the famous chang girls of Lhasa. Normally they are servants of leading Lhasa families, but they are commandeered on occasion by the Tibetan Government. Their duty is to pour out the chang and to see that it is drunk. The chang girls are of better family than the dancers, and their dress and ornaments are similar to those worn by the highest ladies of the land. As the girls are remarkably pretty and the chang delicious, they start with a distinct advantage. The girl fills the glass and hands it to the guest; if he puts it down she repeats the invitation; if he only drinks a little she is still not satisfied and returns it to him with further importunity. Before moving on to the next victim she refills his glass. In obstinate cases she is permitted to nudge his arm and use any form of coercion. The phrase " *Tunda nang-ro-nang* " ("empty it, please"), spoken in persuasively sweet but compelling tone, was an invitation not to be lightly ignored. They say that the chang girl is allowed to stick pins into the arms of guests, even into the Prime Minister himself, if they are slow to drink; but as I liked the beer I never experienced this myself. Usually one girl would pour out the chang from an enamel teapot while another kept her supplied from a larger container. We could usually keep pace with one pair of chang girls moving round the table, but when a rival team worked in the other direction we were forced to protest. The Doctor was even seen to threaten one of the girls with a soda-water syphon. The chang is excellent, but its potency depends upon its age, and until you have drunk a good deal you do not discover how old it is. Sometimes it is very old. Chang is the colour of rather milky lemonade; it tastes of fermented yeast and barley and it is very nourishing. The Shap-pes used to make us drink with each of them in turn, and later we would return the compliment. Their favourite trick was to make us drain our glasses while they only took a sip.

The upper-class Tibetans, unlike the poorer people, do not drink much chang and, except for the Gargantuan Ringang, we could usually outdrink them, from which we gained very greatly in prestige. The Doctor especially, apart from the fame attached to his professional knowledge, will go down in Lhasa history as a champion drinker of chang. I may say I made a considerable name for myself as a trencherman, and as a drinker (purely out of bravado) of a certain spirit called Mongolian whisky, which tastes of burning rubber and rotten goat-skin (from which it is probably distilled), but which is comforting some time after it is swallowed. The Shap-pes luncheon party lasted from midday until six o'clock in the evening, and was said to have been much more intimate and lacking in restraint than the usual Government lunches; I can well believe it.

Now that the close season for luncheon parties was over, we

found ourselves inundated with invitations, and Gould had to make a rule not to lunch with people under the fourth rank, though this limitation did not bind the rest of us. We lunched with each Shap-pe in turn, with the Duke, Trimön, the Prime Minister and the Regent.

The embodiment of God Incarnate (the Regent) gave us a very good lunch at his summer palace. As his greatness did not permit him to eat at the same table as ourselves, he sat on his throne and had each course brought to him in very beautiful silver bowls embossed with designs in gold. At the end of an extensive Chinese luncheon a huge tray of traditional Tibetan foods was brought in; this was for display and not, we were relieved to find, to be eaten. There were joints of aged dried mutton, raw meat in chillies and a towering mass of barley-meal paste decorated with coloured ornaments of butter.

We found the Regent most unaffected and simple, and rather wearied by the greatness that is thrust upon him. He complains that he can get no exercise, as on the rare occasions that he leaves his palace he must be carried in his palanquin.

Having heard reports of various forms of entertainments that Nepean and Dagg had ingeniously fitted up at the Norbhu Lingka, and being unable, owing to his high position, to come and see for himself, we were requested to bring a selection with us. Accordingly the wireless officers rigged up a public-address amplifier. The microphone was set up in one corner of the garden and the amplifiers near the house. Norbhu and Tsarong then carried on a mock quarrel in front of the microphone, and the Regent, sitting in his room, could hear every word. This simply delighted him and he was as excited as a schoolboy. Then some gramophone records were played. Nothing but the loudest possible noise would satisfy the Regent, who made us play record after record at full blast. After this he went over and spoke into the microphone himself, at first rather self-consciously, but gradually finding great amusement at the sound of his own words and laughter booming back at him.

Langchungna, who gave us an unexpectedly excellent lunch, provided a new sort of entertainment. During the meal we had heard distant singing and afterwards, on climbing up to the flat roof as a necessary digestive exercise, we found three men singing and dancing with phenomenal animation. The dance was based on the sedate performance we had often seen given by the women, but these fellows were singing at the tops of their voices, stamping, and swinging their legs in rapid time and throwing their arms from side to side as if demented. Another attraction in Langchungna's house was a prayer-wheel which rotated by radiation. The heat from a butter-lamp was led through a spiral cylinder of parchment, on which thousands of "*Om Manes*" had been written, so that it gently revolved. It was curious that his menials and their children were allowed to gaze at us through the window all the time that we were there.

One day we lunched with the old Lord Chamberlain and, as we took the trouble to discover what each dish was and to write down its name, I shall describe this lunch, as being typical of many others. We were entertained in the living-room of a large house in the city which had at one time belonged to Kumpala, the Dalai Lama's banished favourite. The room was decorated in Tibetan style, but there was glass in some of the windows and we used the European type of table and chairs.

Arriving soon after midday, we exchanged the usual compliments with our host and then sat down to Indian tea with Jacob's biscuits and dried apricots. The latter are grown in Kham, in south-east Tibet; they are so hard that the teeth make little impression on them. When the tea had been cleared away small china bowls were brought in, each containing three sweet rose-flavoured dumplings in warm sugary milk. Chop-sticks, and squares of Tibetan paper on which to lay them were provided, and renewed after this course.

After another interval the following small dishes were put on the table together: stewed mutton in gravy with onion and carrots, tinned herrings, dried prawns, halved green peaches, stewed peaches, tinned pineapple slices, dried dates, Chinese sweetmeats, melon seeds, peanuts, Mongolian smoked ham, sliced yak tongue, pressed beef, plain beef. Small dishes of sauce (perhaps Soya bean sauce), and a small china ladle were given to each of us for the above, and were retained throughout the meal. A continuous supply of chang was provided, but as there were no chang girls it was poured out with less coercion by the four men-servants who waited on us. All this was by way of hors d'œuvres; now the main courses followed in one

or two large and very beautiful Chinese bowls, which were put
in the middle of the table so that each person could pick out
what he wanted with his chop-sticks or spoon. The smaller
preliminary dishes were left on the table for anyone to dip into
until the last (and fifteenth) course appeared, when there was
no longer any room for them. These courses were as follows:

1. Sharks' fins and minced mutton in gravy.
2. Fine mince rolled in batter with vermicelli, celery and
    cabbage in gravy.
3. Mince meat in pastry.
4. Slices of a very firm-fleshed fish (probably tunny) with
    onions, carrots and boiled bacon.
5. Sea slugs in soup with boiled pork.
6. Round meat dumplings.
7. Green peas and mince in gravy.
8. Hard-boiled eggs quartered and attached to a similar
    quarter of mince in sauce.
9. Damp pastry dumplings.
10. Bamboo roots with boiled pork in soup.
11. Eels in gravy with pork and onion.
12. Rice with raisins, cherries and other fruit in syrup.
13. Small squares of sweet fried bread dipped in syrup.
14. Jam dumplings with sponge-cake.
15. (a) Shark's stomach; (b) boiled pork and carrots; (c)
    minced yak beef; (d) pieces of mutton; (e) steamed rice
    with varieties of wet bread-pastry in the form of flowers,
    peaches, horse-shoes; and also soup.

One is not expected to sample all the preliminary dishes, but
each major dish should be tasted. The dumplings (courses 3,
6, 9, 14), two or three on a small dish, were brought round to
each person. The food was extraordinarily good, being very
rich and highly flavoured. My great criticism is that there
was always so much to eat that one could not do justice to the
meal without going into training for some time beforehand.
At the end of the lunch the cook—a short Tibetan in a very
grimy shirt—came in to receive our congratulations as well as
a more substantial reward for his skill.
Many of the above dishes are Chinese, and such delicacies

as sea slugs and sharks' fins are imported dried from China (usually, I believe, through agents in Calcutta). Such meals are for formal occasions, and as most Tibetan cooks cannot prepare this food, a few experts are shared among many households.

In the course of these visits we entered most of the residences of Lhasa. Tibetan houses are built very much in a set pattern. Take, for instance, a typical mansion in the city. Between two stalls in a squalid Lhasa street is a large and heavily carved wooden gate, the upper part of which is protected from the sun by a striped and chequered valance rippling in the wind. A white-washed stone incense-burner stands on one side of the door. Inside there is a large cobbled yard with several fierce mastiffs tied, all too insecurely, to granite posts, there are many mules laden with wool, and riding-ponies standing in covered stalls which run along one side of the courtyard. On the other side are outhouses and storerooms, for the yard is entirely surrounded by buildings. Opposite the entrance gateway is the front of the house with the living-room windows on the first floor, gay with flowers as a rule but now hidden by canvas and yak-hair curtains because the family are using a smaller room while the weather is warm. Brown and white pleated valances protect the paintwork above each window. In the centre of the flat roof is a vase-shaped whitewashed incense-burner, and behind it a cylinder draped with bright silk skirts of the lucky colours—blue, white, red, yellow, green. In addition there are usually " banners of victory " on the corners of the roof. These are small turrets about six feet high draped with black yak-hair, and banded by a white cross of cloth. Often they are surmounted by a trident of brass. On some roofs are wind prayer-wheels, resembling the cup anemometers used by meteorologists. There are also bundles of sticks with fluttering prayer-flags attached. The walls of the first storey are built of courses of square granite blocks bordered by small fragments of stone. Above the first storey the walls are often of sun-dried bricks, though sometimes they are built entirely of stone.

Passing the square granite mounting-blocks one enters the main doorway, which has a protecting stone porch or screen on the inner side. On the plaster of the screen is a large fresco called " Mongolian Leading Tiger ". This is a sign of welcome, and is found in the porchway of almost every house. The man is in Mongolian dress, and there is plenty of action, as his long ear-ring is flying and the tiger strides fiercely at the end of his chain. As a symbol of welcome it becomes less convincing when it is seen that the man crushes small mortals beneath his feet while the tiger treads on representatives of the animal world; but this is intended to be symbolic of the victory of virtue over vice.

Another painting that is usually found on a wooden door-screen or beside a window is known as " the Four Friends ". It shows an elephant—usually with engagingly pink ears—and a monkey sitting on his back; the monkey carries a hare, which in its turn supports a magpie. These four creatures are supposed never to quarrel.

The lower rooms are just offices and storerooms, so we climb a steep wooden ladder to the first floor. On the landing is a row of prayer-wheels which are turned by everybody who passes. The chief room is the private chapel of the house, where there are gilt images of Lamaist saints and deities in ornate glass-fronted cases, rows of small brass Buddhas, gold or silver butter-lamps, holy books in pigeon-holes, and vessels of holy water. There are several religious banners hanging on the walls, which are ochre-coloured and surrounded at waist level by bands of blue and scarlet, bordered by thin gold lines. A frieze re-sembling pleated cloth hangings is painted at the top of the wall. One side of the room consists entirely of windows, two rows of detachable shutters being formed by stretching yellow waxed canvas over a carefully carved trellis-work frame. In the centre of each upper window is a small pane of glass. The square pillars and beams supporting the roof are elaborately carved and painted, and these in turn support innumerable smaller cross-beams used in lieu of plaster and arranged in herring-bone pattern. The ceiling is usually painted a bright matt-blue, except for the main beams, which are red.

The smaller room, in which the family are living at the moment, is built up above the level of the rest so that its windows open out onto the flat roof, on which are rows of flowers in pots. This room has a floor of beaten gravel, stamped and polished to resemble marble. A row of square silk-covered cushions, or rather mattresses, line one wall, and in front of them are low

Tibetan tables lacquered red and gold and deeply carved with dragon or lotus designs. In front of the door is a wooden screen running from floor to ceiling. At the top it is carved in an open-work petal pattern. Lower down is a panel on which there is a painting in low-relief, depicting the eight lucky signs or glorious emblems combined in a design. They are : (1) The Victorious Wheel of an Empire on which the sun never sets. (2) The Lucky Diagram called by the Buddhists " Buddha's entrails ", but really a symbol of endless rebirths in worldly misery. (3) The Lotus Flower of heavenly birth. (4) The Vase of divine ambrosia of immortal life. (5) The two Golden Fish of good fortune, the mascots of Yamdrok Lake. (6) The White Umbrella of Sovereignty. (7) The Conch-shell trumpet of Victory. (8) The Victorious Banner.[1] Another favourite screen-panel shows a gold-painted dragon supporting on his head a bowl of the lucky jewels, which are of such size that they resemble fruits. There is also an altar and a few images in this room, and several banners. Two long-spouted chang jars stand in front of the altar together with a pair of Ming cloisonné vases.

Other rooms are locked with the ponderous and complicated Tibetan padlocks, but the steward gets the keys from the lady of the house and opens them. One is full of stored furniture—square Chinese chairs, tents, small folding tables, and carpets rolled up. On the wall are bows and arrows and masks such as are used in the lama dances. Another room is full of bales of wool. Yet another is used for brewing barley beer, and from the roof are suspended large joints of meat which, in the dry Tibetan air, will keep until the following year. In another up-stairs room is the house latrine. At each end of a bare earth floor are two slits about two feet long and four inches wide. These are usually built up in wooden frames about a foot above the ground and are covered by wooden lids. Beneath this room is a cesspit on the ground floor. Ashes from the yak-dung stoves are poured down from time to time so the place does not smell unduly, though it would be intolerable in a warmer climate. The contents of the cesspit are removed at rare intervals —for in winter everything is frozen solid—and heaped in the less frequented streets. The granaries occupy a large part of the house

[1] I am indebted to Waddell's *Lhasa and its Mysteries* for this list.

and contain wheat, barley and peas. Grain is poured in through an opening at the top and drawn out from a trap-door below. Grain in the dry Tibetan atmosphere, and in the absence of rats, will last for as long as a hundred years. Outside one room an old woman is weaving woollen cloth on a primitive loom, and near by is the kitchen—a smoke-blackened room with stone grates and rows of huge copper pans. A heap of mustard-straw is being used for fuel, but there are piles of dung-cakes too. Servants are continually passing to and fro; they are extremely dirty and clothed in filthy grease-stained garments. Only on high cere-monial occasions are they properly clad. From a closed door comes the monotonous rising and falling of a monk's voice as he prays for the dead of the household, thus ensuring that they shall have the best possible rebirth. Now and then he rings a bell, beats a gong or clashes small cymbals. Half the rooms in the house seem to have some religious significance, and several monks are always in residence. This house is typical of many in Tibet, though as a rule the better houses have three stories.

In return for all this hospitality we used to have equally for-midable luncheon parties at the Deyki-Lingka; but whereas each official had to ask the Mission to lunch, we could invite several at the same time. In this way we avoided complete inundation.

At the end of September we gave a luncheon party to the officials of Cabinet rank. These were the three Shap-pes (the Kalön Lama being away from Lhasa), Trimön Shap-pe (retired), Tsarong Dzasa, the Lord Chamberlain, and the Duke. Un-fortunately the Duke almost forgot the engagement and only arrived in time for tea. Ringang came as additional interpreter, and our lay and monk guides attended *ex officio*. For entertain-ment we hired the town orchestra, the dancing girls and the chang girls. Great features were the microphone and loud-speaker, which Nepean had rigged up so that people performing in his tent behind the house could be heard in our upstairs room or in the luncheon tent. Our guests insisted on having songs from the dancers and chang girls several times as loud as normal, and gramophone music equally blaringly played. Then Tsarong and Ringang had a long argument before the microphone, much to the delight of our guests. After tea and liqueurs in our sitting-room we sat down to lunch under an awning in the garden. We provided a solid six-course luncheon of " English " food, starting with hors d'œuvres and working through soup and asparagus to roast mutton with vegetables, and then subsiding to cold tongue and fruit salad. The Shap-pes showed less obvious enjoyment in sampling our food than we had theirs, but they did their best, and the party was an undoubted success.

A more fortuitous entertainment was provided by a chang girl trying to deal for the first time in her life with a soda-water syphon. Having poured some whisky into a glass, she pressed the handle of the syphon with such enthusiasm that the whisky was shot entirely out of the glass, most of it into her face. Luckily she agreed with us in seeing the humorous side of it. It took the girls some time to learn that whisky must neither be poured out nor drunk in the same way as chang. It was their natural inclination to fill the glass with neat spirit and to make the unfortunate guest drink it straight off. Before our guests departed—at five o'clock in the afternoon—all the servants, including the all-important cook, who is usually overlooked on such occasions, were lined up and presented with scarves and a small bag of rupees. Similar largesse was distributed to the orchestra, the dancers and the chang girls.

Two days after we had returned the hospitality of the Shap-pes we invited the Prime Minister to come to lunch. He showed considerable interest in the wireless, and a message was transmitted on his behalf to the Chief of Signals at Jubbulpore. We sometimes wonder if the latter thought somebody was having a practical joke at his expense! A few days later we gave a lunch to eighteen guests who were mainly fourth-rank officials; many of the more important ones could not come, as the Regent was at this time preparing to leave Lhasa in order to visit Samye Monastery. On the following day, making our seventh party in a single week, we gave the last of our big luncheon parties. This time the guests were all below fourth rank. They included the secretaries of the various Government departments, Tendong, the Gyantse Dzongpön who had been our guide from Gyantse to Lhasa, the monk telegraphist, and many younger sons of noble families.

Although there were rumours that the Tashi Lama, together with his controversial Chinese escort, had reached Jyekundo on his way to Tibet, the Regent set off on 6th October to visit Samye Monastery, to the south-east of Lhasa, on the Tsang-po river. This incident is only too typical of the happy-go-lucky Tibetan outlook. The political situation was as bad as it could be, yet he took two of the four Shap-pes with him and—to take photographs—the only depön who had any knowledge of machine-gunnery. So that during his absence—and he was away for six weeks—no important decision could be made; the army was even weaker than usual, and, for all the Tibetans knew, the British Mission might have had to return at short notice to India. But this religious pilgrimage had been planned for some time and could not be delayed any longer. Possibly the Regent, who was at this time in a state of great uncertainty and vacillation, hoped that events would tend to settle themselves in his absence and thus save him the trouble and responsibility of making difficult decisions.

CHAPTER SEVEN

HISTORICAL INTERLUDE

THE early history of the Tibetans is obscure. Their own " Book of Genesis " tells how a certain monkey who was an incarnation of the God of Mercy or the Compassionate Spirit (Avalokita in Sanskrit, Chen-re-zi in Tibetan) met a she-demon who had been born in misery owing to the wickedness of her former life. She inveigled him into marrying her, and they produced six children, who are the ancestors of the Tibetan race. Although the early writers are at pains to explain how their saintly ancestor succeeded in getting rid of the tails and long hair of his children by bringing them up on a diet of sacred grain, yet this traditional explanation of the origin of the Tibetan race is not accepted by the anthropologists, who declare prosaically that they are a branch of the ancient Mongolian stock which has inhabited the high plateau of Asia from time immemorial.

The earliest monarchy is supposed by Tibetans to date from the fifth century B.C., but little is known for certain of the rule of the early Kings of Tibet until in the seventh century of our era King Song-tsen Gampo came to the throne. Although Buddhism was first introduced into Tibet in the fifth century it had made little headway against the earlier Pon religion of pure animism, whose chief activity was the propitiation of innumerable malignant devils. The new King, by introducing a reformed system of laws and by other acts of general enlightenment, prepared the way for a more adolescent faith. Moreover, after great military successes in Burma, China and Nepal, he took two queens, one from Nepal and the other from the palace of the Emperor of China, and it was these two Buddhist ladies who inspired the vigorous introduction of the more theistic development of Buddhism which was then prevalent in India, China and Japan.

The original faith of Gautama Buddha (who lived in the sixth century B.C.) was essentially a fatalistic doctrine of negation and despair based on the less nihilistic tenets of Jainism and Brahmanism. It held, as Waddell summarizes it, "that man's sole Salvation was strenuously to try to escape finally and completely outside Life and Existence in any form, with its supposed endless cycles of rebirths after death for the same individual soul, into the haven of Total Extinction of all Existence in Nirvana (literally ' blown out ' like an extinguished candle flame) ".

A faith which demanded that its adherents must abandon wife, home and worldly goods, and live as a mendicant upon the charity of others in order to accumulate sufficient merit to attain Nirvana in a remote future birth, was hardly likely to become a popular religion for the many. Moreover, woman was only capable of salvation if, in a future rebirth, she should be born as a man. However, the great ruler Asoka (whose grandfather had successfully kept Alexander the Great out of India in 327–325 B.C.), by adopting Buddhism, in its more humanized form, as the State religion for his vast Indian Empire in 261 B.C., saved this faith from probable extinction. And it was this Asoka who, for the first time, caused to be recorded the life-story and sayings of Gautama Buddha and, by dispatching missionaries, propagated the faith throughout the Orient.

From these foundations sprang a theistic development which created a less remote Buddha who was called Amitabha, " The Boundless Light " (Öpa-me in Tibetan), but who was still so far removed from mankind that he was provided with an archangel in the form of Avalokita, the Saviour, or the God of Mercy. This more popular form of Buddhism flourished in India during .the early centuries of our era and was, as has already been recorded, introduced to Tibet by the wives of Song-tsen Gampo; but it will be seen that present-day Lamaism has in many ways reverted to the earlier form, in which half the population lived parasitically on the working laymen, who had little hope of salvation. An alphabet of Sanskritic characters was brought from Kashmir so that the Scriptures could be translated and written down, and these have survived in Tibet while their originals in India were totally destroyed by the iconoclastic Mohammedan invaders in the twelfth century. Monasteries were erected and the country ceased to be a land merely of nomadic herdsmen, for now the ancient civilizations of China, India and Nepal were introduced by Buddhist missionaries and the returning soldiers of Song-tsen Gampo. This King also built himself a palace on the hill where the Potala now stands.

One of Song-tsen's successors possessed communistic tendencies; he ordained that every Tibetan should have an equal share of the country's wealth. But it was found that the poor, finding themselves suddenly rich, became indolent and soon lost all they had. Three times he ordered the equal distribution of wealth, but at this stage, we are told, the King was poisoned by his mother. The priests astutely ascribed the failure of the scheme to the doctrine of the transmigration of souls, by which men do not start equal in this life but bring with them a heritage of good or bad from previous existences.

The Buddhist faith gradually extended during the eighth and ninth centuries, and Tibetans went down to study in Nepal and India. It was at this time that Ti-song De-tsen and Ral-pa-chan reigned; these two, together with Song-tsen Gampo, are revered by the Tibetans as " The Three Religious Kings, Men of Power ". That they were men of power is attested by the fact that Tibet was then at the zenith of her military power. Having subjugated Turkistan, Nepal and the western part of China, only the hatred of hot climates and the fear of disease can have saved India from the incursions of these conquering hordes from the north of the Himalayas.

When Ral-pa-chan was only forty-eight years old he was slain by his brother Lang-dar-ma, the head of the anti-Buddhist party, and for nearly a hundred years religion suffered a severe set-back, although the fratricide himself ruled for only three years before he was slain by the Black Hat Dancer. After this the famous line of kings ended, and for some three centuries the country was ruled by petty chiefs whose forts can still be seen dominating the villages over which they held sway.

When Buddhism again asserted itself it was in a changed form known as Lamaism, much influenced by the more mystic teaching of India and Nepal, where the purer faith of Gautama had degenerated to mere sorcery and the practice of black arts.

In the twelfth century the grandson of the great conqueror, Jenghiz Khan, invited the chief monk of Sakya monastery, who was then the most important man in Tibet, to visit his Mongolian court. The Mongol armies of Jenghiz Khan, and later of Kublai Khan, in their victorious progress across high Asia did not molest Tibet; due possibly either to the comparative poverty of the country, or to some racial or religious affinity.

In the thirteenth century Kublai Khan had conquered the Chinese Empire and established a Mongol dynasty. In the year 1270, wishing to receive the blessing of the Pontiff of the greatest Church in Asia, he, like his predecessor, invited the then ruler of Sakya, whom alone in all Asia he admitted as an equal, to visit his court; and his history records that the Emperor, adopting Lamaism as the State religion of the Mongols, gave the temporal sovereignty of Tibet to this hierarch, who thus became the first priest-King of Tibet.

This hierarchy lasted for some seventy-five years until it merged into the second monarchy, which, now that the Tibetans had lost something of their martial ardour, was more or less dependent on China. This dynasty lasted for nearly three hundred years, that is, until 1635. During this latter period came a much-needed religious reformation. Tibetan Buddhism had absorbed too much of the later debased form of Indian Buddhism, which had been further adulterated by the devil-worship already prevalent in the country. The reformer was Tsong-kapa, " The Man from the Land of Onions ", who was born in 1358 in Amdo in north-eastern Tibet. His followers, who became known as the Gelugpa, or Yellow Hats, to distinguish them from the Red Hats of the existing priesthood, were not allowed to marry and were expected to lead a life of devotion and simplicity. It was Tsong-kapa who founded the great monasteries of Ganden and Sera on the outskirts of Lhasa, and his successor founded the Tashi-lhünpo monastery of Shigatse, which was destined to become the residence of the Tashi Lamas.

Tsong-kapa's successor died in 1474, and some years later it was claimed that his spirit had passed into the body of a child; and it was this infant who received the title of Dalai Lama from a Mongolian ruler, a title that was held by each subsequent reincarnation of the head of the Yellow Hat sect. Thus was solved the difficulty in finding a successor to a celibate ruler; and the system of reincarnation has become so popular that there are now about a thousand incarnate lamas in the Tibetan priesthood.

The fifth reincarnation was Lob-sang Gyatso, a man of peasant origin. He set himself to subdue the decadent Red Hats, and for this purpose called in the help of the Mongols, who, as a reward for his energy and piety, gave the Dalai Lama the temporal sovereignty of Tibet. Lob-sang then started to build the Potala Palace on the rocky hill-top where lay the ruins of the earlier edifice of King Song-tsen Gampo. The Dalai Lama's old tutor was made Grand Lama of Tashi-lhünpo and was considered to be an incarnation of Amitabha, "The Boundless Light". The Dalai Lama himself was from this time regarded as an incarnation of Avalokita (The God of Mercy). As Amitabha is on a superior spiritual level to Avalokita, it follows, metaphysically speaking, that the Tashi is senior to the Dalai in spiritual affairs; and many Tibetans, especially those from the Shigatse district, consider this to be so. But as the Dalai Lama lives at Lhasa, the religious and political capital of the country, he has always tended to take the lead in secular affairs. The Dalai is the active and the Tashi the passive element of the Godhead.

Soon after the Manchus had forcibly replaced the Ming dynasty, Lob-sang visited Peking, and was received by the Emperor with all the honours of an independent sovereign. But this desire for recognition by the Emperor was destined in the future to disturb the peaceful isolation of Tibet and to draw her into the vortex of world politics. For both China and Mongolia recognized their responsibility to the Dalai Lama as the spiritual head of their Church, and from time to time found it necessary to interfere with the conduct of his affairs. After reorganizing the government of Lhasa, Lob-sang died in 1680. During the latter part of his reign he followed the custom of leaving secular affairs in charge of his Chief Minister while he devoted himself to religion. The

Potala, much in its present form, was completed a few years after his death. Until the reign of the last Pontiff he was considered the greatest of the Dalai Lamas, and is known in Lhasa as " The Great Fifth ", while others are referred to merely by their numbers.

The next Dalai Lama was not interested in religious matters and spent his time carousing and love-making. He was also a great poet, and some of his songs are still sung in Tibet. Naturally many of the Tibetans, and more especially the Chinese and Mongols, thought that there must have been some mistake in the selection of this incarnation; and during the dissensions that arose the Dzungarian Mongols swept across Tibet, and the Chinese took the opportunity of increasing their influence at Lhasa. They annexed parts of Eastern Tibet, garrisoned the Tachienlu–Lhasa road, and in 1706 put the young Dalai to death and substituted another whom they declared to be the true incarnation. But the Tibetans, backed by the Mongols, refused to recognize the Chinese candidate. Already they considered the incarnation of the God of Mercy to be beyond the machinations of worldly conquerors. Fearing a Mongol–Tibetan combination against China, the Emperor dispatched an army in 1718 which, though defeated at first, eventually entered Lhasa; and from that time until the Chinese revolution in 1910 the Emperors have endeavoured to station representatives, called Ambans, in the capital. In 1750 the Ambans murdered the Regent. In revenge all the Chinese in Lhasa were put to death by the Tibetans, but this merely resulted in the arrival of another Chinese army to strengthen the power of the unpopular Ambans.

Towards the end of the eighteenth century the warlike Gurkhas had gained the ascendancy over the other minor kingdoms of Nepal. Having attacked Sikkim, they occupied parts of southern Tibet and in 1791 sacked Shigatse, the second largest town, which lies just beside the Tashi Lama's monastery at Tashi-lhünpo. At this a large army of Chinese and Tibetans marched across the high passes and desolate wind-swept plateaus of northern Tibet in the middle of winter, and in one of the most remarkable campaigns in history defeated the Gurkhas several times and followed them down to within a few miles of their capital, Katmandu.

After these victories the Chinese increased the power of the two Ambans, who were given equal rank with the Dalai and Tashi Lamas and were even to take a prominent part in selecting the incarnations of the more important Lamas; moreover, the Dalai Lama could now only approach the Emperor through the Ambans. But there has always been a wide divergence between the edicts of the Emperor at Peking and their enforcement at remote Lhasa, where the independent nomad blood of the Tibetans still resents any interference. From the time of the Chinese ascendancy until the birth of the present Dalai Lama in 1876 the Dalais invariably died young; for the Ambans found it easier to control a Regent who was dependent on their favour than one who was the spiritual head of the whole Buddhist Church and a God-King in Tibet.

In the nineteenth century there was further trouble between the Tibetans and the Nepalese. A tribe from Nepal overran northern Sikkim, which was then a Tibetan dependency, and were only expelled with the aid of Tibetan troops. In 1855 the Gurkhas again invaded Tibet and gained the right to establish a Nepalese Agency at Lhasa, and various other concessions.

So far we have only considered the relations of Tibet with other Asiatic powers. It is now time to see how the Tibetans were forced, in spite of their policy of exclusion, to meet the representatives of European civilizations.

In 1626 a Portuguese Jesuit priest entered Tibet, but did not penetrate far. (Marco Polo, by the way, had crossed the Pamirs but never set foot in Tibet.) In 1661 two Jesuits, an Austrian and a Belgian, left Peiping and passing by the Koko Nor Lake travelled south-west over the Chang Tang until Lhasa was reached. They spent a month there and then went on to Katmandu, the present capital of Nepal. It was one of them who described the fifth Dalai Lama as " Devilish God-the-Father who puts to death such as refuse to adore him ".

When Warren Hastings was Governor of Bengal, and the power of Britain was making itself felt in India, he decided that we could no longer tolerate the Bhutanese raids on the borders of Bengal. During the consequent subjection of Bhutan the Tashi Lama wrote to intercede for the vanquished country, which was at that time under Tibetan suzerainty. So it was in 1774, to follow up friendly relations instigated by the Tashi Lama, that Hastings sent George Bogle, a young writer of the East India Company, to visit Bhutan and then to proceed to Tashi-lhünpo to meet the Tashi Lama. Similarly, in 1783 Samuel Turner went up to Shigatse. In 1811 an eccentric Englishman, George Manning, who was a friend of Charles Lamb, went to Gyantse and, owing to his knowledge of medicine, was allowed to go on to Lhasa. Unfortunately he was a very poor observer, to judge by his inadequate account of the journey; though his much-quoted verdict on Phari: " Dirt, dirt, grease, smoke. Misery, but good mutton ", is worth recording.

After the Gurkha campaign of 1792 the Chinese, thinking that we had assisted the Nepalese, encouraged the Tibetan policy of exclusion. In 1850, having annexed Sikkim, we found ourselves neighbours of Tibet and in control of the trade route between Lhasa and India. But it was found impossible to open up any sort of communication with Lhasa. China was at that time the suzerain of Tibet, and the Chinese Ambans at Lhasa found it in their interests to encourage this policy of exclusion, which was almost fanatically maintained by the Tibetans. Suspicion of the intentions of the Government of India was further increased by the remarkable secret explorations of the Bengali, Sarat Das and others. The adventures of these famous surveying " Pandits " make fascinating reading. Recording distance with the beads of their rosaries, and hiding instruments and records in their prayer-wheels, they were able to visit and map Lhasa, even receiving a blessing from the Dalai Lama, whose omniscience fortunately failed to penetrate their disguises. But this was achieved at the daily peril of their lives. The village headmen were held by the Lhasa government as personally responsible, under penalty of death, that no foreigner should pass their village. This responsibility and threat were passed on by the headman to every villager; and fearful were the tortures meted out to the incarnate lama who, after much importunity, assisted Sarat Das to reach the Holy City of Lhasa in disguise. This was only sixty years ago.

In 1885 Macaulay, a secretary to the Government of Bengal, obtained Chinese permission to conduct a Mission to Lhasa; but when the Tibetan authorities refused to allow it, the project was abandoned. Soon after this the Tibetans, instigated by the State Oracle at Nechung, occupied part of British Sikkim. Protests addressed to the Chinese and Tibetans remained unanswered and peaceful messengers were maltreated, so in 1888 General Graham attacked the fort, expelled the Tibetans and advanced up the

Chumbi Valley. At last, in 1890, the Sikkim Convention was signed by China and Great Britain, recognizing a British Protectorate over Sikkim, delineating the boundary between Tibet and Sikkim, and stipulating that the question of trade facilities across the Sikkim–Tibet frontier should be discussed at a later date. As a result of the last clause a trade mart was established at Yatung in the Chumbi Valley in 1893. But the Tibetans, who had not signed these treaties, refused to recognize them and obstructed all attempts to develop the trade mart at Yatung and to mark out the frontier between Sikkim and Tibet. When, in 1900, we tried to treat direct with the Dalai Lama, letters were returned unopened, for the Lhasa Government feared that the British desired not only to increase their territory at the expense of Tibet but to undermine the influence of the monasteries and generally to counteract their cherished policy of seclusion.

The late Dalai Lama, born in 1876, was two or three years old when he was identified. A few years later he was brought to Lhasa, where he took up his residence at the Potala. His four immediate predecessors had all died under mysterious circumstances before they were old enough to exercise any power, so that Tibet had been administered by Regents for a hundred years. As the Dalai Lama grew up the power of China seemed to be waning. True, the Amban remained at Lhasa, but his power was chiefly nominal; this was especially brought home to the Tibetans when the results of the Sino-Japanese war became known in Lhasa. At this time the young Dalai Lama had a Russian tutor, one Dorjieff, a Buriat monk from Siberia, and this man persuaded the leading Tibetans that Russia, since her recent advances in Mongolia, was embracing the Buddhist religion more and more, and that it was therefore to powerful Russia that Tibet should turn for help against British intrigues. Consequently in 1900, and again in 1901, Dorjieff escorted an envoy from the Dalai Lama with letters for the Tsar of Russia. When they returned they brought to Lhasa a supply of Russian arms and ammunition as well— paradoxically enough—as a magnificent set of Russian Episcopal robes as a personal present for the Dalai Lama. There were rumours—even reports in the Chinese press—of an agreement between Russia and China, by which China had transferred to Russia all her interests in Tibet. Although these rumours were officially denied, the British Government was very anxious for the safety of the northern frontier of India from Kashmir through Nepal, Sikkim, Bhutan and Assam to Burma. This was before the Russo-Japanese war and the Anglo-Russian agreement: Russia was still looking eastward to fulfil her troubled destiny. The North-West Frontier had been a continual source of trouble and expense, but hitherto, relying on a Tibet governed under the comparatively peaceful suzerainty of friendly China, we had maintained no garrisons on the malarial north-east frontier of India. Now the integrity of this frontier was threatened.

So it was that in 1903 Lord Curzon, the Viceroy of India, proposed to dispatch a Mission accompanied by an armed escort to deal directly with the Dalai Lama at Lhasa, and to discuss the commercial and diplomatic relations of Britain and Tibet. Assurances were at the last moment received from Russia that they had no designs upon Tibet, but that if we increased our influence in Tibet, Russia might find it necessary to advance elsewhere (in, as it proved, Mongolia). However, as our relations with Tibet, especially in regard to trade, were most unsatisfactory, Lord Curzon persuaded the Home Government to send Colonel Younghusband with an armed escort as far as Kampa Dzong, a few miles north of the Sikkim–Tibet frontier. The Mission went up to Kampa Dzong in 1903 and stayed there for five months, but the Tibetans refused to have anything to do with it and vigorously urged its immediate return to India. The Chinese disclaimed any coercive power over the Tibetans, and what had started as a peaceful Mission was forced to become a military expedition.

Younghusband, joined by reinforcements, marched up the Chumbi Valley, occupied Phari Dzong, and advanced towards Gyantse, halting at Tuna, beside Dochen Lake, until March 1904. In spite of considerable opposition from the Tibetan soldiers the expedition captured Gyantse Dzong and, crossing the Karo La, a pass over 16,000 feet high, fought its way to Lhasa. The Tibetan authorities, while continually urging the return of the Mission, for a long time refused to consider coming to terms. Although the Tibetan soldiers had no sort of modern equipment they showed great courage, partly because this was their first experience of modern warfare, nor had they any conception of the strength of their foe. The lamas, who were really behind their stubborn resistance, had given them charms which would, they assured them, afford protection from the British bullets. So the Tibetan soldiers, armed with antiquated muzzle-loading guns and broad-swords, advanced with complete nonchalance against our service rifles and machine-guns. There were of course many casualties; but the lamas decided they had only given them spells for copper bullets, and as the British ammunition was of some other metal the magic had not worked!

The Dalai Lama, advised by Dorjieff, fled to Mongolia and eventually reached Urga, 1500 miles, as the crow flies, to the north-east of Lhasa. Later he returned southward to Sining and at last reached Peiping, where he stayed until the end of 1908. The Chinese issued a proclamation deposing the Dalai Lama, but this was completely disregarded by the Tibetans, who have always ignored any Chinese interference with the power of the Dalai Lama. They continued to refer all important matters to him. Meanwhile, on the twenty-seventh day of the seventh month of the Wood Dragon year (7th September 1904), a treaty was signed in the Potala Palace at Lhasa between the representatives of Britain and those of the Dalai Lama's Government, the Chinese Amban and the Nepalese and Bhutanese representatives. Apart from the payment of an indemnity by Tibet and the British occupation of the Chumbi Valley until this was paid, the treaty was concerned with strengthening trade relations and guaranteeing the mainten-ance and safety of the trade route between Tibet and Sikkim. With this object a trade mart was to be established at Gyantse, half-way between Sikkim and Lhasa, in addition to the existing mart at Yatung.

From this time onwards the relations between the British and the Tibetans entirely changed. Before the 1904 expedition they had regarded us with extreme suspicion : from then on they came to realize that we had no desire to subvert their religion or to occupy any part of their territory. We wanted a strong indepen-dent Tibet, possibly under the suzerainty of China, but free from the interference of other countries. The Tibetans were also favourably surprised that having captured the Holy City—which they had considered impregnable—we should almost immediately have retired. The behaviour of our troops and our treatment of the wounded also created a very good impression. The Tibetan administration was not interfered with and the monasteries and other holy places were not desecrated or looted. When grain and other supplies were bought, a liberal price was paid.

In 1906 the 1904 convention was ratified by the Emperor of China with modifications which gave the Chinese a practically free hand in Tibet while we guaranteed not to annex any territory or to interfere in the internal administration of the country. In the following year an agreement was signed by Great Britain and Russia imposing a policy of non-interference in Tibet and binding both Powers to negotiate through China in Tibetan affairs. The Tibetan Government, however, were not consulted in either of these matters.

Apart from fostering trade between India and Tibet, the object of Great Britain in the 1904 Mission and the subsequent agreements had been to assure the territorial integrity of Tibet and to safeguard the northern frontier of India by maintaining her existence as a peaceful autonomous State; but the chief result, paradoxically enough, was to put Tibet more and more under Chinese domination, and to give her cause for complaint in that we had once again concluded a treaty with China concerning her without consulting the Lhasa Government. The 1907 agreement between Great Britain and Russia further weakened our position in Tibet by binding both Powers to negotiate in Tibetan affairs through China alone.

China immediately set about reasserting her power in Tibet, wherein she was helped by this treaty and by the apparent lack of interest in Tibetan affairs shown by the British Government of the day. While the Dalai Lama was still absent a Chinese Amban came to Lhasa. The Tibetan indemnity to Britain was paid off by China, and we accordingly evacuated the Chumbi Valley. The Tibetans were persuaded that it was only fear of China that had induced the British to withdraw so soon from Lhasa and to leave no representative there. Trouble broke out once more on the eastern marches of Tibet, in those turbulent semi-independent States inhabited by people of Tibetan blood but under more direct control of the Manchu Emperors than the rest of Tibet.

In 1727, as a result of the Chinese having entered Lhasa, the boundary between China and Tibet was laid down as between the head-waters of the Mekong and Yangtse rivers, and marked by a pillar, a little to the south-west of Batang. Land to the west of this pillar was administered from Lhasa, while the Tibetan chiefs of the tribes to the east came more directly under China. This historical Sino-Tibetan boundary was used until 1910. The

K

States Der-ge, Nyarong, Batang, Litang and the five Hor States—
to name the more important districts—are known collectively in
Lhasa as Kham, an indefinite term suitable to the Tibetan Government, who are disconcertingly vague over such details as treaties
and boundaries.

In 1860 the aggressive Tibetans of Nyarong invaded and conquered several of the neighbouring States who were also under
the nominal protection of China. But when they appealed for
assistance against the warlike chief of Nyarong the Chinese Government were unable to help them, but the Dalai Lama sent a Tibetan
army into Kham and the power of Nyarong was broken. This
State, although to the east of the 1727 boundary, was henceforward
administered by the Lhasa Government with the full acquiescence
of China.

After the 1904 expedition to Lhasa the Chinese started to
impose their domination over Tibet, not only diplomatically in
Lhasa but forcibly in Kham. Chinese troops entered by Tachienlu
on the Szechuan frontier and attempted to interfere with the
powers of reigning chiefs and lamas. As a result of this the
nomads and lamas of Batang rose and drove out or slew the
isolated Chinese garrison.

In 1905 General Chao Erh-feng was put in charge of punitive
measures. His policy was to reduce Tibet to the status of a
Chinese province, with the Dalai Lama as a merely spiritual
figure-head. Great monasteries were besieged and razed to the
ground, monks were killed and local chiefs beheaded. Chao
Erh-feng's relentless and harsh measures led to a renewed and
fiercer revolt. But the Tibetans lacked organization and modern
methods, and were, especially in Der-ge, torn by internal dissensions. Kham was gradually overpowered. By the end of 1909
Batang, Der-ge and Cham-do were occupied by Chinese troops
and the road to Lhasa lay open.

In spite of Tibetan protests, the Chinese continued to advance.
Resistance to them was sporadic. The Lhasa Government,
realizing the power of China, wished to avoid direct conflict.
They were also beguiled by the diplomatic persuasiveness of the
Amban at Lhasa, who assured the Tibetans that no more than 1000
Chinese troops would come, and that their real object was to
police the frontiers and roads. So, in February 1910, for the third
time in history, a Chinese army marched into the Holy City of

Tibet. It is interesting to note that on each of these three occasions China was stimulated by the inroads of other Powers—the Mongols in 1720, the Nepalese in 1790, and the British in 1910.

Let us return now to follow the fortunes of the unfortunate Pontiff of the Buddhist Church. In the summer of 1904, as the British expedition entered Lhasa, the Dalai Lama fled northwards from the Potala Palace. After a long journey he at last reached Urga, the capital of outer Mongolia, nearly 1500 miles north-east of Lhasa, a city regarded by the Buddhists of High Asia as a Holy City second only to Lhasa. After a year at Urga, and two more at a great monastery near Sining, he at last reached Peiping in 1908, having been invited to an audience with the Emperor. But whereas the Great Fifth Dalai Lama had visited the Chinese Emperor as an equal, now great care was taken to stress his position as a vassal of the Manchu throne. In addition to his title of Great Good Self-Existent Buddha of Heaven, an additional title of honour—Loyal and Submissive Vice-Regent—was conferred upon him as well as an annual allowance. Leaving Peiping in December 1908 and travelling by way of Kansu, Sining and Jyekundo, he reached Lhasa in December 1909, after an absence of five years.

Two months later 2000 Chinese troops appeared at Lhasa. The Dalai Lama had once more to flee from the Potala Palace. The efforts of the British Trade Agents at Gyantse and Yatung to promote friendship between Tibet and Britain had not been in vain. During his long exile the Dalai Lama had had much time to think. He did not forget the manner of his reception at Peiping. Now he fled for his personal safety, and this time it was to British India that he fled.

The advance-guard of the Chinese army had had special orders to capture him, but they were just too late. In the middle of the night the Dalai Lama, accompanied by six ministers and a small escort, fled southward across the Tsang-po to the Chumbi Valley. The escort were left at Chaksam to deal with the pursuing Chinese soldiers. In the ensuing fight—according to the Dalai Lama's own letter—two Tibetans and seventy Chinese were killed. At Yatung the Chinese soldiers were only a short distance behind His Holiness.

Nine days after leaving Lhasa the exiles crossed the border into Sikkim, having ridden almost 300 miles and having crossed passes of 15,000 and 16,000 feet—a phenomenal achievement for men of advanced age who normally took little exercise. The party proceeded to Darjeeling, where they were given sanctuary and hospitably entertained for nearly two years. During this time the Dalai Lama and his Ministers went down to Calcutta at the invitation of the Viceroy, Lord Minto. This further augmented the feelings of friendliness between Britain and Tibet.

Sir Charles Bell, with his great knowledge of the Tibetan language and affairs, arranged for the accommodation and entertainment of the Dalai during his exile in British India. His was the unpleasant task of telling the Dalai that the British Government would not intervene between China and Tibet, and that they could only recognize the government set up in Tibet by the Chinese. To such an extent were our hands tied by treaties that we could do nothing to interfere since the Chinese had guaranteed not to alter the administration of Tibet, or to convert it to the status of a Chinese province. It seemed that as long as China kept her hands off Nepal, Bhutan and Sikkim, we were prepared to abandon Tibet to the Chinese. His Holiness, realizing that the recent Chinese aggressions had been brought on—however unwittingly—by the British Mission to Lhasa and its subsequent retreat, was speechless with distress. He and his Ministers even denied any sovereign rights of China over Tibet; and they repudiated the 1906 Convention, which, indeed, they had never even been invited to sign. It seemed that Tibet had no friend to whom she could turn. It was at this juncture, in 1911, that the revolution against the Manchu Dynasty broke out in China.

Once again the tables were turned. General Chao Erh-feng, a great man in spite of his ruthlessness, who had become Viceroy of Szechuan, was treacherously beheaded by the revolutionaries, and the Chinese lost control of most of the frontier districts.

In June 1912 the Dalai Lama and his Ministers returned to the Holy City and Tibet became once more an autonomous State.

In eastern countries which have had spiritual rulers the power has usually been in the hands of a chief minister, while the religious head lived a life of contemplation and seclusion. But the late Dalai Lama, being a man of exceptional character and ability, set himself to follow the example of the " Great Fifth " and to rule the country himself. Not only did he control the organization of the monasteries and the religious life of the people, but he took under his personal supervision more and more of the details of secular government. Perhaps it was these centralizing tendencies of the Dalai that, more than anything else, aroused the alarm of the Tashi, and led to the long and unfortunate quarrel between these two mysterious figures.

In 1904, after the Younghusband Mission had returned from Lhasa, Captain (now Sir Frederick) O'Connor, who had been the chief interpreter to the Mission, was left at Gyantse as the first British Trade Agent in Tibet. One of his first duties was to visit Shigatse, the second town of Tibet, to make the acquaintance of the Tashi Lama, who lives half a mile away in his walled monastery at Tashi-lhünpo which houses 4000 monks. As O'Connor was the first European ever to visit him, he was somewhat surprised when His Serenity said what a pleasure it was for him to renew his previous friendship with British officers. O'Connor suddenly realized that he was referring to the reception afforded more than a hundred and thirty years previously to the two officers sent up by Warren Hastings. The Tashi Lama was identifying himself with one of his previous incarnations.

Captain O'Connor found that the Tashi was then a young man of twenty-two years of age, very friendly, straightforward and intelligent, but at the same time very spiritually minded and strangely aloof from worldly matters, living a cloistered life given up to prayer and meditation. He was much interested in what O'Connor could tell him about the outside world and accepted the invitation of the Government of India to come and meet their Royal Highnesses the Prince and Princess of Wales (later King George V and Queen Mary) on their forthcoming tour of India.

In 1905 His Serenity, with a suite of some 300 monks and laymen, set off with Captain O'Connor for India. As His Serenity was carried in his palanquin the Tibetans came from afar to line the route in the hope of touching his palanquin and receiving a blessing. It is recorded that these villagers, who are not easily moved to tears, were so overcome that they wept with emotion. Although the Tashi Lama had never before spoken to any woman except his mother, he conversed for some time with their Royal Highnesses and impressed everybody by his quiet spiritual voice and charming natural manners; at the same time he met Lord Kitchener, Lord Minto, the Viceroy of India, and other important figures. He also witnessed a review of 60,000 troops at Rawal Pindi. Before returning to Tibet he made a pilgrimage to the holy places of Buddhism, and held a service beneath the famous tree at Boddh Gaya, where his great predecessor, Gautama Buddha, of whom he is believed to be the earthly personification, obtained enlightenment some 2400 years before.

In 1906 Sir Charles Bell was invited to visit His Serenity at Tashi-lhünpo and found him extremely friendly and much interested in the political situation. He feared that the Chinese, who were regaining their hold over Tibet, might have been annoyed by his visit to India. He also feared the Lhasa Government, who suspected that he was trying to secure the aid of Britain to help him to set up independent rule at Tashi-lhünpo. For the Tashi Lama has temporal power over three small districts, though not over Shigatse itself, which is administered by a dzongpön appointed from Lhasa.

It is unfortunate that there is considerable jealousy between Lhasa and Tashi-lhünpo. When the Chinese troops were in control of Lhasa the Tashi Lama's Ministers, several of whom were openly pro-Chinese, had secret relations with them, and refused to take up arms against China until compelled to do so. When the Dalai had been deposed by the Chinese in 1910 the Tashi had been invited to take his place. Though he had wisely refused to do this, he actually went to Lhasa and is said to have sat on the Dalai's throne. In 1912, when the Dalai returned from his exile at Darjeeling, it was arranged that the two Lamas should meet and discuss their differences at Ralung, but nothing came of this.

In 1912 the new republican government dispatched an army from Szechuan to Tibet to restore the Chinese position there; and Yuan Shih Kai issued a Presidential Order that Tibet was to be regarded as on an equal footing with the provinces of China proper.

In 1913 Russia concluded an agreement with China whereby the former recognized China's suzerainty over Mongolia, but Russia was allowed privileges which would give her a large measure of economical and political control over the country. Tibet has always been on very friendly terms with Mongolia, and now that that State was controlled by Russia it became all the more necessary for us to insist upon a strong and autonomous Tibet. Dorjieff had become active again and, using the authority of a letter given to him years before by the Dalai Lama, he engineered a "treaty" between Tibet and Mongolia. The

Kalön Lama was sent to Kham to drive back the Chinese, and from now on the border skirmishes developed into a frontier war between China and Tibet. The power of Lhasa at this time extended east to the Mekong, and north to the southern watershed of the Yangtse.

In order to settle these various differences a conference was arranged in 1913 at Simla between representatives of Great Britain, China and Tibet. The Dalai Lama wanted for Tibet complete control of internal and external affairs; to consult with the British only on more important external relations; to have no Chinese representatives or soldiers in Tibet, and for Nyarong Der-ge, Batang, Litang and the country up to Tachienlu—that is, all the regions inhabited by persons of Tibetan race—to be included in Tibet. The National Assembly, and later the Dalai Lama, also desired a British representative at Lhasa. The Chinese entered the conference with the hope of recovering the position they had held in Tibet at the conclusion of Chao Erh-feng's conquests. The object of Great Britain was to restore Tibet to the position of an autonomous State under Chinese suzerainty; to establish at Lhasa a stable and friendly Tibetan government free from all outside interference, and to restore peace between China and Tibet.

The Simla Convention was initialled in April 1914 by the three parties. Chinese suzerainty over Tibet was recognized, on condition that China did not convert Tibet into a Chinese province. A Chinese Amban with a suitable escort was to be re-established at Lhasa, and the British Agent at Gyantse was authorized to visit the city if necessary. The British Government promised the Tibetans diplomatic support, and reasonable help in securing munitions. But as regards the boundary question the Chinese and Tibetan points of view were so divergent as to make agreement seem impossible. Both sides ignored the 1727 Manchu boundary and, while the Tibetans claimed all the States up to Tachienlu, the Chinese wanted to push the boundary to within a few marches of Lhasa. Eventually Tibet was divided into two zones, " Outer Tibet " (as visualized from China) and " Inner Tibet ". The automony of Outer Tibet, which included Lhasa, Shigatse and Chamdo, was recognized. Inner Tibet, including Batang, Litang, Tachienlu and a large portion of Eastern Tibet, was to remain under the nominal control of Lhasa but the Chinese were to be allowed to send troops and officials there and to plant colonies.

China objected to the frontier which had been established between herself and Tibet, but otherwise agreed to accept the Convention in all respects. At this stage the Great War broke out, and there was an armed truce pending the resumption of mediation by Great Britain. During this truce the Tibetans had time to increase and modernize their army, but the worn out Chinese forces, owing to internal dissensions, were neglected and left to live off the country, so that they deteriorated into brigands and military adventurers.

A Chinese General broke the truce and made a sudden attack while the Tibetans were celebrating one of their many religious festivities. The Tibetans, however, soon rallied and drove the Chinese practically back to Tachienlu and thus recovered the greater part of Eastern Tibet. At this stage the British Consular Agent at Tachienlu was called in to mediate and the truce was re-established in 1918, with a provisional boundary through Batang, and one therefore much more favourable to the Tibetans.

A year later, in 1919, the Chinese proposed to resume the frontier negotiations, but for various reasons nothing was done. The Tibetans were by then running out of munitions, being now prohibited, in spite of our promise to help them in this respect, from importing them through India; and, feeling that we had not given them adequate support, they were forced to agree to receive a Chinese Mission in Lhasa. In 1920 this Mission reached Lhasa and remained for five months treating directly with the Tibetans in the presence of no British intermediary or witness. However, no definite agreement was made. During the same year, 1920, Sir Charles Bell, who had maintained his friendly relations with the Dalai Lama and who had frequently been invited by him to visit Lhasa, was at last allowed to conduct a Mission to Lhasa to endeavour to clarify the political situation.

Although the Tibetans had repeatedly proved to the world that they were competent to maintain order and peace in their own country, Tibet could not stand alone unless she was left alone. It became increasingly clear that, surrounded by Russia, China and India, and carefully watched by Japan, Tibet must rely on a stronger Power. If we could not guarantee her peace she must arm herself, and if we could not supply her with munitions she must turn elsewhere. The Tibetan reception of Sir Charles Bell's Mission was her final effort to secure our assistance.

Sir Charles Bell, accompanied only by Lieutenant-Colonel Kennedy of the I.M.S., spent eleven months at Lhasa. As both had long experience of dealing with the Tibetans, and spoke the language fluently, they were able to establish far more personal and friendly contacts than had been possible hitherto. The Dalai Lama showed his more than friendly intentions by receiving Sir Charles, at the very first interview, informally, sitting with him at a small table in his private apartment, with no witness present. This was regarded by the people of Lhasa as a special honour, as it was the custom for His Holiness to receive even the highest Tibetan officials while seated on his dais. His attitude was always most cordial: often he asked advice about the Tibetan army, some problem of education, finance or even on matters of justice. It was through a personal request from Sir Charles that the Dalai gave permission for the first attempt to climb Mount Everest, though Nepal had already refused to allow the expedition to reach the mountain from the Nepalese side. When it was probable that the Government of India would recall the Mission after it had been in Lhasa only a few months, the Dalai Lama, the Prime Minister and the Shap-pes begged, with the utmost urgency, that Sir Charles should remain longer; and when he eventually took the road to India the Dalai Lama's last words were: " We have known each other for a long time, and I have complete confidence in you, for we two are men of like mind. I pray continually that you may return to Lhasa." A month or two later His Holiness wrote to the Viceroy of India: "All the people of Tibet and myself have become of one mind, and the British and Tibetans have become one family ".

CHAPTER EIGHT

LHASA CITY

BEFORE visiting Tibet I had read of the horrors of winter travel, of the unmitigated grimness of the scenery, of the filth and benightedness of the inhabitants, and the squalor of their dwellings. After spending seven months in Tibet I had to amend my preconceived conclusions. True, in winter the high plateaux are swept by relentless dust-storms, and the thermometer falls below zero; but if one starts before dawn, has the good sense to follow the Tibetan way of dressing, and reaches one's destination before midday, when the storms usually start, even winter travel can be enjoyable. The country is bleak and forbidding at first sight; the hills as bare as the rocks of Aden, the valleys frequently sand or stone deserts—but what depth of colouring, what marvellous contrasts! The silver-gold barley rippling in the wind, the tremulous willow-groves, the dun and olive hills swept by deep violet shadows as the heavy cumulus clouds sail across the pale turquoise sky. And, for those who have eyes to see, the hills, bare at a casual glance, are bright with gentians, primulas and delphiniums, and teeming with innumerable species of rare and brightly coloured birds.

It is true that the common people do not wash, that their houses are, by our standards, filthy, and that they live in a state of serfdom—but what delightful folk, nevertheless! What finer men are there in the world than the nomads of the Chang Tang?

So far, I disagree with many of the earlier writers; but when it comes to describing Lhasa itself I am bound to say that they are right. Manning, the first Englishman to visit the Holy City, wrote of it in 1811: " There is nothing striking, nothing pleasing in its appearance. The habitations are begrimed with dirt and smut. The avenues are full of dogs, some growling and gnawing bits of hide which lie about in profusion and emit a charnel-house smell; others limping and looking livid; others ulcerated; others starved and dying, and pecked at by ravens; some dead and preyed upon. In short, everything seems mean and gloomy, and excites the idea of something unreal. Even the mirth and laughter of the inhabitants I thought dreamy and ghostly."

Though I disagree with his impression of the cheerlessness of the people, Manning is right; and Lhasa, the most conservative city in the world, is the same today.

For instance, suppose one were to follow the progress of a religious devotee who, having followed the weary track from India, enters the city and rides to the heart of it to visit the great Jo-kang, the Mecca of Lamaism, the holiest building in all Tibet. As the pilgrim approaches Lhasa along the main trade route from India, the city is completely hidden by the two rocky excrescences

on whose summits are the Potala and the Medical College. With
what excitement does he first see the sun glittering on the golden
roof-pavilions of the Potala wherein are enshrined the mortal
remains of former Dalai Lamas. On either side of the road are
lingkas, park-like enclosures, which are one of the most attractive
features of Lhasa. These belong to the Government and are controlled by special officials. Graceful white poplars and willows
are grown in these lingkas, the latter being pollarded every three
or four years to provide wood for building purposes. The road
now enters the western gateway (Pargo Kaling), built in the cleft
where the ridge connecting these two rocks drops to the level of
the plain. This gate is in the form of a magnificent chorten
through which an archway has been pierced. There are subsidiary
chortens built on the rocks at some distance on either side; and
strings of bells tinkling in the breeze, which connect the three
summits.

Beside the gateway are always swarms of beggars sitting against
the wall and, with obtruded tongues and upraised thumbs, whining
for alms. Many of the beggars are strong and healthy and could
easily work for their living, but in Lhasa begging is a privileged
profession, and a beggar would consider it far beneath his dignity
to accept any kind of work. Others are aged and loathsome,
blind, crippled and diseased. They just sit there all day, nodding
in the sun, only waking up to start their thin whining as somebody
rides by. Lhasa is full of such medicants: any child will come
and ask for money; any monk will surreptitiously hold out his
hand. Beyond the chorten, on the eastern wall of the Iron Hill,
are some attractive little houses precariously built into the vertical
wall. They seem to be fairly clean, and all manner of flowers
are growing there—nasturtiums, stocks, petunias and phlox
predominating.

Just inside the gate is a wooden sentry-box where a " policeman " sits sewing a yak-hair boot-sole or telling his beads. As
we splash through the flood-water he takes no notice, then rather
shamefacedly remembers that he is on duty and gets up to salute.
He wears a tattered and ancient khaki coat, a battered topee and
ragged trousers and boots. His face is extremely dirty.

Floods cover the waste ground beside the road, in some places
flowing right across it; the water is dark and slimy and stinks to
heaven. The Tibetans have no idea of sanitation; you see them,

men and women, just squatting down in the street like dogs. Were it not for the cold climate they would surely be afflicted by every variety of epidemic. On the other side of the road, between it and a pleasant-looking park, are great piles of offal eight and ten feet high. The women of Sho, the hamlet across the road, empty every sort of garbage on to this heap. Amongst the filth, some of which is indescribable, are two semi-decomposed dead dogs which are being torn at by others of their species and by three ravens, which are remarkably tame.

These dogs are one of the most disgusting and pathetic sights of the city. They seem to have no owners; nobody cares for them except for a few devout old women, who throw them scraps as an act of piety. In a Buddhist country it is not permitted to take life, so when an unwanted litter of puppies is born they are just turned out to fend for themselves. Domesticity, while providing no food for them, has yet robbed them of the power to hunt. These dogs are of no recognizable breed; in one you see a resemblance to a fox-terrier, in another to an Eskimo husky, but most of them are like nondescript sheep-dogs with prick ears and medium coats. Some of them, usually those that are regularly fed, dislike the smell of foreigners and bark furiously whenever we pass; but the majority have not that much strength, and lie motionless, perhaps in the middle of the road. There was one wretched animal that we saw day after day, with one eye, or rather the place where the eye should have been, swollen up to many times its normal size, completely raw and discharging.

In front of the hamlet of Sho there are several stalls, kept by women whose faces have been daubed with black pigment to protect them from the sun and wind. Most of them have black patches of plaster, the size of a halfpenny, stuck on to their temples to cure headache. They wear dusty homespun robes and greasy striped aprons. Their tousled hair looks as if it has not been washed or combed for months. On the right wrist a bracelet made from a white conch-shell is worn. One or two wear the triangular Lhasa head-dress, but there is no false hair hanging from it, and it merely looks like a distorted halo. These women are selling meat, yak-meat judging by the size of the joints; and there, towering behind them, is the Potala, the palace of the Vice-Regent of Buddha, the very essence of whose teaching is that life should not be taken.

Some children are flying kites; this was a favourite craze during the late autumn. Others, most of them women, are playing another street game which requires considerable skill : a shuttlecock is made by sticking a few feathers into a piece of wood and this is kept in the air by kicking it with the side or back of the foot. The girl usually removes her boot to play this game; hopping on one foot and holding her skirts out of the way, she kicks the shuttlecock either in front of her or behind her back. Some of them could in this way keep it in the air for five or ten minutes on end.

Just beyond Sho there are two small pagodas on the left of the road; these shelter stone inscriptions recording Chinese victories. On the other side of the road is a four-sided stone edict pillar erected by the Chinese with inscriptions in Tibetan, Chinese and Manchu. Raised on several stone steps, it is about twenty feet high. The inscription refers to the Tibetan conquests in China during the eighth century A.D. It can be seen that in some places words have been obliterated, and the Tibetans state that the Chinese, having obtained permission to make a copy of the inscription, effaced the names of the places in China which Tibet had conquered. Near the monolith is a well where the women stop to gossip as they bring earthenware or wooden vessels for water. There is, at any rate, one point in favour of these townswomen—unwashed though they may be—they are always laughing.

Soon after this the road divides : the left-hand fork, completely under water, leads past park-lands and monasteries to the northern part of the city. In this fork, beyond a small flooded park, is the mansion of the Yuto family, represented at present by the spruce young general who came to call on us. As the original house was burnt down some years ago the present mansion is very fine and up to date. It is a solid-looking square four-storied house with a courtyard and outbuildings on the southern side. The windows are of the casement type, and fitted with small panes of glass—a convenient size this, when glass has to be brought from India on the backs of yaks and mules. On the summit of the roof is a cylindrical banner draped with successive layers of the lucky colours.

The right-hand fork, just before it meets a chorten, turns to the right and crosses a stream by the famous Yuto Sampa, usually

known as the Turquoise Bridge, as it is roofed in the Chinese
manner with tiles of a greenish (but not turquoise) colour, and
has golden dragon-heads at the corners, and conical ornaments
along the sides. At each end of the bridge there are always
beggars to be found; usually the same ones sit there day after day
—a blind man with a thick black beard and a small yellow dog,
a wrinkled white-haired old woman, and two youngish men
revolving prayer-wheels. After turning to the left the road runs
through a plain Chinese gateway leading to a large open space.
To the north (left), across some unpleasant-smelling flooded land
and heaps of offal, are the ruins of Tengyeling monastery, which
was destroyed after it had sided with the Chinese in 1912. In
part of the remains of the building is the Post Office, run by an
intelligent English-speaking monk who was trained at Kalimpong.

Having passed this gate we are really in the city. To the south
is a ruined gateway and part of the old city wall. Along the
eastern side of this square in former times was the residence of the
Chinese Amban, with its considerable barracks, theatre, restaurant
and gardens. The place is completely ruined, but two Chinese
lions of granite still stand in front of the ruined wall, eloquent of
their vanished power.

The city itself is surprisingly small, a compact square of buildings
only two or three miles in circumference. The houses are all
flat-roofed and two or three stories high. They are whitewashed
for the most part, and have the usual Tibetan window narrowing
at the top and shaded by wide carved lintels usually valanced with
cloth of striped or diamond pattern. The windows are surrounded
by a dull black plaster border. Little glass is seen, usually a piece
of canvas is stretched across the frame. The window-sills and
balconies are gay with flowers, and often with singing birds in
cages. At each corner of the roofs are square towers holding
bundles of sticks with prayer-flags attached. The beams along
the eaves below the parapets, and over the windows and doors
are often carved with an intricate chequered pattern and picked
out in bright colours with red predominating.

The centre of the town, both in position and importance, is
the Jo-kang, the most holy place of pilgrimage in all Tibet,
the real Lhasa, the Place of God. This is usually referred to by
Europeans as " The Cathedral ". Unfortunately it is so surrounded by other buildings that it is impossible to obtain a com-

prehensive view of the outside, which is little higher than its neighbours, though its golden roof-pavilions rise above the drab sea of surrounding roofs, like the snow-capped peaks of a distant mountain-range. The Jo-kang was built in A.D. 652 to enshrine the images brought by the two Buddhist wives of the great King Song-tsen Gampo. Since that time the original shrine has been added to considerably, until some three centuries ago it attained its present dimensions.

Just outside the main gate, at the junction of two squalid streets, are two ancient weeping-willows which, having been struck by lightning in 1924, are now much reduced in size. They are supposed to have sprung miraculously from the hair of the Buddha. The Tibetans considered the breaking of the branches a most inauspicious event, and the Government ordered special prayers to be said in all monasteries to avert the suspected evil.

Beneath the shade of the willows' branches is a somewhat mutilated tablet, put up at the end of the eighteenth century by the Chinese, giving instructions how to combat the dread scourge of smallpox, which in the past has frequently decimated the population. As recently as 1925 some 7000 died from this plague in Lhasa alone. Near by is another stone monolith bearing record of a treaty between Tibet and China. The main gate is set back between two blocks of Government offices. The first thing that strikes one is the crowd of beggars in front of the doors, for nowhere else does the gift of a coin reflect so meritoriously upon the donor. There must have been nearly a hundred of them, some diseased and decrepit, exciting unutterable pity, others able-bodied and clamorous, needing nothing so much as a good whipping. As we approached they set up a piteous wailing, bowing up and down, sticking out their tongues, and stabbing the air with up-turned thumbs.

Several immense fluted pillars of wood support an overhanging roof. In this stone-flagged portico a number of pious beggars and pilgrims are continually prostrating themselves, muttering prayers all the time. They stand facing the Temple, go down on their hands, which are protected by wooden " shoes " studded with nails, lie flat on their faces with their hands stretched out in front of them, draw in their arms, stand up once more and bring their hands together in readiness for another obeisance. Sometimes several thousand prostrations are made in a single day, either to wipe out some personal crime, or, in return for a fee, to earn by proxy good reward in Paradise for some more wealthy worshipper. They were so absorbed in this muscular devotion that they hardly noticed our approach. Above the pillars is a deep maroon-coloured band such as is found along the top of the roof of nearly every Tibetan monastery or important house. It is made by laying willow twigs horizontally and then cutting them vertically to form such a surface as is found in a half-used haystack. These osiers are stamped down with mortar which has been mixed with a reddish dye. The resulting matt surface, in the Cathedral as in other buildings, forms an ideal background for the golden mono-grams and emblems which are usually placed there. The flat roof is higher at the sides, and from the lower central portion hangs a very ragged brown yak-hair curtain. On the walls of the portico are vast paintings of the four Celestial Kings of the Quarters. Their faces are of different colours and one holds a stringed instrument. Two massive wooden doors with engraved bosses and hinges lead to an outer courtyard which is open to the sky and surrounded by a dim cloister. The stone flags are rutted to a depth of six or seven inches in some places, not only by the feet of pilgrims but by the activities of the " prostraters " which are being carried on within as well as without the gates. The whole courtyard is extremely dark and dirty; huge frescoes can just be distinguished on the walls. On one side is a prayer-barrel eight feet in height, which, turned by an impassive-faced old woman, rings a bell at each revolution. This outer court leads to the main temple, which is also open to the sky and of great size. In the central part of the court many flowers, lit by slanting rays of sunshine, grow in pots : hollyhocks, coreopsis, phloxes, antir-rhinums, asters and even two rose bushes.

The chief shrine is at the far or eastern end of this temple ; it is protected from thieves by an iron curtain before which several monks are always stationed. On each side are gilt images of the Coming Buddha, who is always depicted seated with his legs hanging down in the European attitude. One of these figures is of colossal size. The central image is a life-sized figure of Gautama Buddha, which Landon considers to be " beyond question the most famous idol in the world ". It is supposed to have been brought from Peiping by the Chinese wife of the builder of the temple. The features of the Buddha are gross and unpleasing, but the figure is thickly encrusted with precious stones, which represent the accumulated offerings of the faithful for more than a thousand years. On the head is a large golden diadem containing enormous uncut gems. Innumerable butter-lamps, many of them of solid gold, light up the shrine, which with its riot of dimly seen gold and fabulous glinting gems gives the impression of some fantastic treasure-house from King Solomon's Mines.

The main hall is surrounded by a cloister from which many smaller shrines open. We followed our guide into one dark evil-smelling chamber after another, each guarded from thieves by hanging curtains of iron chain-work. One small shrine is devoted to the pacification of the Water-Demon of the lake on which Lhasa is supposed originally to have been built. In another are a thousand small images of Buddha in different attitudes. Before one altar is a loose stone, and prayers uttered while standing on this are certain to be answered. Nearly all the images in the temple have been self-created, miraculously transported, or are credited with supernatural properties.

We were then taken to the shrine of Palden Lhamo, the Buddhist equivalent of the Hindu god Kali, the wife of Shiva. It is this goddess that is supposed by the Tibetans to have been incarnated in the person of Queen Victoria. There are two images, showing her in angry and unpleasant mood. In one she appears as a frightful black monster, clad in the skins of human victims and eating the brains of others from a human skull. Surrounding her are emblems of disease and death, hideous masks, and a strange collection of antiquated weapons of war. Her face is so horrible that it is usually covered, but we were allowed to gaze upon her distorted and hideous features. Near by she is depicted in more amiable mood, wearing clothes of rich brocade and adorned with gold and precious stones, necklaces and innumerable charm-boxes.

It was curious that these two shrines were infested with small pale-brown mice, which ran in and out among the egg-cup shaped butter-lamps and over the monks who were on guard. I was anxious to put one in my pocket, in case they were of some rare species, but as they are supposed to be incarnations of former guardians of the shrine, I decided that it would be unwise.

These shrines were dimly lit by the smoky flames from the butter-lamps; and after the continual stooping, the heavy fetid smell of the damp and greasy floors, and the general rancid airlessness, we were glad to go up on to the roof. There is something repellent and sinister about the place, as if at any moment one might come upon priests performing barbaric rites and offering sacrifices of human blood before their sardonic inscrutable idols.

To the south of the Cathedral is the main square, which is used as a market-place. To the north of this square—and therefore built right against the Cathedral—is the Kashag, the meeting-place of the Tibetan Cabinet, from which its name is taken. Here also is the Government Treasury and other official buildings. For some distance in front of the Kashag the ground is set with cobbles, and there is a large incense-burner. It is here that the Dalai Lama, or Regent, preaches a sermon to the people on the occasion of the Tibetan New Year.

Round the Cathedral buildings are the main shopping streets of Lhasa. Some of the shops are in the form of wooden trestle-tables out in the middle of the square; others are simply collections of wares spread out on the cobbles of the street and protected by an umbrella. The larger shops consist of basement rooms opening on to the street, often with tables just outside, displaying a selection of more attractive wares. The better shops are kept by Nepalese and Ladakis; those in the open air are usually Tibetan and are almost invariably in the charge of women. This is customary; the women look after the retail trade and the shops, while the men carry on the larger commercial ventures and the journeys connected therewith. Almost everything you can imagine is sold on these stalls, and a good deal besides. The cloth-shops sell bales of coarse woollen cloth such as is made in most Tibetan households, squares of silk from China, cheap printed material from India. Often all the permanent shops in a certain district will sell the same commodity, and this is true to a certain extent of the movable stalls. The butchers and tanners, who carry on trades connected with the taking of life, are segregated to special streets, usually on the outskirts of the city. In one place are the food-shops. Here you see trays of different sorts of grain, including maize and rice from Bhutan; fresh vegetables—usually peas, potatoes, cabbages, turnips and radishes all grown near by; spices—trays of red chillies, cloves, nutmegs and all kinds of dried roots and leaves; and always the dried bricks of tea from China in varying grades usually pressed into balls about the size of a grapefruit.

One man sells holy-water vessels to place before the house altars, together with rows of shallow brass cups and a few libation jugs for storing and pouring out the sanctified liquid. In one place is a jeweller's stall. Necklaces of amber, coral and agate are there, as well as cheaper imitations; gold filigree charm-boxes with small brocade-clothed Buddhas inside, such as are worn across the back or chest of those undertaking journeys; gold and turquoise charm-boxes for the women, threaded on necklaces of large beads; turquoise ear-rings and uncut pieces of jade and amber. Here, again, is the street of the bootmakers; one man sits at his work surrounded by pairs of the scarlet-and-black cloth Kham-pa boots; another sells the black or brown leather boots from Mongolia which are often ornamented with an appliqué pattern in green leather; and always there is the bright scarlet-and-green women's boot with a thick sole of leather or woven yak-hair. Other stalls sell small china bowls for tea or rice, polished birch or maple tea-cups such as are carried in the flap of almost every Tibetan's coat, assorted cartridges, electric-torches from Japan, candles, damascene stirrups, sticks of incense, mirrors, toys—one could go on indefinitely. And always beside the stall-keeper is the earthenware teapot, the cup, and tsamba bag.

All Tibetans are born traders. The noble families, such as the Surkang and Ra-ka-sha, employ their own traders, who make long journeys to Mongolia and India. The courtyard of the family mansion is often stacked high with bales of wool, bags of borax or salt, and other articles for export. Similarly the great monasteries, as well as private monk officials, indulge in com-mercial ventures. Wool forms by far the most important export of Tibet. Yak-tails (as used in Hindu temples), hides, salt and borax, are also sent down to India, and musk, horn and various medicinal herbs to China. In return come cotton and woollen goods, hardware, glass, sugar, biscuits, dried fruits, tobacco, hoop-iron and a thousand domestic odds and ends. As the total import both in value and bulk falls far short of the export, bullion and coin in the form of rupees are brought back from India. It is common to meet whole trains of pack animals laden with small heavy boxes of silver or coin.

Perhaps the best-known trader in Lhasa is Pangda-Tsang, who lives in a large mansion in the middle of the city. He trades mainly in wool, silk and furs, but anything else from jewellery to horses can be bought through him. He is also the largest transport contractor in Lhasa. I went to his house one day with a friend who wanted to buy some stone-marten skins. Of these he had an enormous stock, as well as skins of snow-leopard, lynx, fox, otter, marmot and many I could not identify. His courtyard was at that time filled with some fifty mules which were ready to set off to Kalimpong with loads of coarse wool, of which he must have had many tons packed all round the yard right up to the surrounding roof.

The Lhasa streets always seem to be crowded, and wherever we went we were watched by innumerable pairs of eyes—but practically always in a friendly way, for the Lhasa crowd is as amiable as could be wished. Only occasionally does a monk gaze at one with sullen malevolence, perhaps realizing that we represent progress, and that progress spells the end of the unquestioned and unquestioning power of Lamaism.

The first thing that struck me, apart from the filth and the beggars, was the extraordinary number of women in Lhasa: some wearing the hooped Gyantse head-dress, some with the triangular Lhasa type, and others with tousled unadorned hair. This is partly due to the monastic system, which draws so large a proportion of the men to a life of theoretical celibacy; and partly to a system of polyandry which in the country districts leaves a surplus of women who naturally gravitate to the town, where they can find employment and contract promiscuous marriages, for the moral level—at any rate judged by our standards—must be as low at Lhasa as in any city of the world. This practice of polyandry is not confined to the lower classes. I once went to photograph the wife and child of a young lay official. He explained to me that the child was not actually his, as his two brothers shared his wife; and that this child was the son of his younger brother—who happened to be a monk official. Another friend of mine, upon being asked who a certain small boy was, replied that one could never really answer such questions; and that in his case, for instance, he had had three fathers and found the problem of relationship very difficult.

But why polyandry should flourish in Tibet of all countries, when so many thousands of men are debarred from marriage, is a problem I could never solve. Tibet is a poor country, and the system probably originated with the idea of keeping the family patrimony intact and undivided. When the Tibetans were still a pastoral people the men were too poor each to support a wife and home, also they would rarely be at home at the same time: one son would till the fields, while another would look after the herds of animals on the pasture-grounds, and the third would join the local monastery.

Among the cosmopolitan Lhasa crowd were always a great number of nomads; these are the finest people, both in looks and character, that we met in Tibet. They are swarthy independent folk with easy swinging gait and the open faces of mountaineers. Many of them, as the weather grew colder, came down from Golok, Amdo, Hor and the Chang Tang—the high wind-bitten plateau that covers all central Tibet. There are many different types, but the Lhasa people just call them Khampas (people from Kham) or Drok-pa (nomads). The men have short tousled hair and do not wear ear-rings. They wear a single rough sheep-skin garment hitched up to the knees, and boots of a design different from those made in Lhasa. They grow no hair on their faces. The women wear a long full robe of sheep-skin with the fur on the inside. Often one arm and shoulder is slipped out of the garment, and it is then clear that nothing is worn beneath. The most remarkable thing about these nomad women is their head-dresses, which exhibit untold variety. One woman (I think from Nagchuka) had her hair tied into innumerable minute plaits, each no thicker than blindcord. These were divided into two bundles and looped up to her belt. Over the nape of the neck and hanging from her hair was a square foot of cloth ornamented with cowrie shells and, apparently, white bone trouser-buttons. Over her forehead was a rosette the size of a saucer, of small blue, white and red beads. Another head-dress was even more remarkable: the woman's hair was again tied into tiny plaits and these were sewn on to a long strip of cloth woven in green and scarlet squares that reached almost to the ground. These squares were ornamented with Chinese dollars, Indian rupees, pieces of coral and turquoise, rows of cowrie shells and carved ivory; and in the centre was a beautifully embossed disc of silver. I wondered how often she washed her hair! Some women wear two lumps of amber as big as plums on top of their heads, and usually a few turquoises or corals between.   Sometimes strips of black, green or scarlet cloth are sewn on to the border and sleeves of the sheep-skin garment.   This is very effective.

The black yak-hair tents of the nomads could often be seen on the Sera plain surrounded by their flocks of yaks and sheep.   The former carry wool and the latter small bags of salt or borax, which is collected on the shores of the great brackish lakes to the north of Lhasa.   Part of this is paid to the Government as their year's taxation; the rest, together with bales of yak-dung, is exchanged for barley, which they cannot grow in their own country.   They do not need much money.   A certain amount of brick-tea, a few odds and ends, such as needles, matches, mirrors and jewellery, are bought in the Lhasa bazaar, and they are off home again—perhaps a five months' journey.

While they are in Lhasa, in fact this may be the primary object of their journey, they visit the shrine of the Dalai Lama and the Cathedral.   The nomads, in the off season, are notorious brigands, making it unsafe for pilgrims or merchants to cross the Chang Tang except in large caravans, which are formed at regular times each year for mutual protection.   They rarely rob their victims of money or valuables that are being taken as an offering to the Jo-king or the Dalai Lama's tomb, for the nomads are notoriously pious, and sometimes they will save up for years and present surprisingly rich gifts to these shrines.   Their language is quite different from that of the Lhasa Tibetan; indeed they can hardly understand each other.

In part of the Cathedral buildings there is a religious cloister, the circuit of which must be made at frequent intervals by the devout.   In the course of this perambulation several hundred prayer-wheels, set in racks almost touching each other, must be turned.   There is also an intermediate circle around the block of buildings of which the Cathedral forms the centre.   Enormous prayer-poles surmounted by yaks' tails and chortens mark the course of this circuit.   The third and outer circle runs right round the entire city and Potala.   It is called the *Ling-kor* or " park circle ".   All Buddhists are supposed to go round this each day, especially on holy days, the fifteenth and last of each month.   And as to walk round it gives one a glimpse of many sides of Lhasa life, I will describe the circuit in some detail.

The Sacred Way runs past the square mud-brick archway leading out of the Deyki Lingka. We have to turn left because the circuit must be made in a clock-wise direction; prayer-wheels are also turned in this way, and when chortens are encountered they must be passed on the right-hand side. To do these things in the reverse direction would stamp one as an adherent of the Pön religion, and would nullify the good work of others.

As we meet the Lhasa-Norbhu Lingka road at right angles there is a pile of stones marking the spot from which the Potala again becomes visible. On the other side of the road are sitting two or three beggars, clad in patchwork garments of filthy rags and wearing necklaces composed of fragments of conch-shell bracelets. Along the main road comes a gang of coolie women carrying a long block of granite to be used in the building of some noble-man's house. As they walk they chant a peculiar and monotonous dirge to keep in step. Sometimes these stones are carried on a wooden two-wheeled cart—the only wheeled vehicle used in Lhasa. The Ling-kor, only ten feet wide here, runs between walls of sun-dried brick striped at regular intervals with splashes of whitewash. Beyond the walls are parks of white poplar and pollard willow trees.

A gateway on the right leads to Gundeling monastery, which can be seen through the trees, with the gable-roofed Chinese temple above. In the latter, behind a wooden balustrade, are two enormous painted figures on mounts like rocking-horses. We overtake a man who is measuring his length round the Sacred Way. As the total distance is between five and six miles, he must make nearly 3000 obeisances per circuit. This man has short hair but does not wear monk's dress. He has a long leather apron strapped over his front and wears on his feet wooden clogs protected with heavy iron nails. He stands with his feet together muttering prayers, brings his hands together in front of him, then lies flat on his face with his arms stretched out beyond his head. He stands up, brings his hands together again, and then walks forward to the point reached by his hands. Sometimes he stops to rest beside the road, marking his progress with a small stone. Unless he is a very notable sinner, I don't think he is doing this on his own account, as I see him at work almost every day. Probably he is wiping out the transgressions of some high official—for a consideration. These exalted people excuse themselves from this form of devotion on the grounds that their presence would distract the other worshippers; they must, however, practise it in the privacy of their own houses. Nevertheless, I have met the Duke and Langchungna Shap-pe in the evening on the Sacred Way. The latter was turning a golden prayer-wheel and wore dark glasses and a flat-peaked eye-shade projecting a foot in front of his forehead; he was followed by two or three servants.

Soon the Ling-kor turns sharp right as it meets the sandy bank of the aqueduct and the main road from India coming in from the left. This aqueduct, called the Kaling Chu, was built in 1721 to preserve the city from the encroachments of the flooded plain to the north and west. It diverts the streams of the valleys on either side of Sera monastery and leads them in a semicircle eight miles in length to join the Kyi Chu below Drepung. The Kaling Chu is several feet higher than the surrounding plain and is enclosed between two immense walls of sand. The Ling-kor, here little more than a couple of yards wide, is constricted by an outcrop of rock. This is being gradually scraped away as it is a remedy for rheumatism if taken internally. It is very sandy here, and fifty or sixty bright-plumaged sacred cocks attached to the Chinese temple strut about in the road. A train of mules laden with wool comes from the direction of the city on its way to India, and a mounted woman, with her head so wrapped up in scarves that only her eyes can be seen, takes the same road, followed by her two servants. Above, there is an unusual view of the Potala; seen end-on from here it looks quite small and is dwarfed by the rock on which it stands.

The track is confined between the steep sandy wall of the aqueduct, here fifteen or twenty feet high, and a row of willows, on the other side of which are Government barley-fields. Several dogs, with their noses tucked under their tails, lie curled up with one eye open for anybody who will give them food. Now there is a stream just beside the road; some goosanders and mallard swim in mid-stream, allowing us to get within ten or fifteen yards. Looking back I can see as many as fifty people following; practically all are turning prayer-wheels or telling their beads. There are very few young people and few men. Old women predominate. It is only when their time in this life becomes short that they seriously start to prepare themselves for the next. They are well muffled up, as it is cold in the early morning. Many of them wear a very practical peaked hood which comes down over the shoulders and buttons across the chin, leaving exposed only the eyes and nose. Some of these women lead small dogs which look like crosses between Lhasa terriers and Chinese spaniels. Others lead pet sheep. Some of these are so tame that they follow of their own accord. Both sheep and dogs have many bells tied round their necks. A good number of the followers are nomads with a look of childlike ingenuousness in their eyes. Every morning of their stay in the Holy City they walk round the Lingkor in the early dawn.

A bridge bearing the road from the Lhalu mansion and the Sera plain crosses the aqueduct on our left, but we turn right, over another small bridge towards the Potala, the back of which is now quite close. There is another lingka on the right, and a row of willows on the left, beyond which is a marshy area where white gulls, bar-headed geese and Brahminy duck are feeding. At the foot of the Potala rock there is a tall prayer-pole and a chorten; but we turn left and follow round the high wall of the Snake Temple lake.

Beyond the chorten is the stable of the Dalai Lama's elephant, which was presented some years ago by the Maharajah of Bhutan. It is used in certain ceremonies but otherwise leads a peaceful and apparently healthy life. Some women are carrying in loads of rushes for its breakfast. The northern side of the walls is in ruins and one catches a glimpse of a small temple surrounded by age-old poplars on an island in the middle of a considerable lake. More gnarled and twisted willows, their trunks often lying on the ground, surround the lake; but in the open water are many varieties of duck—mallard, teal, gadwall, tufted, white-eyed and common pochard, as well as goosander, coot and waterhen.

The temple was considered by the Chinese to be one of the five beauties of Lhasa. We visited it soon after we arrived. There is a causeway of ancient poplar logs, but in September it was submerged and a ragged boatman was there to ferry us across to some stone steps that come down to the water's edge. The ferry is similar in shape to the great rectangular barge at Chaksam, but it is only about six feet by four. As it is cut away at the sides to facilitate getting in and out, it is extraordinarily unseaworthy, and we had to sit very still, as there is only an inch or two of freeboard. At the front—there are no bows—is a wooden model of a horse's head raised on a long neck a yard or so above the water. At the back are some twigs with prayer-flags attached. The boat resembles a floating bedstead and seems to be constructed so as to give the maximum possible resistance to the water. Watching the many-hued dragon-flies, and looking across the untroubled surface of the lake to where the iridescent heads of the mallard drakes scintillate among the bowing rushes, and behind them to the luxuriant willows, it is difficult to believe we are nearly 12,000 feet above sea-level.

In the shade of an enormous poplar is the temple, small and square-roofed, with a curious hexagonal tiled dome and a conventional conical ornament on the summit. Hanging from the six corners of the roof are gilt dragons with raised elephantine trunks; from each a golden bell is suspended with a piece of flat metal attached to the clapper so that they tinkle in the wind. Behind the temple rises the northern escarpment of the Potala, somewhat foreshortened from here but as impressive as ever. The temple, like so many Tibetan shrines, is disappointing inside, nor are there any snakes—at any rate not live ones, though some of the idols have diadems or necklaces of writhing serpents. There is, however, a small chamber with a divan where the Dalai Lama used to come and mediate for hours together.

This temple is the abode of a most powerful demon who is the spirit of the lake on which the city of Lhasa is built. On a certain day of each year all the officials and people of Lhasa must visit the temple in order to propitiate him. Having walked in procession round the city, the Prime Minister and the Shap-pes, dressed in their yellow silk robes, and other officials in all their finery, must present scarves to the water-spirit. Yak-hide coracles are brought in and the officials have to remain for some time afloat. Although we did not see this ceremony, as it takes place in the early summer, we saw a small cinema film that Tsarong had made of it, and though the photography was bad—he had waved the camera about like a hosepipe—it was enough to let one realize what a magnificent sight this must be.

The Ling-kor follows the wall of the Snake Temple and of the flooded reed-covered enclosure alongside. On the left are marshes where grow some of the typical Lhasa willows with gnarled spiral-twisted trunks. This is a favourite haunt for birds; in September we would see flocks of literally hundreds of pintail, shoveller, mallard, pochard and teal, together with the ubiquitous bar-heads and Brahminy ducks. The Sacred Way now crosses some open barley-fields where they are gathering in the harvest and treading out the corn with the aid of a dozen or fifteen yaks, which they drive round and round over a floor of beaten clay. On one side is a pile of grain protected from evil spirits by a brightly coloured prayer-flag. Women are sifting the grain and sorting it by tossing it in basket-work trays, and storing it in striped brown and white yak-hair bags. It has been a good harvest. Luckily there were no hail-storms when the grain was ripening, nor any night frosts. An early drop in the temperature can lay waste acres of barley, though these frosts are unusual in the sheltered and comparatively low-lying vale of Lhasa. Now they are starting to plough up the fields with yaks and dzos harnessed in pairs. This must be finished before the ground is held by the winter frosts.

All at once, close at hand, there is a deep booming noise that sets the air a-tremble; it sounds like a hoarse syren or a large animal in dire distress. It is produced by three monks who are sitting on the ground practising on the twelve-foot-long monastery trumpets. The noise is so great that they have to come out into the fields to practise.

The Ling-kor again approaches the city and skirts the high wall surrounding the Regent's summer palace. On the left of the road are the hovels of the lowest class of Lhasa society, the *ra-gyap-pa*, a community of scavenging beggars whose work it is to dispose of the dead bodies. When Buddhists die, their bodies must return to the elements from which they originated—earth, fire, water, air. In the Tibetan winter the ground is frozen too hard for graves to be dug; where yak-dung is the chief fuel not enough can be spared for cremation; many people drink from the river, so that if the corpses are consigned to water the drinking supply would be contaminated. So the body returns to the air. The ra-gyap-pa may be seen in the early morning carrying on their backs the huddled corpses of the poor. These grisly burdens are taken to appointed places where they are laid out on flat stones and cut into small pieces. These are thrown to the vultures and ravens who crowd round waiting for their share of the loathsome meal. These ra-gyap-pa must also remove the carcases of animals that die in the city. Another of their duties is to seek out thieves and robbers who flee from the city to the surrounding country. At the time of the 1904 Mission they were put in charge of convicts, but the practice has been discontinued. Soon after our arrival a dozen of these ra-gyap-pa came round to the Norbhu Lingka to ask for money, or rather to demand it as their right. For all officials visiting Lhasa must pay them on arrival and departure; similarly when an official is promoted, and on days of festival, these importunate fellows appear. If they are not paid they break into such a frenzied yelling and cursing that it is better to settle up at once and let them go. Some of the ra-gyap-pa are very wealthy and wear the saucer-shaped hat and ear-ring of respectability.

Their dwellings consist of a wall of sods into which are built the horns of animals; over the top is raised a roof of ragged yak-hair tent-cloth. This is often surrounded by an outer wall made of the horns of yaks, cattle and sheep heaped together. In the summer their hovels are gay with nasturtiums and marigolds. Beside the track an aged wizened woman with short white hair raises herself from her patchwork sheepskin bag, in which she lies to keep warm, and in a thin whining voice asks for alms. She lives in a wretched dog-kennel of a hut which is only just big enough to hold her. Children run naked in the road. There are innumerable lean and mangy dogs, too emaciated even to bark at strangers. But these are the lowest of the ra-gyap-pa. Further on, though they must still live outside the city, they have proper houses, built of sun-dried bricks, but still with neat rows of yak horns let into the face of the wall, like a mosaic.

On the right, close to the Ling-kor, appears the single golden roof-pavilion of the Ramoche temple, in which is a huge image of the Chinese wife of King Song-tsen Gampo. Opposite this temple a road from Sera monastery and the arsenal comes in from the left. Already a line of bare-headed, bare-footed monks are entering the city; many of them carry on their backs bundles wrapped up in a flap of their voluminous robes. The Ling-kor crosses another stretch of open-country with the tents of ra-gyap-pa on either hand, and away to the left are open fields with occasional villas surrounded by lingkas. The great walls of Muru monastery appear above the lower buildings on the right. Soon the north-east corner of the city is passed and the road swings to the right over a stone bridge. On the left are marshes and lingkas with a stony road coming in from the north-east. Next the quarter of the butchers is reached, again without the city walls; and the ground is littered with horns, hoofs, bones and scraps of hide. Inappropriately placed among the slaughter-houses and butcheries is the mosque of the Ladakis, rather a mean and neglected-looking building with a wooden lich-gate and enclosing wall. The main road from north Tibet, Ganden and Nagchuka comes in here, and beside it is a small walled pagoda in Chinese style. This is the grave of a member of General Huang-Mu Sung's 1932 Mission to Lhasa who died after being thrown from his horse.

The Ling-kor now turns east and returns between the Kyi Chu and the city. The leather-workers (also outcasts) live here, and there are several coracles stacked against the side of the road. It is a mean quarter of the town, although a few gateways open on the right to the better-class houses which lie behind. Beside the road are piles of dung and all the refuse of the city, with dogs and ravens searching for tasty morsels. There are stacks of kindling wood here, probably the property of the Government, or of Tsarong or the Prime Minister, whose mansions lie to the left amidst groves of trees.

Soon part of the ancient wall of the city is passed on the right, pierced by a ruined gateway where a group of beggars sit turning their prayer-wheels. Beyond this is a large white-washed chorten and a stone bridge which gives access to an open grassy plain stretching to the willow groves wherein are the pleasure-gardens and summer-houses of the monk and lay officials.

It is the picnic season now—Lhasa's favourite pastime—and each official in turn must entertain his colleagues to a picnic, usually followed by a theatrical entertainment. Often canvas tents are put up and pots of flowers brought out for their adornment. The middle and lower classes seem to spend all the day picnicking. Riding through the lingkas we meet party after party sitting round dicing and drinking chang. They bring out a cloth tent, or simply an awning, adorned with blue and red appliqué work. Carved Tibetan tables and padded cushion seats are also brought. The lunch is often cooked in a smaller yak-hair tent. Tea and chang are drunk all day, and in the evening we would meet parties returning, master, mistress and servants all walking together (sometimes arm-in-arm to provide the stability necessary after taking so much chang) and singing songs in harsh Tibetan voices.

The poorer people were usually more abandoned and we would see them returning only just able to walk. Occasionally a man could be seen fast asleep in the gutter beside the road. The doctor found that the number of his patients increased very much during the picnic season, and as soon as he saw what the man's complaint was, he would anticipate his excuses and say: " I suppose you went to a picnic last week? "

"Yes," the man would sheepishly admit.

"And I suppose you fell down? "

" Yes, yes, that's what happened." And the man would receive his injections and go off to another picnic.

In the stream beside the road are shoals of small fish, and it is considered a pious act to feed them with small fragments of barley dough. A little farther on the main river sweeps in to meet the Ling-kor, and quite near in a deep back-water are any number of huge char. Sometimes we saw as many as a hundred in this one pool. The largest would be eight or ten pounds in weight. This pool is the abode of a powerful spirit and the trees near by are festooned with thousands of prayer-flags. Very often there is somebody burning azalea leaves and throwing food to the fishes on the point overlooking the pool. For quite a long while there was a dead baby at the bottom of this pool, for the fish do not seem to appreciate carrion.

Over the tops of the trees of the largest lingka in Lhasa can be seen the long southern face of the Potala and behind it the dun hills on the other side of Sera plain. Just here, where the Sacred Way swings towards the Iron Hill, there is an enormous cairn of stones with the topmost ones whitewashed. This pile is twenty feet high and more than fifty yards in circumference. Each person as he passes picks up a stone from the road and throws it to the top of the heap. The Tibetan has a passion for piling up stones, particularly white ones. A little farther back along the Ling-kor there is a cleft willow which is almost hidden by the stones which have been thrown into the tree.

And now, before completing the circuit, we must cross the precipitous south-western buttresses of the Iron Hill. It is impossible to keep on the level, because a stream washes right against the foot of the rocks. So the path, with steep crags above and below, cuts over the shoulder of the hill. This is perhaps the most remarkable part of the whole Ling-kor. Beside the track are hundreds and hundreds of carved and painted Buddhas. Some are cut out of the rock itself. Others are painted on flat slates and propped up in niches. There are also the horns of animals and innumerable clay castings of the Buddha, which are baked in a primitive kiln beside the track. The Ling-kor here descends so steeply that those measuring their length may cease their uncomfortable progress and walk to the foot of the hill. On the right are three large prayer-barrels built into the wall; these must be turned as you pass. A little farther on is a vertical wall of smooth rock on which are painted several hundred similar Buddhas in red, blue and gold. They are arranged in ranks both vertically and horizontally. Just below the multiple wall painting is a rock which must be touched with the forehead. It is polished to the smoothness of marble. There is also a small hole in the wall forming the summit of a painted chorten; a finger must be placed here. Another devotional exercise is to crawl under a slab of rock which leans against the foot of the main wall. These actions, especially the last two, are often dispensed with. From the top of the wall long strings of prayer-flags are stretched above the Ling-kor to the trees beside the stream. One more chorten is passed and the Sacred Way runs between two willow groves to the Norbhu Lingka gate where we first entered it.

CHAPTER NINE

THE POTALA

WRITING of Lhasa City, it has been difficult not to digress occasionally and to describe the many glimpses that one gets of the Potala, which appears from time to time poised above the flat roof-tops or framed at the end of some squalid street. As Salisbury Cathedral towers above the city and plain at its feet, so the Potala completely dominates the vale of Lhasa.

To me the Potala represents the very essence of the Tibetan people. It has a certain untamed dignity in perfect harmony with the surrounding rugged country; a quality of stolid unchangeableness—it seems to say: "Here I have been for hundreds of years, and here I intend to stay for ever". Yet underneath this beauty, which is reflected not only in the inspired simplicity of its lines but in the exquisite workmanship of many of the smallest details, there is a lurking grimness, personified, perhaps, in the unfortunate political offender Lungsha, who, having fallen foul of the Government, lies with sightless eyes in a dungeon at the foot of the building.

Certainly the Potala is one of the most astonishing buildings in the world, whether it is seen from afar perched on the summit of the eminence which rises from the level plain of Lhasa, with the sun striking flame from the golden pavilions of its roof, or whether, riding out before dawn, you see the moonlight thrown back with unearthly brilliance from the whitewashed wall of the immense southern face. All the supremely great works of art, in literature, painting or architecture, have an indefinable quality of magic which is born from circumstances usually beyond the artist's control; so, in common with the few un-questionably perfect buildings of the world, the Potala has some transcendent quality derived neither from the inspired skill of some master builder or craftsmen, nor from its historical associa-tions, nor from the fact that it is the cynosure of innumerable religious devotees. That it does possess this divine excellence cannot be doubted.

I have sometimes regretted the presence of the Iron Hill and wished that the Potala rock could stand alone as the only eminence in the vale of Lhasa. But it justifies itself by affording what is to my mind the finest view in all the world. It is from here that the Potala, balanced by the flat-roofed village at its foot, is seen to most advantage. It is sufficiently near for detail to be distinguished, and far enough away to be seen as a whole. From the other view-points it leans back unduly; it is stupendous, awe-inspiring, but not in equilibrium. Seen from the top of the Iron Hill it is as near perfection as anything in this world can be. Buildings in other countries may challenge comparison with the Potala; but to my mind no edifice, so perfect in itself, is placed in such incomparable surroundings.

One looks down on to the three chortens of the Western Gate, and on each side of it a sea of tree-tops, with the tenuous green of the willows set off by the darker poplars. Between the trees are pools of water reflecting the blue sky, or level expanses of grass. A mile away to the east, appearing through the greenery as a broken white line, is the city of Lhasa, with the golden Cathedral roofs catching the sun and leading up to the larger mass of gold on the Potala. At this distance Lhasa is indeed a garden city. The fertile plain is bordered by the Kyi Chu, which runs in a great semicircle from extreme east to extreme west. Beyond the river the mountains rise abruptly, spur after spur coming right down to the water's edge. In the valleys between these gaunt ridges are villages surrounded by willow groves and barley-fields, watered by streams that flow from the mountains which tower another 6000 feet above them. The whole plain of Lhasa is surrounded by this ring of great mountains, over whose high passes have flocked for hundreds of years the pilgrims who came from all parts of Asia to tread the Sacred Way around the city and Potala.

Quite unlike anything else in the world, the Potala yet has something of the New York sky-scraper, a faint kinship with Egyptian architecture, and still more of the massive flat-roofed buildings of the Hadhramaut in Arabia. But whereas New York is a city of sky-scrapers, and the Egyptians were prolific builders, the Potala is an isolated example of the perfection which Tibetan architecture can attain. Although some of the monasteries and forts are built in the same style, they cannot be compared with the palace of the Dalai Lamas, standing alone in superb detachment.

Not only does its beauty of form and colour take one's breath away, but it is of such colossal size. This is best appreciated from the Government lingka below the southern face. In front of one is the level turf where a few yaks are grazing. Beyond this is a line of misty green pollard willows through which appear the flat roofs of Sho, the hamlet that nestles at the foot of the Potala. Behind this starts the great rock, strewn with small willows, on which the palace is built. It is difficult to tell where the actual building starts, as the foundation seems to grow out of the rock, and the whitewash on the walls has run down over the lower buttresses. Huge staircases, protected by walls which are themselves cut into enormous steps, zigzag up to the doorways which, as none of them faces south, are not visible from here. As the whole building leans back, and as each " vertical " wall

L

leans inwards, the impression of height is still further enhanced. It is actually 440 feet high and 900 feet in length. Except for the central part, which is of a rich maroon colour, and a small block which is ochreous, the walls are white-washed, and each block of masonry is picked out with a border of deep red along the summit, surmounted in its turn by a narrow white parapet. The form of the whole is reflected in each window, which is broader at the bottom than at the top and is shaded by a wide lintel.

The Potala gives the impression not of having been built by man but of having grown there, so perfectly does it fit in with its surroundings. It has the pleasing lack of symmetry of a great tree or mountain, yet this apparent aimlessness is focused, first by the red central block and then by the golden pavilions on the roof, so that the eye is naturally led from the less important to the essential, both visually and spiritually; for in so much as the gilded roofs over the mortal remains of the Dalai Lamas are the dominant feature of the architecture, so is the incarnate spirit of these rulers the very soul of Tibet.

Over the central line of windows of each block are draped brown yak-hair curtains striped horizontally with white. The roofs of the terra-cotta central portion and of the wing to the east of it, which contains the Dalai Lama's private suite of rooms, are especially beautiful. Here there is a wide strip of dull maroon bordered above and below with white. In the centre of this rich matt surface, which forms an ideal background for them, are four very large embossed monograms of gold, with several smaller ones on either side. These ornaments prepare one for the larger mass of gold on the roof-pavilions. Spaced along the edge of the parapet and at the corners are golden turrets and cylindrical banners of black yak-hair crossed with white. These serve—as well as keeping off devils—to break the severity of the sky-line, which is further relieved by the roof pagodas.

In the seventh century Song-tsen Gampo, the great warrior-King of Tibet, built himself a palace on what was called the Red Hill, where the Potala now stands, but it was demolished in the wars that followed. The word Potala is taken from the name of a rock at Cape Comorin, the southern tip of India, which was supposed by the Indians to be the abode of the God of Mercy, or Chenrezi, who is incarnate in the Dalai Lama. There is another " Potala " on the east coast of China. It was the great fifth Dalai Lama, Lob-sang Gyatso, who started the construction of the palace that is now there, and it is uncertain how much of any previous buildings he incorporated. He died in 1680, and it was completed by his competent Minister, Sang-gye Gyatso, a few years later.

As the Jo-kang is the centre of the purely religious life of Tibet, so is the Potala the focus of the temporal and spiritual powers of this ruler, who so strangely combines the offices of Dictator and Pope. Since its completion it has been the official residence of the Dalai Lamas, though the last Pontiff preferred to spend his time in the Norbhu Lingka, only visiting the Potala when ceremonies demanded his presence.

The Regent, who is not permitted to use the Dalai Lama's suite of rooms, has his own office there, as also has the Prime Minister. Every Lhasa official, monk and lay, must, theoretically, meet in the Assembly Hall once each day at a certain time to drink tea—though the last Dalai Lama usually summoned them to the Norbhu Lingka. This is to ensure that the officials remain at their work and do not leave the city. Nearly all the great ceremonies of the Tibetan year take place within its walls or on its spacious roof: the inception of the New Year; the Lama dances which mark the end of the old year; and the changing of clothes which represents the beginning and end of winter. When a high official leaves or returns to Lhasa he must go to the Potala to report and present his scarf of greeting.

Here are the mortal remains of former Dalai Lamas enshrined in tombs lavishly ornamented with gold and precious stones. Here also, in the strong rooms of the Potala, is the almost fabulous private treasury of the Dalai Lamas, which contains the accumulated wealth of centuries, and possibly the world's finest collection of old Chinese porcelain and cloisonné, ceremonial brocade robes, golden images, exquisite gems and jewellery, and other rare or valuable objects. These were presents from pious pilgrims and others to the head of the Buddhist Church; many of them came from the Emperors and Princes of China and Mongolia. No man knows the extent of this treasure-house of the Dalai Lamas.

The Potala has its own monastery, called the Namgyal Choide, whose 170 monks are usually recruited from the better families, and who have the reputation of being the best-dressed monks in Lhasa. The Dalai Lama takes his place among their number as an ordinary priest. Within the palace there is also a college for monk officials called the Tse-laptra, the School on the Hill. This takes about thirty boys and trains them for three or four years. It is in charge of the three Grand Secretaries, who choose the pupils among boys from the great monasteries near Lhasa. As the choice is made purely by merit, they are frequently of humble birth.

In September they gave the Potala its annual coat of paint. The whitewash was mixed in the well between the stone monument and the small bridge to the south of the Potala. A bag of lime was attached to the middle of a yak-hair rope and dragged from end to end of the well until all the water had been converted into whitewash—a somewhat drastic method of chlorination! This was ladled into wooden or earthenware buckets and carried on the backs of the women to the foot of the Potala walls. Here it was simply thrown up in small buckets or dippers. The areas of wall that could not be reached in this primitive fashion were covered by wash that was thrown down from the windows. Years of this treatment have given the walls a stalagmitic appearance. In September, too, they removed the hanging yak-hair curtains which protected the woodwork from the glare of the sun. The bare lower part of the wall, below the bottom line of windows, is at certain times of the year covered by enormous religious paintings. At the foot of the southern face of the Potala, towards the western end, are the Government prisons and printing establishment. We did not visit the dungeons; report has it that they are unspeakably filthy and that the prisoners are barbarously treated. The printing press, like all others in the country, is in charge of the monks. Tibetan paper is made of the bark of daphne or other shrubs. We would often see it being prepared, usually by a man out of doors. He would pound up the bark with water by spreading it on one flat stone and beating it with another. The resulting mixture was then spread on a wooden frame four feet square, over which was stretched a fine wire gauze. When dry it was removed from the frame and trimmed. This paper is very tough and coarse and resembles cream-coloured cardboard. Troughs are also used in which the pulp is pounded underfoot. Owing to the poisonous nature of one kind of bark used, no insects will attack Tibetan paper; on the other hand, people who have to spend much time with these books complain of severe headaches. Outside the Potala press we saw a line of men sitting in the sun laboriously cutting out wooden blocks in reverse corresponding to each page, for type is not used in Tibet. These blocks were two to three feet long and about six inches wide. Inside, an enormous hall was taken up with racks holding the sets of blocks. There is here a complete set of the Kangyur, or Buddhist Scriptures, in 108 volumes; also of the Tengyur, its commentaries, in 225 volumes.

Although the outside of the Potala is so superb, the inside is disappointing. True, there are certain details—a painting on the wall, a golden butter-lamp, or even a complete room—which are worthy of the palace, but there is no sort of unity; and the various assembly halls, shrines and storerooms are connected by dark and evil-smelling passages slippery with the spillings of innumerable cups of Tibetan tea, while the whole place is anything but clean.

It was 6th September before we could spare a day to go over the interior of the Potala. We rode up the long western causeway and zigzagged to the doorway on the northern side. From here there is a wonderful view to the west and north. We looked down on to the wide road crossing the flooded meadows past Gundeling and thence leading to the Norbhu Lingka. We could just make out our own Deyki Lingka among the trees over the shoulder of the Iron Hill. From above, one can appreciate how very wooded this side is; willow and thorn scrub stretch in a wide green band beside the river as far as eye can see. It was wise of the Tibetans to surround the Potala by a green belt of linghas and fields. Towards Drepung—westward, that is—the greenery is stopped by a wide marshy area on each side of the road; and to the north is the bare Sera plain. The sandy banks of the aqueduct run in a great arc from the front of Sera almost to Drepung. There is also a good view of the Lhalu mansion, where the 1904 Mission were housed. It is surrounded by wooded gardens and water-meadows and has a large private monastery.

We were shown the assembly room where the 1904 treaty was signed. A huge dark room with a flagged floor, and roof supported by square wooden pillars swathed in cloth or hung with strips of silk. In the middle of this a monk was arranging different-coloured powders on a large tray in the form of a geometric design. The walls of many of the audience halls and cloisters were completely covered with frescoes, but it was too dark to see them clearly. Among the many images were life-sized effigies of King Song-tsen Gampo with his two wives from Nepal and China. There were many images from India, including a sandalwood image of Chenrezi, which is supposed to have been miraculously formed as the tree split. Another image of this god was made by the last Dalai Lama. It is of silver, and has eleven heads and a thousand arms and eyes, one eye being engraved in the palm of each hand. We were shown one golden image from the back of which an avaricious monk had stolen a large piece of the precious metal. As a punishment he had had his hands cut off. There is also a special room which was used by the fifth Dalai Lama and which has been preserved exactly as he left it.

The most impressive part of the interior of the Potala is the mausolea of the Dalai Lamas, from the fifth onwards, though the sixth is excluded owing to his dissolute life, or because he died away from Lhasa. Nor are the last four represented, as they were never allowed to grow up. The embalmed bodies are actually there inside chortens which, instead of being made of stone, are reputed to be of silver; certainly they are overlaid with gold plentifully set with turquoise, lapis lazuli, amethyst, coral, onyx, sapphire, and even rubies and diamonds. As the tomb of the fifth is sixty feet high, and that of the thirteenth even higher, they must be worth a vast amount of money. That of the last Dalai Lama had only recently been completed, and in proportion to his greatness it far exceeds all the others in splendour. It is interesting to see that the work done in Lhasa today is apparently indistinguishable from similar work carried out at various times since the seventeenth century, when the palace, in its present form, was built.

Considerable structural alteration has been necessary to fit in this tomb, which rises through three complete stories of the building. It is a great pity that the chorten is not housed in a larger room so that one could stand back and see it in its entirety.

When this saintly ruler died the pious from many parts of the Buddhist world contributed what they could afford to the building of this shrine. The main chorten is encased in gold embossed with different designs and plentifully encrusted with precious stones. In some places valuable charm-boxes, turquoise ear-rings, onyx and coral snuff-boxes, strings of amber and pearls, and innumerable unset gems have been let in to form designs on the gold background. On several shelves in front are displayed more precious presents, gifts from the ancient and noble families of Tibet and from the rich monasteries of China and Mongolia. Here are rare porcelain vases, exquisite examples of cloisonné work, chalice-like vessels of solid gold, meticulously wrought metal-work, alabaster models of temples, and glass cases containing curiously fashioned flowers with leaves and petals of china. On the eastern wall of the room are pigeon-holes containing holy books with carved wooden covers, many small images and filigree charm-boxes such as are carried by travellers.

In front of the shrine burn several enormous butter-lamps of solid silver. They stand four feet high, and the bowls, with a row of burning wicks floating in the fat, are more than two feet in diameter. Each wick has melted a little lake for itself in the congealed butter. White scarves had been thrown up on to the chorten by pilgrims, and there were vases of artificial and real flowers in different parts of the shrine, while the square wooden pillars surrounding the tomb and supporting the roof are covered by long brocade strips of different colours, each hanging over the next like the scales of a fish. Although certain details of the tomb, such as the crystal globes hanging from the ceiling and a coloured biscuit-tin on one of the shelves, struck a false note, the general impression is a fitting tribute to the memory of this revered ruler.

On the upper story of the tomb, which surrounds the chorten like a balcony, some fifteen of the best Tibetan artists were at work on a series of thankas illustrating the life-story of the Dalai Lama. It was interesting to see them at work. They were obviously men of some standing, as each wore the long turquoise and gold ear-ring. They wore white shirts, indigo or purplish broadcloth robes, and black top-boots. They worked on fine canvas, which had been prepared and stiffened with white paint; this was stretched over a wooden frame about four feet high and two and a half feet wide, which they rested on their knees, as they sat cross-legged on the floor. The paints, made of stones and earths (many of them imported from India) ground up with oil, were in separate porcelain saucers. The brushes, of which each painter used several, appeared to be of hog's bristle. The work was extremely fine and they showed great accuracy and skill, though they all painted in the conventional manner, so that it would have been difficult to pick out the work of individual artists. The Potala, considerably conventionalized, appeared in many of the paintings, also processions of monks, street scenes and landscapes, as well as the usual Buddhas, curly clouds and stiff formal flowers. As is usual with Tibetan pictures, every corner of the canvas was filled up. Each artist had his wooden teacup and tsamba bag beside him, and seemed to drink every few minutes.

After tearing ourselves away from the shrine we climbed a crazy ladder to the roof, which is of sand and gravel beaten to the consistency of concrete. It is here that the Dalai Lama, when in residence at the Potala, takes exercise. And what a superb place to take a constitutional! The whole vale of Lhasa lies spread out beneath one, surrounded by its cirque of wild mountain scenery.

Everywhere there are trees—lines of giant poplars, groves of pollard willows, and beside the river acres and acres of thorny scrub.

On the roof of the Potala, surounded by the seven glittering mausolea of departed Dalai Lamas, one cannot help contrasting this superb building with that drab and squalid city with its stinking puddles and rotting heaps of offal; the wealth of the monasteries, and the poverty of the common people. " The Potala ", says Percival Landon, " unconsciously symbolizes the vast erection of power and pride which separates the priestly caste of Tibet from the real truths of the religion they have prostituted." Yet in conclusion he almost forgives this Lamaism that has raised up to its gods so great and enduring a wonder.

CHAPTER TEN

THE NORBHU LINGKA

As Lhasa is approached from the west a great walled enclosure can be made out between the road and the Kyi Chu. Above the wall, which is ten or twelve feet high, can be seen the golden turrets of an attractive-looking building surrounded by tall trees. This is the Norbhu Lingka, or " Jewel Park ", the summer residence of the Dalai Lama.

It is a fairly recent building, having been put up in the closing years of the last century, while two of the palaces are of even later date. A metalled cambered road, the finest in Lhasa, leads from the western extremity of the Potala rock—a stone's throw from the Western Gate—to the main entrance of the Norbhu Lingka, which is just short of a mile distant. Having crossed some willow-clad water-meadows by a low causeway, which is flooded in the summer months, the road cuts between Gundeling monastery and a spur of the Iron Hill. For the rest of the way it runs between lingkas of willow and poplar. Here it is bordered by walls of sun-dried bricks with stone coping pleasantly overgrown with weeds. These walls, as is usual in Lhasa, are ornamented every few yards with broad splashes of whitewash. Half-way along this straight stretch of road the Sacred Way is crossed, and from this point both the Potala and the Norbhu Lingka gates can be seen.

In 1904 no member of the Mission was ever allowed within the walls of the Norbhu Lingka. To such an extent has the Tibetan attitude changed that in 1920 Sir Charles Bell frequently went there to converse as man to man with the Dalai Lama; he also visited the Forbidden Enclosure, which is a privilege denied even to the highest in the land.

As there was no Dalai Lama during our visit, we were most generously allowed to go there whenever we liked; and when Gould was recovering from his illness he was invited to make use of the gardens for convalescence. He took full advantage of this, and, as I usually accompanied him to take photographs, we spent many hours in this delectable place. On such occasions they let us wander where we liked, and it was only when we went into the inner enclosure that a Tibetan came with us.

L 2

The Norbhu Lingka consists of a walled enclosure nearly half a mile each way and more or less square in shape. The Tibetans are skilled wallers, and this is as good an example as any. More than ten feet high, it is built of huge blocks of granite laid in lines and separated by smaller fragments of stone set horizontally. The lower part is whitewashed and is separated from the reddened upper part by a string course. Along the ground at the foot of the wall lie huge coping-stones of granite; these were brought with much labour, often as a punishment for some minor crime, from the mountains on the other side of the Sera plain; but as the strength of the wall was found insufficient to bear so great a weight their use has been abandoned and many of them have lately been broken up for other purposes. On the southern side a branch of the Kyi Chu, held back by a masonry embankment, comes almost to the foot of the wall. For the rest, the garden is surrounded by overgrown park-land and open meadows. A narrow aqueduct, at present in a state of disrepair, brings water to the small power-station in an angle of the northern wall. This was formerly used to supply electric light, but this scheme seems to have been abandoned.

The main gate is most impressive, with a roof of highly glazed tiles and the usual golden medallions on a background of dark red. On each side and above the gate is a system of branching woodwork painted red and picked out with flower-designs in bright colours. A row of grinning white demons look down from beneath the roof. The heavy wooden doors, with metal knockers formed by a ring held in the jaws of a lion, open into a portico, the ceiling of which is richly painted. It is a pity that the square pillars here are of granite which has been treated in the same way as wood, for the stone looks out of place and its surface is little suited for paintwork. The first place to be visited is the Assembly Room, where, when the Dalai Lama was alive, the Ministers would assemble each day and, sitting on cushions strictly in order of precedence, would drink ceremonial tea and receive a blessing before discussing affairs of State. Hanging from the pillars are curious cylinders covered with tiger and leopard skin; these, we were told, are symbols of power and justice.

The Dalai Lama's reception room is magnificently decorated. The throne, on which he used to sit cross-legged, is about six feet

higher than the polished floor. Over the front of it hangs a
wonderful piece of embroidery showing the swastika and sacred
thunderbolt (dorje) symbols. On each side are pillars swathed
in heavy silk hangings. A row of richly coloured thankas framed
in brocade hangs along the back wall. The roof-beams and the
capitals of the pillars are especially beautifully decorated with
gold and bright-coloured flower patterns.

The Norbhu Lingka comprises three separate palaces, houses
for the Grand Chamberlain, Chief Secretary, and other officials
attached to the Dalai Lama's staff, reception and throne rooms,
an inner enclosure including an artificial lake with two summer
pavilions, the royal stables, and the barracks where live the 500
troops of the Dalai Lama's private bodyguard. His Holiness
was accustomed to move from one palace to another just as he
felt inclined, and we were shown several rooms with padded
couches on which he used to sit. Before the low cushions was
always a carved table on which were set ready his jade teacup
with its golden lotus-pattern stand and cover, his prayer-wheel,
and often a bowl of fruit. These rooms, unlike other show
places in Tibet, were always scrupulously clean and tidy. It was
as if they were all prepared for the imminent return of the next
incarnation of Chenrezi. The palaces are storehouses of rich
presents that the Dalai Lamas have received in the past from
different corners of the Buddhist world. Many were locked
away and carefully sealed, but others could be seen in glass cases
or were in use as ornaments. There were cones of holy-water
vessels on tables inlaid with ivory and mother-of-pearl, huge
porcelain vases, innumerable golden images set with turquoise
and coral and wearing great necklaces of amber, holy books with
carved wooden covers, and hangings of priceless brocade. In
one room there were several framed photographs of the late
Dalai Lama, one of the Potala, and another of a Chinese temple.
Most striking of all were several magnificent examples of
cloisonné work : Chinese lions four feet in height, and elephants
bearing vases on their backs. The lions showed the traditional
characteristics of their sex : the male, with his paw pressed
playfully on a ball, depicted gentleness in spite of strength, while
the female, playing with her cub, showed affection.

In one room, which had a floor of polished wooden blocks,
was a life-size image of the Dalai Lama himself, mitred and

swathed in rich vestments like a bishop, sitting on a throne with a silken canopy above his head. The walls of these newer palaces were completely covered in paintings, many of them topical, the work of Chinese artists. There were paddle-steamers crossing lakes, a crowd of people traversing an arched stone bridge, as well as birds, animals and flowers.

The gardens had been skilfully laid out, but since the last Prelate's death they have not been properly tended. The flowers are mainly self-sown, and spring up, together with weeds, in the chinks of the paving-stones. But in spite of this lack of proper care the borders in the autumn were a riot of colour, with red and white hollyhocks, purple phloxes, yellow mari-golds, petunias, coreopsis, asters, roses and chrysanthemums. All the flowers of an English garden seem to flourish perfectly at 12,000 feet above sea-level. The trees here, instead of being gnarled and twisted, grow slim and straight to a great height. There is one beautiful avenue of white poplars leading to the newer palaces; it is only spoilt by a granite arch whose spindly columns look out of place beside the more robust Tibetan gate-ways. In one place a pine tree grows as high as the palace roof; there is a clump of bamboo twenty feet high; there are apple trees, apricots and peaches—though these fruits do not ripen in Lhasa. In the gardens two prayer-barrels are set over streams so that they are made to revolve by water-power.

Behind one of the palaces is the Dalai Lama's garage. Here, beneath a dust sheet, we saw a Baby Austin with a number-plate bearing the words *Tibet I*. There was also a venerable Dodge. These cars were presents to the Dalai Lama from former Political Officers. Some years ago he had a road specially built along-side the aqueduct to the Arsenal (*trab-shi*), some three miles distant, and frequently with his favourite, Kumpala, he would drive down to inspect the troops. But now the road has been largely washed away in the summer floods, the wheels of the car, which are missing, have perhaps suffered a similar fate, and *Tibet I* looks neglected and forlorn.

The Forbidden Enclose of the Norbhu Lingka, which is also surrounded by a high wall, is about two hundred yards square. Here there is an artificial lake overhung by tall trees. A granite balustrade borders the lake, which is square in shape, and a bridge, or rather causeway, leads from a small gated portico to two islands built up with stone walls and surrounded by ornamental granite fencing. On the walls of the portico are some very racy frescoes showing golden pheasants and some dogs like dachshunds. On the islands are two pavilions surrounded by innumerable flowers in pots. These summer-houses, with golden emblems along the ridges of their orange-brown roofs of highly glazed Chinese tiles, represent the inner sanctuary of the Priest King. No official was allowed within the walls of this enclosure, and here he could escape the attentions of the crowd of servants that surround a king, and enjoy the solitude that is so often denied to one in his position. Each day (says Sir Charles Bell, who was privileged to know him intimately) he would spend several hours in lonely meditation and prayer among the birds and flowers that he loved.

His Holiness was always devoted to animals and birds, and had set up what might almost be described as a zoo in the Norbhu Lingka grounds. The Bengal tiger which formerly lived in a corner of the enclosure is no longer there, but a pair of *Shao*, the almost extinct Sikkim stag, are tethered on one of the lawns. The hind is quite docile but the stag very much on the defensive. On the lake are many bar-headed geese and Brahminy duck; there are doves in cages, Demoiselle cranes and Monal pheasants in a wire-netting enclosure, and a monkey chained to a tall pole, up which he climbs. There were also many dogs, but these are now looked after by different ministers. The Abbot of Gundeling one day showed us a pair of dachshunds which belonged to His Holiness, and there was also an Airedale terrier and a greyhound. The granite kennels, built at intervals along the outside wall and beside the palaces, bear testimony to the number of Tibetan mastiffs that he used to keep. These dogs are kept chained up in the courtyard of most Tibetan mansions; at night they are allowed to roam round the yard, from which they successfully keep away thieves. As they are tied up all day they become extremely fierce, and as soon as a stranger approaches they bark furiously and throw themselves to the ends of their all too flimsy chains. Very often they wear thick ruff-like collars of scarlet wool; this is to protect their throats from the attacks of wolves. In colour they are black or liver-and-black; their coats may be either long and shaggy or fairly short; they have massive heads, pendant ears and bloodshot eyes.

In the palace gardens there were also several of the other typical dog of the country, the Tibetan terrier or " Apso ". These lively little animals were brought by the Chinese, but in Lhasa the breed has practically died out. The usual colour is sable. They resemble Skye terriers, but have curly tails like Pekinese.

The Dalai Lama's herd of two-humped camels are allowed to roam at large over the waste land between the Norbhu Lingka and the main branch of Kyi Chu, where they browse on the thorny bushes that grow there. There are seventeen of them now, one of them having been born since they arrived as a present from Mongolia. Each morning and evening the Tibetan who is in charge of them rounds them up and prevents them from straying too far. While doing this he usually sits on the back of one that is used to being ridden. There is also a herd of some fifty mules and ponies which are taken from the stables to graze in the park in front of the Potala. Though these are in magnificent condition they are never used; practically all of them were presents to His Holiness. Some of the mules— who are as fat as butter—are of a curious fulvous colour with a black line down the centre of the back and tail and similar striped markings on the legs. One, the strangest of all, is white, covered all over with small black spots, like a Dalmatian.

Perhaps the most surprising thing in all the Norbhu Lingka is the Dalai Lama's stables. The stalls are arranged along three sides of a cobbled courtyard and around another block in the centre. On each side of the entrance gateway are two paintings, the Mongolian leading a tiger, and, in a style that recalls an Italian primitive, a man followed by an amiable-looking elephant laden with symbolic jewels. These paintings one has seen elsewhere, but over every stall is the most enchanting fresco painted in bright colours on the plaster of the wall. Many of these are of equestrian subjects, beautiful Pegasus-like horses, pink, blue, spotted or white, flying over far hill-tops or gambolling playfully together. One of the most interesting shows the anatomy of the horse. It is intended for veterinary purposes, and shows two horses, a front and a back view, standing on their hind-legs. This displays the Tibetan conception of the position of the bones·and organs of the animal's body: it is naturally somewhat rudimentary. Other paintings illustrate Chinese proverbs and folk-tales: four figures are trying to move something that looks like an enormous peach; a boatload of people cross a lake while an old man sits wrapped in thought, and a wisp of cloud flowing from his brain is developed to form a vision of the Buddha.

All these frescoes, though slightly splashed and discoloured, are marvellously executed and must be the work of first-class artists. The topical paintings on the palace walls are clearly Chinese; the huge richly-coloured figures of the four Kings of the Quarters on the portico opening into the Forbidden Enclosure are as clearly Tibetan, but these equestrian studies exhibit a rare economy of line and colour and are quite unlike other work I saw in Lhasa.

The palaces and grounds are in the charge of the young Prime Minister, who is a nephew of the last Dalai Lama, and nearly every week we used to see him, with his six servants, riding past our house on his way to visit the Norbhu Lingka. Each article is carefully catalogued and entered into books, and he must go and see that none of the seals are broken, and that none of the massive Tibetan locks are undone. However well he may have looked after the treasures, it is a great pity that the garden has so completely gone to seed; it will take many years to restore it to the orderly state in which the last owner kept it. The man directly in charge is a half-brother of Yuto Depön, who is in charge of the bodyguard and has rooms in the barracks.

The nominal strength of this bodyguard is 500, but many of the soldiers were on leave. The barracks face the river and are separated from it by a stony parade-ground where the troops play football. In one corner of this ground was a huge pile of kindling-wood some twenty feet high, and to go and collect loads of this wood from the waste land by the river seemed to be the sole activity of the soldiers, though several of them made remarkable noises with a bugle. There was always a guard in the sentry-box beside the gate. When we gave notice of our intention to visit the palace, there would be a section ready in charge of an N.C.O. They were usually youths, not so tall as the fixed bayonets they carried—it was necessary to have their bayonets fixed, as they carried no ammunition. As we passed they would present-arms and look very ashamed of themselves. The Tibetans are not a military nation.

Going through the quiet rooms and shrines of the palaces,

obviously tended with such loving care, and more especially walking alone in the gardens, with the cooing of turtle-doves and the fragrance of flowers in the air, one could almost feel the presence of the Dalai Lamas, that mysterious spirit of the universe—call it Avalokita, Chenrezi, what you will—which was at that moment being so carefully sought in the person of a young child. But it is the ghost of the Great Thirteenth alone that haunts the Norbhu Lingka.

During our six months in Lhasa we heard so much of this great figure, whose name was mentioned always with respect amounting to adoration, that we were able to form a clear picture of the Precious Protector. Bell describes him as follows:

" The present Dalai Lama has a somewhat dark complexion, which is pitted, but not very deeply, with the marks of small-pox. His form and features reflect his humble parentage, but he moves and speaks with the natural dignity that is inherent in his race and is still further emphasized by the high position to which he has been called. As is natural in one who has perforce to mix much in worldly affairs, his face has not acquired the quiet expression of saintliness that distinguishes his brother Prelate at Tashi-lhünpo. His moustache, high eyebrows, and keen watchful eyes accentuate the impression of worldly cares, so that one who knew him but slightly would be apt to under-rate his spirituality. In actual fact he is in some ways more strict in his devotions than even the Tashi Lama. The quick deprecatory smile that lights up his features when he speaks, and his courtesy, which never failed, even when receiving un-welcome letters from our Government, could not but impress those who conversed with him."

Even the selection of this Pontiff was different and more convincing than that of his predecessors. When a Dalai Lama dies, the method of discovering his successor is most complicated. The child is usually of peasant stock, though during the time of close alliance between the Tibetans and Mongols the child was sometimes the son of a noble or royal Mongol family. The Ambans in Lhasa, when they had sufficient power, used to assist in making the choice. After a certain number of candidates had been chosen, the names and birthdays of the children were written on pieces of wood or paper and put into a golden urn. From this one would be withdrawn by the Amban with a pair of golden chop-sticks.

Often the Dalai Lama before he dies will give some indication to his ministers of the district or even of the house where he will reincarnate. The spirit does not transfer itself to a child born at the exact moment of the decease of the former incarnation; and as it takes several years to find the child, who must in any case pass beyond the age of infancy before he can exert any power, a Regent is chosen to be at the head of affairs. This Regent, or sometimes another incarnation lama, after spending some days in meditation, goes and gazes into the surface of a certain holy lake not far from Lhasa, where he sees a vision which will direct him to where the child is to be found. The Tashi Lama, the Abbots of Sera, Drepung and Garden monasteries, the State Oracle at Nechung, and other important lamas are consulted; and eventually by visions and other mystic means certain information is revealed as to the date of birth of the child and the occupation of his parents; of the type of country, and perhaps an actual description of topographical features in the neighbourhood of the house where the child is to be found.

At this stage expeditions are sent out from Lhasa to the districts of Tibet where it is foretold that the child will be found. They may be away for many years, crossing high passes and searching remote plateau villages for just such a house or hill or family as has been revealed in visions and dreams. In a likely locality any reports of miraculous births or portents and visions bearing on the whereabouts of the child are eagerly looked into by the search-parties. Eventually several possible children may be found, some uncertainty remaining as to which is the genuine incarnation of Chenrezi. The children are then put through various tests. The true incarnation may recognize servants and officials that he had about him in his former life; he should pick out his own teacup, prayer-wheel, bell and sacred thunderbolt from others, and frequently, in spite of his youth, he can indicate occurrences that happened to him in one of his former incarnations. In addition he usually has certain physical peculiarities which Bell gives as follows:

(a) Marks as of a tiger skin on his legs.
(b) Eyes and eyebrows that curve upwards on the outside and are rather long.

(c) Large ears.
(d) Two pieces of flesh near the shoulder-blades indicating the two other hands of Chenrezi.
(e) An imprint like a conch-shell on one of the palms of his hands.

The last Dalai Lama bore the last three signs. On the occasion of his selection the Tibetan Government assured the Amban that the choice was so certain that the ceremony of picking out the name with golden chop-sticks was unnecessary. The State Oracle at Nechung was also quite unwavering in his choice.

Born in 1876, it was not till he was eighteen that he took up the reins of government, the time between being spent in preparation—mainly of a religious character—for his high office. He was taken from his mother at the age of three and brought to the Potala and put in charge of the Master of the Bedchamber and the Court Physician. His four predecessors had all been " removed " by the Chinese before they were old enough to have any power, and this must have caused him considerable concern. It was not long before he discovered a conspiracy to kill him by witchcraft, in which the Regent, Abbot of Tengye-ling monastery, was implicated. It was alleged that he had condoned the preparation of a pair of boots which were presented to the young Dalai Lama. Sewn into the sole of these was a charm which, as he walked, would speedily kill him. As a result of this conspiracy being discovered the Regent was imprisoned and treated so cruelly that he died. The other vicissitudes suffered by the late Dalai Lama have already been described in the chapter on the History of Tibet.

Even in these days of dictators one cannot but be amazed at his unrivalled power. Former Dalai Lamas—with the exception of the Great Fifth—had been pawns in the hands of ambitious and unscrupulous ministers, and for a hundred years prior to the accession of the last Prelate they had been quietly done away with before they were old enough to wield the Double Sceptre. But the last incarnation of Chenrezi, who would have been an exceptional man in any sphere of life, escaped by his own astuteness the dangers of poisoning and witchcraft; and despite certain violent and headstrong elements in his character, and the mistakes and vicissitudes of his early years, he built up for himself a position unique in the history of the Dalai Lamas.

In the sphere of internal administration his power was supreme, and he could and did enforce his will against the combined opposition of the Cabinet and Assembly. In foreign affairs he was supposed to act in conjunction with these two councils, but in point of fact he rarely consulted them; and, as the people of Tibet consider him literally as a God ruling on earth, his very words are inspired. Actually his power is limited by the difficulty of communications in Tibet and by the natural independence of the nomadic section of the population. In their mountain pastures there is no one to enforce the laws of distant Lhasa.

The two most important officers of the Dalai Lama's staff are the Lord Chamberlain (Chi-kyap Kempo), who is the head of all the monk officials in Tibet, and the Chief Secretary (Dronyer Chempo), who has ten under-secretaries in his office. There is a Court Physician (La-me Kempo) and four orderlies, who are usually of enormous size. It will be noticed that all these officials are monks, and as the Dalai is precluded by his exalted position from travelling about himself, it is through them that information is communicated to him; their power is therefore very great indeed.

When living at the Norbhu Lingka he would rise at dawn and spend two hours before breakfast at his devotions, praying not only for humanity but for all the animal kingdom—all " soul possessors ". The morning would be given up to matters of State for he personally settled all important questions of secular and religious administration. There might be a dispute between two landowners, a question of monastic discipline, an appeal against some decision of the Cabinet, the details of a ceremony to be arranged, a junior official to be appointed. All this was undertaken by the Dalai Lama personally. After an hour spent in prayer he would have lunch, and the afternoon would be spent in the same way as the morning. Any spare time would be devoted to walking round the Norbhu Lingka grounds looking at the flowers and playing with his dogs and other animals.

Again in the evening two more hours were spent in prayer and meditation; the hours until midnight or even later would be devoted to any especially serious problem that confronted him. At certain times of the year he would go into meditation for days, sometimes for months together, at the Norbhu Lingka or elsewhere. I was shown a room in the private monastery of Lhalu mansion and another in the Snake Temple where he used to stay on these occasions. A great deal of his time was taken up in blessing his subjects. When the Dalai travels, the whole countryside flock to be blessed. The monks from Drepung, Sera and Ganden must be blessed every year, each individual monk being then touched by the Dalai's hand. He was an indefatigable worker and his attendants used to complain that they rarely had sufficient sleep.

The Dalai Lama was much criticized in some quarters, especially by the envious supporters of Tashi-lhünpo, for mixing so much in worldly affairs. It was remarked that as an incarnation of Buddha he had no right in 1910 to order the Tibetans to oppose the Chinese and thereby cause considerable loss of life. He should, they said, have followed the example of his predecessors and have devoted his life to religious duties while his chief minister carried on the administration of secular affairs. He was also criticized by many for his harsh treatment of the plotting Regent of Tengye-ling monastery, whose rigorous imprisonment was said to be tantamount to murder. Naturally there will always be some who from jealousy or other motives criticize one who has the strength of character to assume such autocratic powers. But when the Dalai started to rule in 1893 some sort of reform was essential. When he died in 1933 a friend and protector had been found in Great Britain.

CHAPTER ELEVEN

MONASTERIES

IN Tibet religion always comes first, and God, says a Tibetan proverb, can only be approached through a lama. The monas-teries are therefore the chief influence in the country. Now that there is a comparatively trained army in Lhasa the power of these strongholds of Lamaism is somewhat curtailed, but it is still incalculably great.

In the vicinity of Lhasa the great monasteries of Drepung, Sera and Ganden, known as the Three Pillars of the State, contain some 20,000 monks. It was with some excitement therefore that I heard on August 30th that we were going to visit Drepung, the largest monastery in the world. I hoped to find some answer to the questions that had continually occurred to me since entering Tibet: "How on earth do all these thousands of monks spend their time? how are they supported? and what good, if any, do they do?"

Drepung is supposed to house 7700 monks, but sometimes as many as 10,000 live there. The name Dre-pung literally means "the pile of rice", which is what the monastery resembles, as its tiers of whitewashed buildings lie one behind the other on a sloping site at the head of a wedge-shaped valley. Looked at from a distance, Drepung resembles a large fortified city rather than a single monastery, and it is only when one climbs the steep mountain slopes behind it and looks down on to its innumerable ramifications that one gets a true idea of its immense size. Looked at from below it is foreshortened and many of the buildings are dwarfed or hidden.

The monastery was founded at the beginning of the fifteenth century by the son of a poor herdsman from eastern Tibet, who was a disciple of Tsong-kapa. It was he also who founded the great monastery of Tashi-lhünpo at Shigatse in the middle of the fifteenth century.

Outside the monastery wall a number of very dirty boys dressed in dishevelled monks' robes were playing among the huge boulders; but in anticipation of our visit the majority of the monks had been ordered to keep to their cells so that we would not be inconvenienced by their crowding round and staring at us. As we entered through a ponderous gate in the long southern wall we were met by two *shengoes* or proctors, who are responsible for keeping order in the monastery. They were dressed in robes more scarlet in colour than the usual dull red of the monk's dress. They wore sleeveless undercoats of red and gold brocade and their shoulders were built up and padded to give them an additional air of importance. These proctors were preceded by two lictors who carried curious square iron maces damascened with golden dragons. Perched on the top of these maces were the proctors' yellow crested hats. As we walked along the narrow ways and steep staircases of the monastery these men preceded us, shouting every now and then in stentorian tones, " Pha gyuk " (get out of the way).

We were first taken along a paved roadway, up a steep hill to the main assembly hall. The heavily bossed entrance door lay at the top of a long flight of stone steps twenty yards in width. Outside the door was an anteroom or portico with its roof supported by several enormous fluted pillars of wood. These were each made of several poplar trunks, the components being held together with iron bands. The walls of this anteroom were covered by vast paintings of guardian deities: one red-faced, with grinning fangs, others pale and terrible. These are the four Celestial Kings of the Quarters who guard the universe against the attacks of the outer demons. Other frescoes depict the tortures of poor mortals in the never-ending lives to come.

The Lamaists are great connoisseurs of hells. They recognize some thousands, of which there are sixteen specially select abodes, eight of which are hot and eight cold. These hells, whose varied forms of entertainment bear a close resemblance to the torments of Dante's Inferno, are carefully graded. As well as a wide choice of punishments for commonplace sinners, there are others worthy of note. There is a hell for doctors who kill their patients through incompetence; in this the victims are scarified and clumsily dissected, only to be reunited and revived so that the process can continue indefinitely. Busybodies are nailed down, black lines are drawn on their bodies as a guide to red-hot saws which cut them to pieces; the tongue, enlarged and pegged out, is harrowed by hot spikes. Those who cast refuse or dead bodies on the public roads are pounded in iron mortars and beaten on anvils. Men who grumble against the weather or obstruct watercourses (an obscure connection!) have molten iron poured down their throats. There is a special hell for stupid people, for to the Buddhist unawareness or wilful lack of perception is one of the major sins. In the cold hells, the sinners are immersed in glacier water and the resulting chilblains are aggravated and torn. There are also hells of tantalization wherein the starving victim is surrounded by choice foods which he cannot enjoy, as his mouth is a mere pinprick; and if the poor starveling does succeed in swallowing anything it is turned to lacerating knives and molten metal.

The celebrated Wheel of Life painting, of which there are some fine examples at Drepung, eloquently depicts the endless birth, death and rebirth of man, which is inevitable unless he can escape this eternal circle and attain Buddhahood. The wheel is clutched by a snarling monster. Outside the wheel are two or more figures of Buddhas who have escaped from the circle. In the very centre, as it were the hub of the wheel, are a cock, a serpent and a pig, each grasping in its mouth the tail of the next. These are symbolic of lust, hatred and ignorance: the three sins necessitating rebirth. The six main segments, divided by the " spokes " of the wheel, show the six worlds of rebirth: Heaven, the home of demi-gods or Titans, the animal world, the various hells, the abode of tantalized spirits, and the realm of mankind. In each region is shown a Buddha, who, like the Dalai Lama, has foregone his right to Nirvana in order to help mortals struggling in the inexorable grip of the wheel. The outer rim, divided into twelve partitions, shows the phases of a man's life as symbolizing the causes of rebirth.

Inside the assembly room there were no windows, and the immense room was only dimly lit through the doorway and by a number of spaces left around the central part of the roof-lantern, which was raised higher than the surrounding cloister. The roof was supported by massive square wooden pillars, the lower parts of which were swathed in dark red cloth. On the floor were long strips of cushioned cloth on which the monks could sit; there were raised seats at the end for the officiating monks. On the walls, as far as one could see in the dim light, were gruesome paintings, recesses containing images, and, higher up, lines of richly coloured thankas framed in brocade. At the end of the hall opposite the door was a row of the usual Lamaist images, some of them of immense size. The smaller images of gold were so covered in white scarves that it was difficult to recognize them. Their head-dresses were magnificently bejewelled. On the shelves in front of the images were rows of butter-lamps, holy-water vessels, libation jugs and curiously wrought shapes in butter and tsamba dough. The hall had a heavy, sickly smell, a mixture of incense and rancid butter from the spillings of the monks' tea. The stone flags on the floor, and indeed everything one touched, were thick with sticky grease from the same source.

Drepung is divided into four colleges, each presided over by an Abbot: it was by the careful appointment of these officials that the late Dalai Lama was able to subdue this turbulent monastery. Each college houses monks from a different locality; one being favoured by Khampas, another by Mongolians, and so on.

We drank tea, or hot sweet milk of a curious mauve colour, with each of the Abbots in turn, and were offered heaped-up dishes of rice, sweet cakes and dried fruits. Before eating any rice it is customary to take a few grains between the thumb and middle finger and to scatter it as a libation to the gods. It took some hours to make the tour of the monastery, and even then we must have left out many of the buildings.

We were shown a room used by the great fifth Dalai Lama; it has been kept exactly as he had it in the seventeenth century, when he left the monastery and set about building the new Potala Palace. This custom of retaining undisturbed a room used by some holy lama is common in Lhasa; we were shown several rooms in private houses, usually furnished as chapels, where the last Dalai Lama had stayed.

We must have seen literally hundreds of images at Drepung, some of them being of gigantic size. They were usually dressed in gold brocade and had a silken canopy above their heads. The expressions of some were formal, of others most life-like. Among the latter was a row of effigies of previous incarnation lamas of the monastery; each was depicted in his monk's robe and crested yellow cap like a Roman helmet. We saw five images of the goddess Drölma (or Mary), each one of which was alleged to have uttered words. In another hall there was a striking image of the late Dalai Lama.

We visited some of the monks' cells. The richer brethren or those of noble family have rooms to themselves or share accommodation with a few chosen friends; the poorer monks live in large dormitories. The small cells that we visited had by way of furniture a simple altar, a padded cushion seat which would serve as a bed, and a low carved table. We saw the kitchen too, a dark smoky hall with a number of copper cauldrons six feet across and three or four feet deep. It is in these that the buttered tea is made which, with a few handfuls of barley meal, forms the daily fare of the monks. It must be an exacting task to be in charge of the catering and cleanliness of so many thousands of men. And although the monks themselves looked and smelled as if they had never washed, yet the streets and byways of the monastery were noticeably cleaner than those of Lhasa. There is an underground sewer running the whole length of the monastery and this takes all refuse to some sort of cess-pit, a settling tank a mile away.

The roofs of the buildings are particularly striking. As a rule they are flat and surrounded by a parapet, at the corners of which, and at frequent intervals between, are cylindrical banners held aloft on long poles. These are to frighten away evil spirits. The roofs of the main halls are surmounted by gilt pagodas of Chinese design, similar to those on the summit of the Potala. To relieve the monotony of the white walls pierced by symmetrical rows of windows, many of the roofs are finished by a layer of dull red willow-twig walling six or eight feet high. These form an excellent background for the circular gold emblems with which the upper part of the walls are ornamented. On the parapets above these red layers are cylinders as much as twelve feet high and a yard in diameter, covered with exquisitely chased gold leaf of considerable thickness. In the very centre of the roof is a similarly worked screen about five feet high and three feet wide which is used as a rest for the long monastery trumpets.

After following the custom of giving a very substantial cash present to the monastery, we departed, carrying with us a confused impression of rows of enormous sardonic images in dimly lit halls; steep narrow alleyways with towering walls leaning back on either side; solid gold butter-lamps; slippery, greasy ladders leading from one storey to another; grotesque but wonderfully richly coloured paintings of hideous demons, and everywhere that all-pervading but indescribable smell—a compound of rancid butter, stale incense, musty age-old buildings and unwashed human bodies.

When we emerged from Drepung we saw that many trestle stalls had been put up just outside the main gate. Nearly all the vendors were women; raw meat was the chief article for sale, but there were also vegetables, dried fruits and cigarettes obtainable. The Tibetans are the most tolerant people in the world. Tobacco is strictly forbidden for the monks—though snuff is allowed; and the ban against taking life goes to the very root of the Buddhist religion. Yet they are sensible enough to realize that in a climate such as is found at Lhasa, meat is practically a necessity. The high lamas satisfy their consciences by saying that the spirit of the yak or sheep that is eaten by them will reincarnate in a higher plane in its next life.

In the middle of October we visited Sera monastery, the second largest in the world, with a nominal total of 5500 monks. Drepung, containing a large proportion of Mongolians, Kalmuks and other aliens, has a reputation for being pro-Chinese and against the Lhasa government, while Sera has a more patriotic record. The arrogant Drepung monks, who had always had too much of their own way, viewed with concern the rising power of the army. They realized that this would limit their power; for in the old days with 20,000 monks in the vicinity of the city, and no one to oppose them, their power was unrivalled. This was especially so at the time of the Great Prayer, the chief annual festival, which lasts for the first three weeks of the Tibetan year. During this time the monks have complete control of the city, and some 30,000 of them billet themselves on the inhabitants.

In 1920, when the Dalai Lama was increasing the army, there was considerable friction, and at the time of the New Year it was feared that the monks would get out of control. Some thousands of the Drepung monks marched to the Norbhu Lingka with certain demands. It was only the prompt and decisive action of the Dalai Lama that averted serious trouble. He put Lhasa out of bounds for the military during the time that the monks were installed there. A few months after this there was some internal trouble in Drepung over a question of discipline, and half the monks came out in open rebellion, threatening to attack Lhasa. The Tibetan Government sent Tsarong, who was then commander-in-chief, to besiege the monastery, which gave in after some resistance. The Dalai Lama, having shown that he would stand no nonsense, treated the culprits with characteristic leniency. It is moreover noteworthy that when the Government troops searched the monastery they found an enormous supply of arms and a complete plant for forging Tibetan currency.

Sera, on the other hand, has always been anti-China and has been repeatedly attacked by Chinese troops. The word Sera probably means " hail ", and is said to have been given to it because the hail of Sera scatters the rice of Drepung; a comparison indicating the abiding rivalry of these two institutions. Another school of thought holds that Sera means " wild-rose fence ", a name given to it by the disciples of Tsong-kapa who founded the monastery in 1419 upon the site of a smaller institution which was surrounded by wild-rose bushes. Sera is supposed to keep a large band of fighting monks who spend their time in continuous training on a secret parade-ground at the back of the monastery. I spent some time searching for this with field-glasses from a convenient station on the steep hill-side behind the monastery, but could see no place where it could exist. But in the next valley to Sera is a long-jump pitch where the monks were often to be seen taking exercise; this is one of their favourite sports. A sloping run is built up so that the take-off is three or four feet higher than the landing pit, the latter being full of sand. The performers that I watched had no style at all; they would go through the air with legs and arms flying in all directions. As with Drepung, it is only from above that one can get a true conception of the great size of this monastery, whose buildings run far back into a deep V-shaped valley. As the slope of the site is only slight, it gives the impression from the front of being about a quarter the size of Drepung.

One of the most cherished possessions of Sera is a sacred dagger which is believed to have been found on a hill-side near the monastery after having been miraculously transported from India. It is the model of the *dorje* (" thunderbolt ") daggers that are used in Buddhist ceremonies for stabbing invisible demons of the air. During the New Year festival this dagger, which possesses miraculous powers, is taken in solemn procession to Lhasa City.

Ganden, the third " Pillar of the State ", lies about thirty-five miles to the north-east of Lhasa. We contemplated a visit there, but it was not till after the main body of the Mission had returned that Richardson found time to go. There are some 3300 lamas at Ganden. The monastery is famous for the tomb of the founder, Tsong-kapa, whose body is embalmed there. It is also the chief seat of learning in a country, where wisdom is considered the highest attainment of man, and where the human mind is credited with such powers as controlling the weather and dealing life and death.

Among the laity it is very rare in this feudal land for a man of low birth to attain to high position; but a monk, if he is sufficiently astute and hard-working, can rise to the highest eminence. Many of the Abbots of the great monasteries are drawn from humble families. These Abbots preside over the National Assembly which is summoned on urgent occasions. And during the absence of the Dalai Lama on the occasion of the Younghusband Mission, the Abbot of Ganden acted as Regent and signed the treaty between the Governments of India and Tibet. In fact the " Enthroned of Ganden ", an appointment that is made purely on qualifications of learning, ranks chief among the non-incarnate lamas of Tibet and next in precedence after the Dalai and Tashi Lamas.

There are several great monasteries in the city of Lhasa. The most famous of these are the four "Lings"—Tengye-ling, Gundeling, Tsomo-ling, Tsecho-ling—which, together with Reting and Murn, have the privilege of supplying a Regent during the minority of the Dalai Lama. Of these, Tenge-ling has been destroyed, its considerable estates confiscated by the Government, and its monks dispersed.

Practically half the revenue of the State is devoted to the upkeep of the monasteries, either in the form of grants of land or in gifts of barley, butter and tea. Up till 1912 the Chinese, as well as paying large cash presents to the monasteries, supplied annually thousands of mule-loads of brick tea. Another source of income is forthcoming in the form of gifts from regular worshippers and pilgrims. Fees are also paid on the innumerable occasions when monks have to be called in, or special prayers offered at the monasteries; when a man sets out on a journey, in case of illness, to avert misfortune, or to celebrate a birth, marriage or death. The monks are not slow to exploit the power that is given to them by the superstitious and credulous Tibetan. The Lamaist mythology, adding the deities and devils of Buddhism and Hinduism to the already overcrowded pantheon of Pönism, is overburdened with an unbelievable variety of Buddhas, saints, Titans, celestial guardians, tutelary demons, she-devils, genii, fiends, furies and familiar spirits. All these must be worshipped, propitiated or appeased, and only the lama, possessing the skeleton key to heaven, hell and all intermediate regions, can act as guide through this formidable maze. Rigidly prescribed offerings must be made, horoscopes have to be cast, auspicious days for journeys and all the events of life must be discovered, prayer-flags and charms have to be correctly drawn up and consecrated, and prayers must be offered. In a thousand ways the co-operation of the lama is needed by the layman to avoid perdition and to give him the highest possible chance of a successful rebirth. It is not surprising that the monasteries are the most wealthy and powerful institutions in Tibet.

Many of the smaller monasteries and nunneries are founded and supported by wealthy families, and the monks and nuns therein recruited from their tenantry. Among the noble families of Lhasa, as their estates are lent rent-free by the Government, the eldest, and often the second son, is expected to go into the service of the State, while the younger son becomes a monk official. For the poorer families the priesthood offers prospects of a career, as any boy with the requisite capacity and energy can rise to the highest positions in the monasteries, or can be nominated to the school for monk officials at the Potala; whereas the lay branch of Government service is almost entirely restricted to the ancient families.

Tibet is a poor country, and the land will support only a certain number of people. If the working families have more children than they can afford to keep, the surplus are sent to the neighbouring monastery or nunnery, where they are brought up at the expense of the State. More than one-sixth of the male population of Tibet are monks. Boys destined for the priesthood go to the monastery when they are seven or eight years old. Sometimes we saw even younger ones there, but these were probably orphans who were being brought up by the monastery from childhood. Not all are eligible. Buddhists, being more consistent in this respect than ourselves, insist that a man's means of livelihood shall be above reproach, so those whose families are connected with trades having to do with the taking of life are not permitted to enter the priesthood. Such are the body-cutters, butchers, tanners, leather-workers and gunsmiths. A high physical standard is also demanded; boys with any deformity of limb or speech are not accepted.

A successful applicant is handed over to the charge of a monk instructor who is personally responsible for his education and discipline. The education consists in learning to read and write and in memorizing passages of the scriptures. At this period he is expected to act as a servant to his tutor. If the boy passes his examinations he is then admitted to a college, and after taking certain vows, he becomes a novice or student monk and is allowed to wear the terra-cotta-coloured robes of the priesthood. Some monks never rise above this stage. After this there are various examinations to be passed, each opening the door to successive well-defined positions. The chief qualification is to be able to memorize page after page of the one hundred and eight volumes of the Buddhist scriptures. Not all the young monks follow a career of learning; at an early stage they can choose a life suited to their special aptitudes. If a man shows outstanding skill in painting, wood-carving or in writing the complicated Tibetan script, his talents can be utilized for the benefit of the monastery. If he shows promise as a healer, he goes to the Iron Hill to study medicine. Should he be particularly agile or graceful, he is trained to take part in the lama dances which mark various religious festivals. He may also be a cook, agriculturist, accountant or even an astrologer or sorcerer. Tibetans are born traders, and many of the monasteries augment their incomes by considerable business enterprise. Some of the monks, therefore, presumably those who find too late that they are unsuited to a life of contemplation and learning, devote their energies to trade.

Many of the larger houses of Lhasa have a special altar-room where several monks at all times of the day are to be heard droning prayers for the benefit of departed ancestors, to avert misfortunes, to advance the fortunes of the house, to bring good health, or for some other purpose. These men are looked after and paid; after a time they return to their monastery and others take their places.

When prayers are being held in the main temple of the monastery the Lamaist liturgies follow traditional lines. On the occasion of our visit to Sera monastery a service was in progress, and we were invited to look in for a moment through the open door of the temple. Errant beams of sunlight percolated through the roof-lantern and slanted across the huge square pillars wrapped in red cloth as though with puttees. A row of richly coloured thankas hung from the edge of the colonnade roof. From the doorway an aisle led to the high altar, where a row of butter-lamps threw a ghostly light on to the images, which were hardly distinguishable from the officiating monk, who was raised on a seat above his fellows.

On either side of the aisle lines of monks faced each other, sitting Buddha-fashion on padded cushions. Row after row of shaven-headed, red-robed monks disappeared into the shadows beneath the overhanging colonnade. As the room was in no way heated, each man wore a heavy pleated cape over his shoulders. Some of them were boys of seven or eight years of age, and these seemed to be in the charge of tutors. Several younger monks came round with teapots, and each worshipper produced a wooden cup from the folds of his robes. After drinking the tea the cup was licked clean and replaced. The service continued. There was a burst of music—shrill notes from the cornets, the clashing of cymbals, the insistent beating of gongs, and then a shattering resonant blast from the long trumpets.

The service seemed to be in the form of a litany: the officiating monk would chant a few sentences, punctuated by the occasional ringing of a bell and the clattering of his skull drum, and then the congregation of monks would return the response, the shrill tenor of the acolytes blending with the preternaturally deep bass of the others. Upon enquiry we discovered that their prayers were to avert a hailstorm whose advent had recently been foretold by the Sera oracle.

Sometimes the monks were simply reciting passages of the Scriptures. This they did in deep complaining undulating voices, the first note of a sentence being spoken in a higher tone. Often they were not all reciting the same passage, for if several chapters are run through by different groups concurrently they naturally cover more ground. At times they swayed backwards and forwards in time to the prayer. The object of their devotion is not only to avert disaster but to heal the sick, to hasten the birth of a child, or simply to pray for all creation—man, animal, bird, fish, insect, all " mind possessors ". When the Great War broke out, for instance, the Dalai Lama, as well as offering us two contingents of Tibetan troops, ordained that in all the monasteries of Tibet part of the time reserved for prayers on behalf of the Tibetan Government should be devoted to praying for the success of the Allies.

The ritual and chanting at once recall a Roman Catholic High Mass. Indeed there are so many points of similarity between the two religions that it has been suggested that Lamaism incorporated some of the ritual of the Lazarist and Capuchin fathers who visited Lhasa in the eighteenth century. Enforced celibacy, the use of the rosary and of swinging censers for scattering incense, the continuous repetition of prayers even though the words are not understood, the method of chanting the services—are points of similarity.

But these are only superficial resemblances. In character the two
religions are fundamentally different. The Lamaist monk does
not spend his time in ministering to the people or educating them,
nor do laymen take part in or even attend the monastery services.
The beggar beside the road is nothing to the monk. Knowledge
is the jealously guarded prerogative of the monastery and is used
to increase their influence and wealth. Another essential difference
is in dogma. The Catholics are bound by strict rules, and what
they must believe is carefully laid down. Not so the Tibetan
monk. As long as he attends the service in the monastery temple
and is subject to the lay discipline of the proctors, he can pursue
any spiritual goal and can endeavour to reach it by whatever
means he chooses. He may follow and teach and believe whatever
doctrine appeals to him. Moreover, he shares in no community
life. If a monk can afford it he keeps his own establishment
within the monastery. If his home is near by he will have meals
sent in to his apartments. Another way in which Lamaism differs
from Catholicism is in its tolerance, which is as admirable as it is
remarkable. Father Desideri, one of the Jesuits who was at Lhasa in
the early eighteenth century, wrote a book in Tibetan rejecting the
tenets of the Lamaist doctrine and defending those of the Catholic
faith; he describes how his house became full of monks, especially
from Drepung and Sera, who came to read and discuss his book.

Each summer the monks leave their monastery and have a
holiday, which varies in length from ten to fifteen days according
to the wealth of each monastic college. One day in the middle
of September (the last day of the seventh Tibetan month) we met
the Drepung monks streaming towards Lhasa to receive the
Regent's blessing before starting their holiday. Mounted in the
middle of the straggling procession were the proctors in scarlet
robes and yellow crested hats, preceded by their stalwart mace-
bearers, whose powerful bellowing rapidly cleared the road.
The Abbots and other dignitaries, including an incarnation lama of
Drepung, followed, each with his retinue of mounted servants in
tall cylindrical yellow hats or the red-tasselled head-dress of the
ordinary lay servant. Many of the monks carried sheeps' carcasses,
cooking utensils, furniture and tents. On this occasion the monks
take their annual bath, being forced to go to the river, wash their
greasy clothes, and at the same time give their bodies the one
immersion of the year.

Once when we visited Gundeling, sometime in early December, a strange ceremony was taking place in a corner of the open courtyard. A bearded monk, wearing a strange fan-shaped hat, was sitting on a wooden throne before an open fire of willow logs. On the other side of the fire were about a hundred monks sitting on the courtyard floor. They were all curiously attired. Some played cymbals, others drums or shrill trumpets. At the side were the long monastery trumpets resting on special supports. Beside the officiating priest was a large table covered with some thirty or forty dishes containing different sorts of herbs and magical ingredients, which would be passed to him in turn by an attendant. He would mutter incantations, make mysterious passes with his hands over each bowl, and then throw its contents into the flames. The chorus would sing, cymbals would clash, drums beat and trumpets boom. Upon enquiry we were told that the object of this strange performance was to prevent disease, which is apt to become rife in Tibet as autumn passes to winter.

As well as the large and famous monasteries there are innumerable smaller institutions. Each village or hamlet has its own monastery, which is usually the most imposing building in the place. And often there are remote monasteries far from the haunts of men, perched up on some precipitous rock-face or away at the extremity of some unfrequented valley. From the earliest times Buddhists, following the example of Gautama, have forsaken, for varying periods of time, the distracting haunts of men and have retired into these desolate hermitages to attain enlightenment or supernatural powers by meditation and self-abnegation. Every Tibetan monk is supposed during his lifetime to spend a period of three years, three months and three days in solitary meditation. Naturally it is not by any means all of them who spend even three days in such confinement.

Near Gyantse there is a hermitage where numbers of monks immure themselves for life. It was founded by Mila-Repa, the great hermit saint, more than eight hundred years ago. At first they retire only for a few months; then after a further period of preparation they are walled in for three years, three months and three days. Once more they emerge before undergoing the final period of entombment, which lasts until they die. The cells are perched among the crags of a rocky hill-side. Once the hermit has been locked into his diminutive stone cell he is in absolute

M

darkness. There is a small drain running through the room, and an opening, closed by a sliding door, through which his tea and tsamba are passed daily. But even the hand that appears to take this food is gloved. Many of these deluded devotees lose their reason before the final lifelong immurement, though they may at any time terminate this self-imprisonment. For a real ascetic to retire into the wilderness or solitary place is a different matter; but these Gyantse anchorites are of a debased type who are capable only of the physical and mechanical part of the hermit's life. This is one of the many ways in which Lamaism has exaggerated the letter of Buddha's laws while being incapable of carrying out their spiritual counterpart.

The Tibetan word for a monastery, *gompa*, literally means "secluded place", and the early monks, like those in our own country, had a genius for choosing the most attractive sites. Unless the building is in the open plain it usually faces south and has its back against the mountains, from which its water-supply is drawn. Often up in the hills above the main part of the monastery is some lonely hermitage where the monks can retire for peace and meditation. Certainly the majority of the monks that one saw in the monasteries or met on the road were anything but ascetic in appearance, but in these remote retreats, far from the disturbing haunts of man, they may have developed that store of occult wisdom for which the Tibetan monk has always been famous.

Lamaism, from the early days of the eighth century when Padma Sambhava preached the debased Tantrik doctrine that had replaced the original pure teaching of Buddha, has always delighted in demonology, oracles and other manifestations of black and mystic arts. Lamaism is still farther removed from pure Buddhism by having adopted many of the practices and beliefs of the earlier Pön religion of pure devil-worship and the propitiation of countless malignant devils both in this life and in the endless cycles of life to come.

The Tibetans have a genius for credulity. They believe implicitly in various psychic phenomena such as are described by that remarkable traveller, Madame David Neel. Though I was never fortunate enough to witness these myself, everybody talked of such things as beyond any possibility of doubt, and many had had first-hand experience of them. Among these powers is that of generating internal heat (*tumo*), which enables ill-clad under-nourished hermits to endure the bitter Tibetan winter at 15,000 feet above sea-level. This power is only attained after a long course of probationary exercises. The breathing must be carefully regulated, and the novice must have the power of dissociating his mind from his body. These men, having once learnt the art, can immerse themselves in icy streams so that the clothes afterwards freeze upon their bodies, and then sit motionless throughout the night, and by concentrating their minds and controlling their breathing can sink into a trance which leaves them oblivious of anything so mundane as the temperature. It was this power that sustained the great Tibetan hermit saint, Mila-Repa, when he was cut off by deep snow and had to winter among the glaciers of Mount Everest.

There are other saintly men who can so control their breathing that they can cover immense distances in a very short time. Men who have met these *lung-gom-pa* declare that they progress in a series of rhythmic bounds with their eyes gazing into the far distance. Their bodies sometimes become so light that they have to be weighted down to prevent them floating away. Other of the supernatural accomplishments of the Tibetans are to send messages by telepathy and to read thoughts. The theory of levi-tation is also understood : maintaining the cross-legged Buddha attitude, certain men can rise into the air as if they were floating, or perch on the summit of a pile of rice without disturbing a single grain.

To what extent these mysterious powers are really possessed by Tibetans I would hesitate to assert. The power of mind over body is being more and more demonstrated by the study of *Yogi*. It is almost certain that if one *has* the necessary faith, one can, literally, remove mountains. It must be borne in mind that to become possessed of these supernatural powers a course of study lasting for many years is necessary, and then it is not all who can succeed, even when taught by eastern ascetics, who maintain an age-long tradition of psychic research and experience. In any case, it is interesting that many of the holiest lamas believe that these psychic exercises are a waste of time and interfere with the search for true enlightenment.

CHAPTER TWELVE

FESTIVALS AND PROCESSIONS

THE Tibetans, in common with most Orientals, are very fond of ceremonial processions and the observation of festivals and saints' days; and during our six months at Lhasa we were the fortunate spectators of several such celebrations, for the Tibetan officials and people, in spite of their general policy of seclusion, were anxious that we, as their guests, should be given full opportunity to witness these scenes of gorgeous pageantry and ceremonial. If we were not formally invited by the Government we would usually receive a special message from Tsarong or from some other official telling us what was toward and where we should with most advantage station ourselves. Apart from the New Year festivities, which are of such importance that they demand a separate chapter, the most spectacular procession was on the occasion of the Regent going on tour.

Although Tibetans in general, being a nomadic people, are great travellers, the Lhasa officials are a strangely sedentary class: the Prime Minister had never ventured farther from Lhasa than Trisum Bridge, about eight miles to the south-west. Many of the officials, unless they had held office away from Lhasa, had never been more than a day's journey from the city. This was partly a matter of custom, and partly due to the difficulty of getting any leave from an official job. But the Regent, by these standards, was a great traveller, and this saved him from the narrow-mindedness which must inevitably limit the outlook of one whose whole life has been spent in a single city. The Regent originally came from Reting monastery, sixty miles to the north of Lhasa, and now he was about to visit Samye, fifty miles to the south-east, on the Tsang-po river. Samye is the oldest of the larger Tibetan monasteries, having been founded by Padma Sambhava, who was summoned from India in the eighth century by one of the early kings of Tibet. Some portions of Samye had been rebuilt and the Regent's consecration was necessary, his presence being of special importance, since he had to preside over the ceremony of replacing the golden ornaments on the roof. On such an occasion the officials who are remaining behind have to present scarves of leave-taking to the Regent after accompanying him for a few miles of the way. As the Kya Chu had to be crossed some four miles to the east of Lhasa, this formed a convenient place for leave-taking, and a large tent had been put up on the bank of the river, so that the officials could present scarves and drink tea there. Gould had intended to present a scarf himself, but in the end it was diplomatically decided that Richardson should deputize for him; so he and Norbhu took their places in the procession while Nepean and I accompanied them to take photographs. We took several clerks and half a dozen scarlet-coated retainers to compete with the Chinese who would also be there. In the eyes of the Tibetans these things are of considerable importance: an official has as many servants and wears as sumptuous clothes as his rank and means will allow.

The procession, which was over a mile in length, was the most brilliant and splendid pageant I have ever seen. Although there were heavy clouds over the mountains, the sky above was clear and the sun shone on an endless variety of exquisitely beautiful costumes. The cavalcade—there must have been about five hundred horsemen—started from the Regent's summer palace between the western end of the city and the Potala, and passed through the whole length of Lhasa. Everywhere the streets were crowded with people trying to catch a rare glimpse of the *Po gye-tshap rimpoche*, " the precious one instead of the king ". Monks holding silken banners suspended from long staffs lined the route, while servants dressed in homespun robes and saucer hats kept the crowd back with whips, and drove stray cattle and inquisitive dogs from the roadway.

In the front of the procession was a horseman holding aloft a sacred painting hanging from a pole: this was to ward off evil. Behind him rode half a dozen others carrying staffs surmounted by cylindrical silk hangings. These men were dressed in Mongolian robes of gold and silver thread, and wore tall conical witches' hats. They were followed by a hundred or so officials riding two or three abreast. There were monk officials in mulberry-coloured robes edged with silk, gaily embroidered undercoats and wide-brimmed papier-mâché hats lacquered with dark gold, or yellow woollen hats shaped like legionaries' helmets; Shap-pes in scarlet-tasselled wide-brimmed hats and robes of heavy flowered brocade; tiny incarnation lamas or sons of noble family sitting in bucket-saddles from which it is almost impossible to be thrown. Depöns, Dzasas, Tejis, Dzongpöns—all the officials of Lhasa vying with each other to wear the brightest silks, the richest turquoise and coral ornaments, the most gorgeous horse-trappings.

In the middle of the procession came the Regent himself, carried in a highly ornamented palanquin of dark red-gold lacquer. His six bearers wore wide, flat, scarlet hats, vivid green coats, white trousers and black knee-boots. Beside him, in attendance, walked several high officials, one of them with his hand steadying the palanquin, and a servant with an immense valanced umbrella of State held precariously aloft on a long staff.

The procession passed the Muru monastery, skirted the Mohammedan quarter of the town, and then crossed some level marshy land by a very stony track, lined all the way by people. There were many walled lingkas here between the road and the river, with fine poplar and willow trees and green grass beneath. About three miles from the city, just where the track and the river converged, a company of the Tibetan Army had been drawn up as a guard of honour. Beyond these, just short of some rather fine country houses resting solidly among trees, several tents had been put up. The largest of these was sheltered by a deep canopy ornamented with a blue and scarlet dragon pattern in appliqué work. In front of this tent, open to the sky, was a canvas enclosure wherein the officials would take tea. Under the awning was a pile of silken cushions and a wooden lacquered tea-table for the Regent; in front of this were seats of different height according to rank.

In the smaller tent near by, the tea was being brewed in earthenware kettles over yak-dung and juniper-wood fires. Here were four massive silver-gilt teapots used for taking the tea to the officials.

Nepean and I had ridden ahead of the procession so as to photograph its arrival. Although there were several hundred officials and servants on horseback, at least a hundred had been sent ahead to prepare the tent, and they were already waiting, sitting in groups on the grass or standing about gossiping. All the officials were wearing special ceremonial dress; the higher ones, instead of their saffron-coloured silk robes, wore dresses of a heavier brocade embroidered with blue and gold dragons. There was considerable variety of pattern and material and some of the dresses seemed to be very old. The junior officials wore a most attractive dress called *Geluchey*. This consists of a short jacket of very thick brocade with long sleeves made up of several transverse strips of different-coloured material. Here again there was much variety, and some of the jackets were extraordinarily beautiful. Over one shoulder and across the chest lay a voluminous roll of silk made up of small rectangles of every imaginable colour, and wide sashes of varied colour and design were tied so that their frilled ends hung over the long pleated black satin skirt which came down to high claret-coloured boots decorated with a white crossing pattern. On their heads they wore comic little white cockle hats designed to protect the top-knot and charm-box. On each shoulder, set towards the front, were turquoise and gold ornaments, one shaped like a whelk shell and the other a flat rosette. In former times these were suspended from the top of the head and worn as ear-rings. The monk officials wore special robes with a wide border of red-and-gold brocade to the skirt, and sleeves of the same material as their mulberry-coloured robes. As always, there were innumerable servants and attendant monks; the former in dark broadcloth robes and wide scarlet hats, the latter bare-headed and wearing the flowing monks' robe and heavy clumsy boots with turned-up toes.

The Regent's palanquin was halted near the reception tent and he walked the last hundred yards through ranks of bowing officials. He was bare-headed and dressed in embroidered silk robes of vermilion and gold. He moved with the awkward shuffling gait of one unused to much walking. When the Regent had taken his seat all the officials prostrated themselves three times before him, touching the ground with their foreheads. Then, carefully shepherded by two of the gigantic monk orderlies, they came forward in order of precedence and each offered a white scarf, which was taken by an attendant. According to rank each was blessed either with both hands or one hand, or with a tassel on the end of a stick.

When all the scarves had been offered the company sat down and tea and rice were handed round. Norbhu and Richardson sat apart from the Tibetan officials directly on the right of the Regent; while the Chinese, who had arrived thirty strong with flying banners and an armed escort, sat in a place of less honour on the Regent's left. After half an hour the Regent left the tent and was carried the short distance down to the river-bank, where two yak-hide coracles had been lashed together and completely covered with yellow cloth.

I had taken up a commanding position on a stone breakwater overlooking the embarking place. I shall never forget that scene: the turbulent green and blue of the rushing Kyi Chu, still swollen from the summer rains; the pale blue sky edged with heavy masses of cumulus cloud casting dark shadows on the surrounding mountains; the milky emerald green of the willow trees fringing the river-bank; a large flock of goosanders flying overhead; the chattering crowd of women coyly pretending to avoid my cameras; and the fantastic coracles sitting right on top of the water like empty boxes, swathed even to the paddles in bright yellow cloth. Suddenly the crowd became silent and, through a gap in the flood-bank, the palanquin appeared and was borne down the sandy slope to the water's edge, making a wonderful mass of colour in the clear Tibetan sunlight—the scarlet, green and white of the bearers, the glowing red-gold lacquer of the palanquin, the mulberry-coloured dress of the Lord Chamberlain and Chief Secretary walking in front, the scarlet-tasselled hats and blue and gold robes of the Shap-pes walking alongside.

The Regent, a small, ascetic, almost apologetic figure, stepped from his palanquin and was helped into a seat of embroidered cushions in the stern of one of the coracles. The more senior ministers got in beside him and, sacrificing the dictates of safety to those of propriety, stood up for the whole crossing. The boatmen pulled out into the current and the light coracles were immediately swept away to land on the farther side nearly half a mile lower down. In another boat a young official—presumably a bad sailor—stood with his arms held above his head in prayer. Farther down, where the river was narrower, they were swimming the ponies across. On the far side another tent and, presumably, more tea were awaiting the party.

Those officials who were staying in Lhasa rode slowly homeward, preceded and followed by their servants in the Tibetan manner. Tsarong joined us, and we had a breakfast picnic on the banks of the river.

On 23rd November the Regent returned from Reting. As he came by Chaksam ferry and Chu-shur he approached the city from the other direction, along the main road from the west by which had we originally reached Lhasa. I take the account of his return from my diary:

November 23rd.—While Richardson and Norbhu go, officially, to present scarves of welcome to the Regent, Nepean and I ride out to photograph the procession. Rising at 6.30 A.M. (with a temperature of 18° F. in our tents), we set off in the chill morning air, riding as far as Shing-donka, the butchers' village four miles to the west of Lhasa, to a place we carefully chose yesterday.

There is not a cloud in the pale dawn sky; already the sun is reddening the snow on the western mountain-tops away beyond the Trisum river. In the valley the early-morning light is still more attenuated, having to pierce a pall of smoke over Lhasa city where housewives are already lighting their dung fires and burning fragrant incense to Buddha. Looking eastwards we are amazed to see the Potala looming mysteriously above the coppery haze which hides the outline of its massive foundations; unsubstantial it seems, like some fairy castle conjured up by a magician and poised precariously above the earth. All at once the sun's rays light up the golden shrines on the summit, and the outlines of the building emerge, now to assume, by contrast, the solidity of a vast medieval castle.

Even at this hour can be heard the deep droning boom of the ten-foot-long monastery trumpets, and a monotonous beating of drums and cymbals. As we ride along we pass many of the pious at their morning devotions. Although it is scarcely seven o'clock the beggars have already reached their stations—unless they slept there all night. From one patchwork of rags a goitrous face appears with protruding tongue, while an emaciated arm, with fist clenched and thumb raised, importunes us for alms. Here are the usual line of worshippers taking the holy walk around the city. A group of swarthy nomads gaze at us with wide ingenuous eyes—perhaps they have never seen Europeans before; a man with leather apron and wooden protectors for his hands prostrates his way round the city; some Lhasa women, with dark pigment protecting their complexions, wearing robes of dusty black homespun cloth, turn their prayer-wheels and mutter the sacred formula.

Today there seems to be more traffic than usual; much of it is the Regent's baggage sent on ahead. Here is a train of sleek

M 2

mules with his tents and camp furniture; farther on, the road is blocked by a herd of sleepy, slow-moving yaks returning to Lhasa for more barley-meal or wool. Respecting their sharp horns, we leave the track and canter along on the grass where the hoar-frost glitters like amethyst in the thin sunlight. On the marshes bordering the road are immense flocks of bar-headed geese, Brahminy duck and mallard. Skeins of geese, with their lavender and black and white plumage set off by orange beaks and legs, flash in the sun as they circle round with harsh cries. The dark bottle-green of mallards' heads can be picked out among the dun marsh grass.

In honour of the Regent a line of stones has been put down on each side of the road, and every few hundred yards improvised incense-burners have been built of sods and painted white. As he passes azalea and artemisia leaves will be burnt to produce clouds of fragrant white smoke.

Passing below Drepung monastery we reach Shing-donka at eight o'clock. We have been told that the procession will pass the village at about half-past eight; but as time means very little in Tibet we expect to wait an hour or two before anything happens. We set up our cameras on a flat roof overlooking the village. The track rises sharply here to cross a rocky spur of the mountain as it comes down to the loop of the Kyi Chu on which the village lies. On our left, stretching for several miles across to the main channel of the river, lies a level sandy waste covered with thickets of willow and thorny scrub. At this time of the year it affords some scanty grazing and is a source of firewood; in the summer it is under water.

On the ridge above us are many small shrines and bundles of sticks from which prayer-flags flutter; on the rocks Buddhas and prayers are carved. The bare hills, of which the tops are powdered with snow, rise four or five thousand feet. As a rule the outlines of the Lhasa mountains are gently modulated and smooth, but above Shing-donka there is a mountain crested like one of the Dolomites with huge pinnacles of rock. Up above, quick to realize that something unusual is about to happen, are lammergeyers and vultures wheeling in great circles with apparently effortless wings. Shing-donka, at any rate in the summer-time when the river valley is flooded, must be a strategic position, guarding as it does the main approach to Lhasa from the south and west. We could see that

the village had once been fortified by the Tibetans; there was still
a ruined wall of mud and stone, while below the village was a
modern square Chinese fort and barracks unused since 1912, when
the Chinese troops evacuated the city.

For two hours there are no signs of the procession, but many
evidences of its approach. Lines of mules pass, their loads
covered with cloths of the Regent's colours—golden-yellow
bordered with scarlet. Then a group of servants in wide red
hats appear in a cloud of dust and, dismounting hurriedly, go into
what is apparently the headman's house to see that all the necessary
arrangements have been made. These servants are mounted on
fine ambling ponies or mules. A little later a group of monk
officials come by, in mulberry-red robes and gold-lacquered hats.
Monks seem to ride mules in preference to ponies. More officials
pass, hurrying on to see that the tea will be ready at the required
time. The small son of the Kung rides by with a group of his
father's servants, some of whom wear silk. The child is only four,
but he sits in a high criss-cross saddle of wood from which it is
impossible to fall. He wears long boots, a yellow silk robe and a
conical hat, with a coral-and-turquoise brooch on the front.
After this comes a tiny incarnation lama similarly mounted, but
led by a monk servant. The child wears miniature monk's boots
with turned-up toes and brocade sides, a claret-coloured robe and
yellow hat. Slung across his back is a gold charm-box containing
an image of Buddha almost as big as himself. The child looks
portentously solemn.

At last a cloud of dust heralds the approach of the procession
itself. Women who were flailing barley beside the river drop
their wooden flails and hurry to the roadside; a dozen incense-
burners on the house-tops and beside the road start belching forth
smoke; another party of mounted servants hurries past to clear
the road ahead.

It is difficult to see the procession clearly because of the cloud
of dust it raises—the standard-bearers, the long line of monk
officials, the green-coated palanquin bearers, the fluttering State
umbrella, the brocaded senior ministers, more monk officials and
always scarlet-hatted servants. The Regent is in a special light
palanquin with a movable hood; a less pretentious conveyance
than is used away from the city—a touring model, so to speak. I
notice that two spare teams of bearers ride at the back of the pro-

cession. We pack up our cameras and, giving the procession a
respectfully wide berth, overtake it and are ready again when the
Regent stops at a gaily coloured tent for tea and rice. The officials
leave their mounts with grooms who have suddenly appeared.
The monks dispense with their hats—which are only worn on
horseback—and form into bowing ranks as the Regent, leaning on
the arms of his intimate monk officials, walks from his palanquin to
the tent. I notice that the Regent's own horses, gaily caparisoned
with strips of brightly coloured silk and gorgeous saddle-cloths,
are led by scarlet-robed grooms in case he gets tired of being carried
and wants to ride.

Although the route of the procession led only a mile below
Drepung monastery, I was surprised to see that none of the monks
came down to pay their respects to the Regent. He was educated
at Sera, and perhaps this is an unfriendly gesture symbolizing the
age-long jealousy between the two institutions. Or possibly the
Abbots, realizing that the presence of some thousands of monks
would increase the dust-clouds, ordered their charges to keep to
their cells.

After one more halt for tea and rice, the procession went on
to the official reception, which took place a mile from Lhasa in
the Garden of the Mystics, where our Mission was received on its
first arrival in Lhasa. Scarves were presented by those officials
who had not accompanied the Regent. The Chinese representative, who had also come to present a scarf, joined, indeed for a
time actually led, the homeward procession. He was escorted by
several mounted standard-bearers, a section of heavily-armed
Chinese soldiers, and the local bazaar band disguised as his retainers.
The guard of honour, drawn up on the open plain to the west of
the city, was the centre of a great crowd of people who had come
out from town to watch the procession. Thus does the representative of God on Earth return to his Holy City.

On the fifteenth day of the tenth Tibetan month, November
28th by our calendar, there was a great procession in the city. An
enormous image of the goddess Palden Lhamo was taken from the
Cathedral and carried through the streets. This all-powerful
goddess is the guardian of all Tibet and especially of the Government. She is the deity of whom our good Queen Victoria was
supposed by the Tibetans to be an incarnation. The eloquent
Landon describes her as follows:

" Palden Lhamo is a dark-blue lady with three eyes who sits upon a chestnut mule drinking blood from a skull and trampling underfoot the torn and mutilated bodies of men and women. Her crown is composed of skulls, her eye-teeth are four inches long, and the bridle, girths, and crupper are living snakes kept in position by the dripping skin of a recently flayed man."

I had been invited to watch the procession from the house of my friend Surkang Se. The goddess was to be taken out of the Cathedral and escorted round the inner road of the city. She would be halted in front of each important house and the owner would have to make some contribution.

It is always difficult to obtain exact information from the Tibetans, whose accounts are so often contradictory. A Tibetan told me that this powerful goddess, when the world was young, was about to destroy all creation, but at the last moment a husband was found for her, and he, apparently, appeased her wrath. On the day that she is taken for her annual tour of the city, her husband, who is kept in a monastery on the other side of the Kyi Chu, is also taken out, and they are allowed to behold each other at a distance of several miles.

The streets were densely crowded; the luckier ones, like myself, watched from the flat roof-tops. Several hundred monks took part in the procession; many of them wore special pleated cloaks and a strip of rainbow-coloured brocade hanging from a diamond-shaped turquoise and gold ornament between their shoulder-blades. They also wore the yellow woollen hat shaped like a fireman's helmet. A group of very youthful monks, hardly yet in their teens, walked past with drums on their shoulders. Others carried golden chargers, swinging incense-burners and silver teapots. Several trumpet-stands, carved in the likeness of dragons' heads, were put up for half a dozen long silver and gold trumpets. A way was cleared for the goddess, who appeared, grotesquely ugly, among a group of monks wearing masks representing different animals. The invisible man who was supporting the goddess took short quick steps so that she appeared to be tripping along with mincing tread, mopping and mowing as she went. This accorded ill with the hideous fixed expression on her face. A few white scarves had been thrown up on her head and shoulders. As the goddess approached the main gateway of the Surkang house there was a deep blast from the long trumpets, a clashing of cymbals and a sustained beating of drums. The goddess was put down in the middle of the road and I saw that a chair was pushed under her skirts, so that the man supporting her could rest. Soon afterwards cups of tea were passed in for his refreshment. The masked monks performed various dances in front of the goddess, and in a side street a large pile of straw surrounding an image of butter and barley-flour was set alight. After more chanting and music the goddess was carried onwards, followed by an immense crowd of people. When she returned to the open space in front of the Cathedral an image of coloured butter and tsamba—which is always prepared by the monks of Muru monastery, who seem to be in charge of the whole ceremony—was broken into small pieces and thrown to the crowd. These fragments are much prized as amulets against the attacks of evil spirits.

Ten days after this ceremony, on December 8th, there was held the Festival of Lights in memory of Tsong-kapa (literally, " the man from the onion country "), the celebrated reformer who established the Yellow Hat sect. He also founded Ganden monastery in the first decade of the fifteenth century, and inaugurated the Great Prayer festival in Lhasa.

The anniversary of the reformer's death, the twenty-fifth day of the tenth Tibetan month, marks the official ending of summer and the beginning of winter. Before this day all officials wear their silks and clothes of summer; only after it, however cold the weather may be before, are they allowed to wear the fur hats and fur-lined robes of winter. (On the eighth day of the third Tibetan month, about April 20th, winter ends and the thin silks are once again worn.) In the morning all the officials of Lhasa collect in the Potala dressed in their thin silks. After prostrating themselves three times before the Regent and presenting scarves, they retire into dressing-rooms and return in a few minutes wearing the wide fur hats and fur-lined robes of winter. After drinking tea, they return to their homes. Norbhu told me that most of the officials wear fur under-robes if they find it cold, but anybody who is caught is heavily fined and may even be degraded.

That night, in memory of Tsong-kapa, all the monasteries, State buildings and private houses were lit up with innumerable tiny lights. There were rows of butter-lamps along every window-sill and along the parapets surrounding the flat roofs. Lhasa itself was completely transformed, and as one had no criterion by which to judge the size of the lights, it resembled some immense distant city with regular lines of lamp-posts marking its long thoroughfare.

Drepung was similarly illuminated. From the Deyki Lingka we looked across to it from a distance of some three miles. An island of a million twinkling lights in the surrounding blackness of the hills, it had an unearthly aspect, like some fairy city floating in the frosty night.

CHAPTER THIRTEEN

OUR LIFE IN LHASA

WE soon found that the Deyki Lingka in summer was a very pleasant place, except for innumerable black and ravenous mosquitoes, which appeared each evening from the surrounding marches; there were also many flies and bluebottles. But once we had cut the long grass that grew in our garden their numbers decreased.

This small walled garden, the haunt of turtle-doves, great tits and hoopoes, was a great boon to us. A row of tall double hollyhocks grew in front of the house and there were rose bushes, peach trees, a few ornamental conifers and a fine walnut tree. Beyond the wall grew white poplars, and one looked between their slim grey trunks to the olive-green hills across the river. The house was surrounded by groves of willows and poplars and was therefore free from the infected dust of the city. Just over the other side of the garden wall ran a small branch of the Kyi Chu, with the blue sky and an overhanging clematis mirrored in its still surface.

Leaning over the bridge, one could always see some char swimming idly amongst the undulating water-weed. Parts of this river resembled a Hampshire trout stream, and I continually regretted that we could not fish. But as water is the purest element, so the body of a fish may be the temporary resting-place of some holy lama, whose hope of immortality one would not willingly jeopardize. Beyond the stream a strip of sandy waste-land covered with thorny scrub ran down to the Kyi Chu.

We found the actual house somewhat small for our requirements. Gould and Neame occupied two minute rooms upstairs; the doctor took possession of an even smaller ground-floor room opening off the tiny kitchen courtyard, while Richardson and I put up our tents in the walled garden. There was one rather gloomy downstairs room which we used as a dining-room, and a more cheerful one above with a veranda that we roofed in with canvas and used for receptions. Neame's bedroom afterwards became Gould's office, while the five Sikkimese clerks had a large office a hundred yards from our house. .The kitchens and stables were part of the main building. Norbhu found quarters just outside our main doorway between the kitchens and the stables. We were looked after by the staff from the Gangtok Residency, augmented by some of Richardson's servants from Gyantse and a few local recruits. As is usual in the East, they were all men, though a few coolie women were recruited as water-carriers. The chief pivots of this most efficient staff were two Mohammedans, the " Butler ", Mir Khan, and cook, Jakob Khan, both of whom had been with Gould for many years. Although they were elderly they never complained of the height or climate, though they had a great deal to say about the laziness and lack of cleanliness of the Tibetans. There was a Hindoo " sweeper " who always looked unutterably miserable, a " dhobi " or laundry-man, of the same religion, and another dozen or so servants who were all Lepcha orderlies from Sikkim, and therefore Buddhists.

One very serious misfortune that beset us soon after we had settled down in the Deyki Lingka was the illness of the Political Officer. On September 2nd, a little more than a week after our arrival, he went to bed with a chill, which steadily got worse and developed into serious gastric trouble. Day after day he could take no food and was tortured by continuous hiccoughs and vomiting which precluded his getting either sleep or nourishment. Morgan sat up with him at nights and tried every sort of remedy, but he became ever weaker and weaker.

This was especially serious because Mr. Williamson, the last Political Officer, had, under tragic circumstances, actually died in Lhasa, also from internal troubles. Had the same fate befallen Gould it would have been the end of our prestige in the country. For so superstitious are the Tibetans that if two successive representatives of Great Britain had died in the Holy City they would have taken it as a sure sign that the gods desired them to have no more dealings with Britain.

The Tibetans, with the quiet fatalism of the East, were quite certain that he would not recover; and the Doctor looked more and more worried. It seemed that in the rarefied atmosphere of Lhasa he was not going to get better, and then the question was whether he had strength enough to survive the long journey down to India. We even borrowed a small sedan-chair from one of the officials, so that if necessary we could at any moment set off from Lhasa.

Each night from our tents in the garden we could hear him racked by the interminable hiccoughs. He became so weak that he could barely lift a glass of water to his lips. And there was nothing we could do. To fly him down to India was impossible; we knew that there was no machine in India capable of crossing passes of 17,000 feet and carrying enough fuel for the return flight, though the landing conditions in Lhasa are more than adequate. After a week of this distress the Doctor's efforts were rewarded: the hiccoughs gradually stopped. In a few days Gould was able to get up, and on September 13th he was strong enough to receive the Shap-pes, though he still looked terribly ill and haggard.

Apart from this we kept extraordinarily well, except for occasional chills and colds in the head. Living at 12,000 feet, we found, had no ill effects on our health or spirits, though most of us lost weight, becoming somewhat desiccated by the dry Tibetan air. Occasionally we got on each other's nerves, but that would have happened to the same extent at sea-level. We were a well-assorted party—an Irishman, a Welshman, a Scot, and three Englishmen. I can only say that if I ever had the chance of repeating the expedition I should be happy to go with the same companions.

People often say to me: " What on earth did you manage to do with yourselves during those six months? Weren't you awfully bored?" Yet in point of fact we had remarkably little time to ourselves. In the first place, a tremendous amount of time was devoted to receiving visitors and returning their calls, and subsequently in luncheon parties and cinema entertainments.

For me many hours were taken up by such pleasant occupations as sight-seeing, photography and natural history work, and though I do not complain of overwork, I have never known so little spare time for reading or writing as there was on the Lhasa Mission.

Gould was occupied with the major policy, expenditure and organization of the mission, which involved the exchange of long cypher messages with the Government of India, Army Headquarters and other departments. He was therefore engaged in those telegraphic duels which seem to be necessary before the powers that be will take any sort of decision that might possibly place them in a compromising position. The North-West Frontier looms always so large in the minds of Foreign Office and Army officials that they shelved or indefinitely delayed issues that were all-important and urgent to us in Tibet. Gould, too, spent many hours in involved conversations with Norbhu—involved because Norbhu has such an intuitive knowledge of Tibetan affairs and people that his conclusions, however fantastic they may appear, are practically always right; but when he comes to justify them, his arguments are inconsequent and contradictory. Even in a dead calm he knew which way the wind was going to blow. Gould had also to supervise, through Norbhu, the work of the five Sikkimese clerks (though two of them were from the office of the British Trade Agent, Gyantse) and the twenty or so servants from his Gangtok house.

A man of tremendous mental activity and with an unbelievable capacity for work, we found Gould took a great deal of living up to. Struck with a sudden idea, he would, during dinner and afterwards, write out a long telegram to the Government of India; Richardson and I would spend many hours of the night laboriously putting it into the incredibly intricate double cypher that His Majesty's Government seem to consider necessary to outwit the ingenuity of hypothetical foreign agents. At breakfast Gould would appear with an entirely new draft, having been awake since four o'clock reading up all available information on the subject, in a dozen bulging files. I would then spend the morning re-encyphering the message.

Brigadier Neame, alas! could only be spared from his military duties in India long enough to allow him three weeks in Lhasa, and during that time he was naturally very busy finding out all he could about that remarkable organization, the Tibetan Army. One of our earliest acquaintances in Lhasa was the Yuto Depön, who came on the day of our arrival with presents from the Cabinet. He was one of those young officials who had been chosen to be sent down to Quetta to receive training as an artillery officer. We then made the acquaintance of the other moving spirit in the modern Tibetan Army, Jigme Tering, who had been at St. Paul's School, Darjeeling, and who, unlike Yuto, spoke flawless English. Both these young depöns were dressed in extremely smart khaki tunics with well-cut riding breeches and shining field-boots. Tibetan officers can choose their own badges, and so both wore several stars of dark orange-coloured Tibetan gold. These, together with their long turquoise earrings and charm-boxes, added greatly to their attractive appearance. We also received calls from Changra Depön, the lay Commander-in-Chief, and Chapay Depön, his assistant, and, as already described, from the monk Commander-in-Chief.

Changra was made depön at the age of forty-eight, having previously held only civil appointments. Two years ago, at the age of fifty-six, he was made Commander-in-Chief, and although he knew that many reforms were needed he did not know where to begin. Chapay, his assistant, had been for many years a depön in Kham. All these officials spoke very freely to Neame and he was able to discover much useful information. It appears that since the death of the late Dalai Lama all military training has lapsed, and only now, with the threat of the Tashi Lama's Chinese escort and further outbreaks in Kham, were the Tibetans becoming anxious. Although they still possess the natural courage and endurance of their Tartar ancestors, a thousand years of Buddhism has undermined their military ardour.

The higher command is often in the hands of officials who have absolutely no knowledge of military affairs, and who have been pitchforked from civil appointments. In Kham the organization is such that each of the four depöns works independently and takes his orders from the Lhasa Cabinet, except when the Kham Commissioner happens to be on the spot. The instruction of the troops is in the hands of a few officers who were trained at Quetta or Gyantse several years ago and who have since forgotten

all they ever learnt.   Yuto, for instance, was actually given a civil
appointment after his training at Quetta.   Experienced soldiers
cannot rise beyond the rank of *rupön* (theoretically major, but in
practice more like a sergeant-major in charge of about 250 men),
all higher appointments being made from the ranks of the civil
officials.

The army is recruited on a feudal basis, each landowner having
to supply so many recruits; there are also several purely military
estates.   In this way some 3000 regulars were raised, but after
the troubles with the Chinese in 1910-12, and the subsequent
clashes with Chinese and communists on the Kham frontier, the
size of the army has been trebled.   The new levies, however, are
unreliable and badly officered.   The soldiers are ill-fed, and paid
practically nothing; they are forced to batten on the civil inhabitants, amongst whom they are consequently unpopular.
The regulars, to save the expense of feeding, are frequently
allowed home on leave; and during service are often used as
navvies for civil undertakings, instead of being allowed to train.
As of recent years all available regulars have been sent to Kham,
in Lhasa itself there are only a few thousand infantry, including
the bodyguard and a battalion of armed police, and many of
these are away on semi-permanent leave.   They are all equipped
with fairly modern service rifles, but live ammunition is so rarely
used for practice that their marksmanship is necessarily poor.
The ammunition is sealed in strong-rooms and none can be
issued without the personal attendance of the Prime Minister,
the Cabinet and the two Commanders-in-Chief.   Some years
ago the Tibetans started manufacturing rifle ammunition in
Lhasa.   A depön told us that it looked all right, weighed the
correct amount, and fitted perfectly, but when fired it frequently
burst the barrel of the rifle and seriously injured the soldier.
There are also a few mountain machine and Lewis guns, but the
men are not fully trained in the use of them and have rarely
practised with live ammunition.   Naturally, too, they become
somewhat weary of cleaning weapons that are never fired, and
many of these are said to be badly corroded and even dangerous.
The troops, as we noticed when we passed the guard of honour
on entering Lhasa, wear battered Wolseley topees, ill-fitting
khaki drill uniforms and European boots.   Naturally the effect
is ludicrous and is further exaggerated by their long pigtails and

enormous ear-rings. The Commanders-in-Chief have just introduced a new uniform which is eminently sensible and most
attractive to look at. A khaki felt hat is worn with ear-flaps
normally tied together on top of the head with blue ribbon.
The tunic, of khaki homespun cloth, buttons on one side in the
Tibetan fashion, and comes down to the knees. Locally made
high boots are worn instead of stiff leather ones.

Having heard so much in disparagement of the Tibetan army,
we were much interested to hear that a review of all available
troops, about five hundred, had been arranged near the Trab-shi
(a building incorporating the barracks, arsenal, and mint) so that
Neame could see them drilling and carrying out range practice.
Yuto and Jigme explained that many of the gunners would be
firing their weapons with live ammunition for the first time,
and they were afraid that the Brigadier would find the whole
display merely ludicrous.

It was a great day. Gould was indisposed at that time, but
the rest of us, including Nepean, who had arrived the day previously from Gyantse, rode out alongside the aqueduct to the
arsenal, some two miles to the north of Lhasa. This roadway,
in the days of " Tibet I," had been carefully built up on a causeway above the surrounding flooded land, but the granite bridges
over the rivulets had broken down and it was nobody's business
to mend them again. It was a blazing hot morning with a
scorching sun and heavy cumulus clouds over the hills. Lammergeyers and kites circled languidly above us, while ravens and
magpies gaped with open beaks on the dry sandy banks of the
aqueduct.

We were received in the barrack square outside the Trab-shi
by a guard of honour, officered by Yuto, by the Commander-in-
Chief, and later, in a reception room, by the Cabinet. Soon
afterwards the Prime Minister arrived—in Tibet, as in other
countries, the higher the official the later he arrives—surrounded
by servants and retainers. As his horse was led through the
barrack square the Shap-pes stood and bowed to the waist. It
took some time for the Prime Minister to drink his tea and to
receive the various military officers, for this was the first time he
had inspected the army or visited the arsenal.

On the dry stony plain outside the Trab-shi stood a row of
white tents ornamented with patterns in red and blue appliqué

work. In the central tent sat the Prime Minister on a high dais with the Shap-pes on one side of him and the Commanders-in-Chief on the other, all of course, on lower seats. There were several tents for other officials, while our tent was on the right of the " royal " one.

Practically all the inhabitants of Lhasa had turned out to see the fun, including several thousand monks. They stood or sat in a wide circle, protected by umbrellas from the scorching sun. The more enterprising women had opened small stalls, where they sat beneath umbrellas selling apricots, greasy-looking cakes, tea and cigarettes. The crowd, which was fairly orderly, was controlled by junior officials and several of the gigantic monks armed with whips.

Soon a column of troops appeared with their colours held high above them. Both the bodyguard and police had bands which made a very creditable noise. One was an ordinary military band with a big drum (the drummer complete with leopard-skin) and the usual bugles and kettle-drums, while the other was a bagpipe band. I am neither military-minded nor musical, but I was greatly impressed by these Tibetan bands, although I must admit that when they played the one tune I *do* know (" God Save the King ") I did not recognize it until I saw the others standing to attention.

The company drill was very ragged, the dressing and marching being bad; while on one occasion a platoon commander got lost and had to sprint vigorously to recover his position. The orders were given in English. After Neame, looking very smart on his white pony, had ridden round watching the drill, he got off to inspect the rifles, some of which were over thirty years old and definitely unfit for firing. The next item was rifle target practice, but as no Lhasa soldier had fired his rifle for the last six years, the sights seemed to have got out of adjustment, and not a man failed to register several misses out of his five shots. The machine-gun fire was more successful, although one gun frequently jammed and only Jigme could persuade it to work, while the others frequently ran across its line of fire in their enthusiasm.

After this we adjourned for a Tibetan lunch in a small room of the barracks, which was decorated in true military fashion with large Chinese drawings of beautiful women.

After lunch there was some Lewis-gun practice, and then two

mountain guns were unloaded from mules, put together and fired at a whitewashed wall over a mile away on the plain. This was the most popular feature of the day. After the report of the gun there was a moment of breathless excitement, and if a direct hit was scored it was greeted with cheers from the crowd, who had converged in their eagerness so as to leave only a narrow channel for the line of fire. At the end of the day the Prime Minister received all the military officers, from the Commanders-in-Chief to the N.C.O.'s, and presented them with white scarves in appreciation of their gallant efforts.

In another section of the Trab-shi is the Government mint, which we visited one day with Tsarong and Langchungna, who are in charge of it. We saw silver and copper coins being stamped out, and paper notes being printed, mostly by up-to-date electrically worked machinery from England. There were two or three venerable home-made hand-power stamping machines with vast wobbly brass fly-wheels. We also saw a new machine made entirely of brass (for they cannot work steel) in process of construction under Ringang's expert direction. In the forge, where women worked marvellous skin-bellows, they were melting bars of silver, mixing in 10 per cent of alloy, and recasting. We were all presented with a set of newly minted coins. It was odd to see Tibetans at work like this, but they seemed to be very skilful. I had heard that owing to the fact that the paint on the paper notes will dry only during the three months of summer, the Tibetans are saved from the dangers of inflation; but this story, attractive though it is, is not true. Owing to the debasing of the coinage and lack of backing for the notes, the *tranka*, which twenty-five years ago was three to the rupee, is now twenty-five. The *tranka*, together with its Chinese and Nepalese variants, was formerly the only Tibetan coin; if smaller amounts were needed the coin was cut into pieces. The Indian rupee, being more stable and harder to cut, is used very largely for more important commercial transactions.

Richardson, as British Trade Agent, Gyantse, maintained a separate office with his own confidential adviser (Sohnam Kazi) and clerks. His job was not only to work with Gould in the straightening out of Tibetan problems and the laying down of a more definite line of policy, but to establish personal contacts with the officials so that when they passed through Gyantse, or if he were again in Lhasa, they would call on him to ask his advice or to supply useful information. The Political Officers of Sikkim have practically always served their apprenticeship to Tibetan affairs by being posted as British Trade Agents, Gyantse; and as they seem to spend the intermediate period in places as far away from Tibet as possible, they must rely on this early training for their subsequent knowledge of the country and people.

Both Richardson and I spent much time learning the language, but it is extremely difficult to acquire. In the first place, in a country where communications are so poor there is a great variety of dialects, though that spoken at Lhasa is the purest and the most widely understood. There is also a great difference between the literary and spoken language. The grammar is very complex and bears little relation to that of European languages; it is said to be most akin to Burmese. Apart from ordinary difficulties of pronunciation there are various tones, so that the same word said in different pitches of voice will assume as many entirely separate meanings. The order of the words in a sentence is exactly the opposite of what it is in English. But the chief difficulty is the use of honorific terms, which necessitates the learning of three vocabularies instead of one. If I talk to a servant or man of muleteer class, or of myself, I use the ordinary language; if I speak to equals or people of higher rank I use the honorific language, but when I speak to members of the nobility or the highest lamas I use a still more exalted form of honorific. These changes are not merely in prefix or suffix, for usually the whole words change. To come, for an equal is *dro-wa*; for a superior, *phep-pa*; for a high official, *chhip-gyu nang-wa*. And as all these verbs mean to go, as well as to come, it will be seen that the language is no easy one.

Some of the words are rather delightfully derived: thus a chair (a non-honorific one) is *kup-kya*, bottom-prop; the word for distance is *tha-ring-thung*, way-long-short; a bribe is *pak-suk*, secret push; an office is *yik-tsang*, nest of letters. The sentence, "Thank you, I have enjoyed looking round the monastery, now I must take my leave", would be, "*La thu-je-chle, te-ring chho-je yak-po she-tra chung; ta gong-pa shu-ki-yin*".

Gould had had a considerable knowledge of the language

twenty-five years before when he had been British Trade Agent at Gyantse, but having had to learn many Indian dialects since then he had forgotten how to speak it, though he remembered enough of the peculiarities of the language to enable him to teach Richardson and me. Gould had, in fact, spent much time over the problem of the language and had compiled a number of stock honorific conversations to be learnt by heart. (One of these sentences is given above.) In a language with such complicated grammar and vocabulary as the Tibetan this is an excellent way to start and gives much confidence.

It was always a source of gratification to the officials that we had learnt enough to carry on a conversation with them. The Chinese, who always considered the Tibetans as mere barbarians, made a point of never troubling to learn the language, relying on their temporary Tibetan wives as interpreters. We did not trouble to learn the Tibetan letters; there was little enough time to spend on the spoken language. Personally I did not trouble about the honorifics, except to learn by heart a few pages of stock compliments and salutations. If we wanted to talk to officials there was always an interpreter available. My object in learning the language was not only to talk to my servants but to be able to carry on a conversation with any muleteer or nomad that I met in the hills. And this I was able to do. Though I had little grammar, I could chat for half an hour with any fairly intelligent fellow-traveller and discover all his history and anything else I wanted to know.

One morning towards the end of our visit I had to go round to see the Regent and explain to him the workings of a Zeiss camera we were going to present to him as a New Year's gift. Unfortunately, Jigme, who was supposed to be coming as interpreter, mistook the time, and I was left alone to explain the intricacies of range-finders and exposures in the highest honorific terms! The Regent was extraordinarily kind and helpful, and what might have been a most embarrassing interview turned out quite successfully. It so happened that we were all lunching with the Prime Minister that day and I had been asked to go earlier in order to photograph his wife and small child. Here exactly the same thing happened; Sonam, who was going to interpret, was delayed with the rest of the party, and I spent another half-hour struggling with high honorifics.

Captain Morgan, assisted by the genial Rai Sahib Bo and two native orderlies, set up his surgery and hospital in a curious square outbuilding half-way up our drive. This barn—for it was little more—consisted of a square room which relied for lighting on a large uncovered opening in the roof. Once it had been whitewashed all over and furnished with an operating-table and a neat shelf to hold the bottles demanded by the profession, it looked most business-like.

It has always been part of the policy of the British Missions to give free medical attention to the Tibetans, and every morning a motley collection of patients could be seen awaiting treatment. The majority of these came for inoculations for venereal diseases, complaints that are almost universal in Lhasa. These must, together with the systems of polyandry and monasticism, account for the decreasing birthrate. But the Tibetans are a hardy race, and they seem to be establishing a national immunity. Venereal diseases were by no means confined to the lower classes, still less to the lay population. One day Morgan was asked to go and give injections to a certain high official and his wife. Two other brothers, who shared the wife, came in for similar attention, and then, while they were still all in the same room, the official and one brother asked if they might bring in several other of their "wives". The family seemed to be living in complete promiscuity, and no one seemed the least embarrassed.

There were broken limbs to be set, sores and cuts to be dressed, glasses to be fitted, and teeth to be extracted. For dentistry cases Morgan was assisted by a Nepalese dentist who practises in Lhasa; he used to visit our surgery every day. There was little accommodation at the hospital, and patients who needed continuous treatment or who had come from a distance had to bring their own tents; it was no uncommon sight to see a dozen cloth or yak-hair tents pitched beneath the trees around the hospital. For several weeks there was a tent containing a cheerful small boy who had broken his leg; another child had fearful wounds owing to a thrashing from his monk employer. Most amusing was what we called " the ophthalmic ward ", which consisted of a single piece of yak-hair sacking stretched between two trees, and affording shelter for a grimy old beggar-woman who was being prepared for a cataract operation. This complaint is very prevalent in Tibet, and Morgan must have operated successfully on at least thirty patients whose sight had practically gone. Monks and nuns were conspicuous amongst these cataract cases, and one would see these aged people, supported on the arm of a friend, hobbling around with their eyes swathed in bandages—for the eyes must not be used after the operation until the skin of the iris has healed. This was indeed a miracle for them; and patients, hearing of the Doctor's fame, would come in many days' journey for attention. Luckily for them, Morgan, unlike the majority of men in the Indian Medical Service, had behind him many years' experience gained in a busy practice in England, where he had done his own surgery work and dispensing.

In Tibet a doctor sees many cases which have advanced much further than they would be allowed to do in a country where medical attention is always available. Sometimes patients would come only after the monks had already failed to cure, or even aggravated, the ailment. Occasionally they would interfere with his treatment of a case, forbidding the patient to take his medicine and reversing all his orders. For in Tibet the lay practitioner has little following and the art of healing is a pre-rogative of the monks, who abuse it in no uncertain way. These meddlesome quacks were a continual exasperation to the Doctor's quixotic Welsh temperament.

Just behind our house rises the sharp peak called the Iron Hill (*chak-po ri*). On the summit of this is the Medical College of the monks, which is supplied with students by each of the large monasteries. The course of instruction takes about eight years and consists chiefly in learning by heart long spells and incanta-tions. Except for a certain knowledge of herbs, the Tibetans seem to be completely ignorant of medicine; and of the func-tions, or even the positions, of many of the organs of the body they have the most fantastic notions. A certain holy lama once said that a woman's heart is on the right-hand side of her body, and as far as they are concerned on the right side it is; no amount of argument and practical demonstration will make them change this opinion.

If a patient is suspected of having an infectious disease his pulse is felt at the end of a long string. If the lama cannot lay hands on the required medicine he will write the prescription on a piece of paper, burn it, and make the patient swallow the ashes; probably it is just as efficacious, perhaps it is more so, since the most revolting concoctions are used for medicines, including the excreta of animals, land-crabs, powdered stone, as well as aconite, musk, camphor and other preparations known to Western medicine. In some cases a cure is sought by getting a high lama to spit upon an affected part. Pills made from the excreta or urine of the Dalai and Tashi Lamas are also considered a sovereign remedy for any sort of complaint.

In the afternoons Morgan would ride out to see private patients; either those who were too ill to visit his surgery, or officials who did not want to advertise their ignominious afflictions. In this way he got to know more about the homes and private lives of the people than any of us, and some of his experiences were staggering revelations of the abuse of monastic power and of the complete lack of any moral sense in a large section of upper-class Lhasa.

Morgan, who was once a well-known rugby footballer, is one of those very large but extremely gentle people who are so beloved by children; and his popularity among the Tibetans, who themselves have all the charm and many of the faults of children, was immense. And, as Gould himself recorded, Morgan's unremitting and skilful work as a doctor and his genial personality contributed very largely to the success of the Mission.

Of the activities of the wireless officers I lack the technical knowledge to write with discrimination. It will be remembered that at Gyantse we discovered that the wireless charging motor would not work owing to the great height above sea-level, so Dagg returned to Calcutta in order to procure a hand-power charging-set while Nepean remained at Gyantse to sort out other wireless gear. It was not until 6th September that Nepean reached Lhasa. Dagg arrived three weeks later with a hand-charging motor that he had had constructed in Calcutta. This was to be operated by coolies, who turned its handles and thereby charged the accumulators. The advantage of this was that if we went beyond Lhasa to meet the Tashi Lama we could provide our own power for wireless transmission. In Lhasa itself the accumulators were usually sent along to Ringang to be recharged. There was not enough wire in Lhasa for the town electricity supply to reach the Deyki Lingka, and we had to rely on accumulators for wireless transmission and for working our cinema projectors.

Our transmission station was capable of sending the cypher messages to Jubbulpore or Rawalpindi, so that if necessary we could be independent of the Lhasa land line. The wireless officers worked on a regular programme with stations in India, and in this way we were always in touch. In addition to this official work a large amount of experimental transmission and reception was done. Once they did a twenty-four-hour test to find out at what time of the day conditions were best. They were also in communication with amateurs in China, Hong Kong, the East Indies, Assam, South Africa, Mauritius, Brazil, Australia and many countries of Europe. A great deal of their time was taken up in devising entertainments for our guests. The cinema projection had to be adapted to run off accumulators; and they were always rigging up transformers, loud-speakers, microphones, telephones and other subtle devices. Most of us had sets by our bedsides. At seven in the morning I used to lie in bed and listen to the midnight news from London. It seemed absurdly incongruous to lie there as the sun rose and listen to Big Ben striking midnight, and to hear the announcer's synthetic voice wishing me good night.

We were able to supply much current news to the Tibetans: Gould, listening in at three o'clock one morning, heard that Marshal Chiang Kai Shek had been released, an item of news that the Tibetans would not otherwise have discovered for weeks.

It was by this means that we first heard scattered rumours of the abdication of Edward VIII. At first we were incredulous, but then, long before there was any official declaration from home, we read the whole distressing story in a Chinese-American weekly. We were apprehensive as to how the Tibetans would receive this news; but they considered it the most natural thing in the world that a King, having reached the age of forty without providing an heir, should abdicate in favour of his brother.

I, being Private Secretary to the Mission, had a variety of duties and considered myself much overworked! Telegrams arriving at any hour of the day or night had to be decyphered; a single message might take as long as four hours to disentangle. Cypher work is much quicker if there are two people on the job, so anybody who happened to be free at the moment was

called in to assist. I also kept a meteorological log; collected and
pressed some six hundred species of flowering plants; dried a
number of seeds, some of which we had been asked to collect for
His Majesty the King; made notes on the bird-life of Lhasa; and
kept a general diary accompanied by photographs, which was
sent off each week to the Government of India. But it was
photography that took up most of my time. During our seven
months in Tibet I took, on behalf of the Mission, some 2500
still-photographs, most of which I developed in Lhasa; 13,000
feet of standard 35-mm. film (all silent), 6000 feet of 16-mm.
Kodachrome colour-film and 3000 feet of 16-mm. black-and-
white. I used the following cameras: a 35-mm. Bell Howell
Eyemo with 2-inch and 6-inch lenses. This was invariably
operated from a panotilt tripod, as at Lhasa's altitude it is almost
impossible to hold the camera steady, especially if one has been
walking just beforehand. I had three 16-mm. cameras: a Model
K Kodak with 1·9, 30- and 6-inch lenses, an ancient Model A
Kodak that Gould had bought for £10 some years before, and
a Siemens' magazine ciné of my own.

Of still-cameras I used five. A quarter-plate Zeiss Nixé film
or film pack camera, two 6 × 9-cm. Zeiss Super Ikonta II, one
of which was always loaded with colour-film, and two Contax
cameras with 2·8 and 3·5 lenses, with a 6-inch 4·5 telephoto lens
which would fit either. As I wanted to keep some check upon
exposure and general results I used to do all my own developing
of still-photographs. The Lhasa water was suitable for this if
strained through a handkerchief. I used to do this after dinner;
and often it would be long after midnight before the films were
fully washed and hanging up to dry.

The cutting and splicing together of cinema film occupied
many complete days. Sometimes 1000 feet of film would
come back from Calcutta, and it all had to be cut and edited
before it was fit to be shown to our discriminating audiences.
On one occasion I had two miles of 35-mm. film carefully cut
and hanging in lengths from the wires I had rigged up at one
end of our dining-room; but in the end we decided not to
project any full-sized film as the light from our accumulators
was not sufficiently strong to throw a bright enough picture.

Sometimes I would be using all this formidable battery of
cameras more or less at the same time.

If we visited a monastery and knew we would not go there again, or on such an occasion as the visit of a high official, we needed a record in big film, colour and still-photography. Take, for instance, the occasion when the Shap-pes came on a ceremonial visit. I would carefully choose my position with due regard to the angle of the sun and the probability of dust, and then, as the Tibetans have no idea of time, I would set up my cameras an hour before they were expected. More usually they were an hour late. As soon as they came into view I would "shoot" them with the 35-mm. telephoto, then take a medium 16-mm. colour "shot", return to the big camera again and take a near shot, repeat this with the colour-camera, meanwhile firing off any still-cameras that I had been able to fix in the right position. Luckily Nepean became fairly skilful with the 16-mm. cameras, and we used to work together.

When we visited some important place it was a fearful mental strain to use all these cameras, each of which requires a different technique and uses film of different sensitivity or colour value.

Luckily the Tibetans did not object to these activities. At first they were a little suspicious, especially the poorer people, and more particularly of the big cinema camera which made a formidable noise and, with its long telephot lens, resembled some new-fangled automatic gun. Once we had shown them photographs of themselves they were delighted and did all they could to help. The Kodachrome colour-film, as soon as possible after exposure, had to be sent down by post-runner and baggage animal, and finally by train to Calcutta, thence it was sent by air to London, which was the nearest place where it could be processed. It was returned to Lhasa by the same expensive means. But the results were worth it. Except for some of the film that passed through Calcutta in summer and deteriorated owing to the heat, the results were extraordinarily successful; and when the officials saw themselves and their wives in all the finery of their gay clothes, in natural colour, moving on the screen, they were simply delighted. This was by far our most successful form of entertainment. They were also anxious to receive enlargements of themselves and their families; so, like a court photographer, I used to receive requests to go round and photograph many of the higher officials at their homes.

These cinema parties were a great feature of our life in Lhasa, especially during the last few months. I shall describe a typical evening.

One day in December, Tsarong with his two wives, Jigme, Mary, the Dele Rabdens (who stay with Tsarong), and eight children aged from four to seventeen years old, are invited to dinner. They arrive an hour early—at five o'clock—but Norbhu keeps things going and gives them tea until we have finished changing. The big lower room is needed for projection and Nepean is busy there with transformers and a network of wire, so we assemble upstairs for preliminary drinks. Tsarong has whisky and the others rather reluctantly take a glass of Cinzano or crème de menthe—Tibetans are not great drinkers. Then we go downstairs and our older guests sit in chairs while the children crowd on the floor in front. Then some of Tsarong's senior servants come in, together with a number of monks attached to his private chapel, and a few of his retainers who have heard of the show, and with their children stand round the room or sit on the floor. Our own servants crowd in at the back. By this time there are sixty or seventy people in a room that would be licensed by the London County Council to take twenty at the very most. The smell is indescribable—the clinging musty smell of old silk robes, smothered by the rancid pungence of monk and servants' butter-sodden garments.

We start with a black-and-white film of the Potala and the Lhasa bazaar as a curtain-raiser; some of the audience have never seen films before, and we break them in with something they know. The bare white walls of the Potala shine with a strange radiance against a dark velvety sky—a simple matter of yellow filters, but the effect transcends the original, and the audience make sharp exclamations of delight, " Ha-le ! ha-le ! " Anon the scene changes to the city, and they see some familiar shop-wife standing, oblivious of the camera, behind her stall. Suddenly she wakes up to what is happening and becomes grotesquely self-conscious, hiding her face with her hands, and eventually bolting indoors. The crowd is delighted, and Tsarong makes some ribald remark which convulses the males of the audience.

Crowd scenes are always popular, as the individuals are known to everybody. This is followed by a colour-film of the army, by request of Tsarong and Jigme, and the latter sees a close-up of his handsome face and smart uniform, enlivened by his long turquoise ear-ring. There are comic incidents too: a soldier with ludicrously battered topee and long pigtails pulls a cord to fire one of the mountain-guns. The cord breaks and he falls over backwards. A group of four Ladakis, wearing red fezes, are revealed sitting on the grass gambling. After a short colour-film of the Political Officer's Residency and garden at Gangtok, it is time for dinner, and our guests, after a stroll in the garden, reluctantly go upstairs.

It is difficult to accommodate some twenty-five people in so small a room, so we sit round with our backs to the wall on padded cushions, and eat from Tibetan tables. Norbhu, Doctor Bo, and Sonham are there as interpreters. The Jigmes can, of course, speak English. The cook deals with the problem by serving a number of hors-d'œuvres-like dishes on the low Tibetan tables. Cups of soup, potato salad, sardines, tinned salmon, sausages and then a substantial dish of rice and curry, is followed by fruit-salad, and anything they like to drink; usually lemon-squash for the children, Cinzano for the ladies, and whisky for the men. But they don't really like our food and drink. Why should they? their own is so much better.

Suddenly Gould, who had slipped out of the room, reappears with an armful of crackers, and the spirit of the party, flagging for a moment under the weight of all this food, suddenly revives. We are amazed by the perfect manners of our guests. They laugh without reserve and yet they avoid becoming boisterous. The children never seem to cry, and without ever being fussed by their parents they behave perfectly. A Tibetan mother never says, "Don't"; yet the child doesn't. A four-year-old girl fearlessly holds a firework, while her brother, aged six, who had previously been told to behave exactly like his father, smokes a cigarette with apparent enjoyment. They are all so obviously delighted that it is a joy to entertain them. The Doctor walks down the room to talk to a child who is sitting, quite happily, alone; but he is so belaboured about the head with balloons that he cannot pass, and pretends to burst into tears; the girls, non-plussed, stop for a moment, and by the time they have discovered his subterfuge, he is at the other side of the room. At eight o'clock, bedecked with paper hats, and Tsarong adorned with a false nose, we go downstairs to continue the film show.

We were going to show a film I had taken in Greenland, but

N

there are shouts of, " Shepada, Shepada," and we weakly give in.
" The Shepada " is the Tibetan version of the Shepherd Dog, a
name they have given to " The Night Cry ", a five-reeled Rin-
Tin-Tin film that has made a tremendous hit in Lhasa; it is
simple, moving and of a subject with which they are familiar,
nor does it leap inconsequently from scene to scene in the way
of more modern films, which are almost incomprehensible to
any but the most assiduous picture-goer.

The story is that the hero's dog, Rinty, is accused of slaying
the lambs of the rival gang. The latter insist that the hero
shoot his dog. He pretends to do this, but actually hides
Rinty in a cellar. Lambs continue to disappear, so the villain,
in the absence of the hero, enters his house and insists on
searching it. In spite of the gallant efforts of the hero's wife
Rinty is discovered, but puts up a terrific and realistic fight
before. . . . But meanwhile the hero has revealed to the rival
gang that the raider is an enormous condor. This bird, tiring
of a diet of lamb, approaches the hero's house and carries off
(on wires) his small child that has toddled out of doors while
its mother was struggling to save Rinty's life. Locked by the
villain into a room, she sees this happening, but it is an agonizingly
long time before she can work the bolt loose. Meanwhile
Rinty, having slain his assailant, also sees the dread bird gradually
approaching the baby, but by the time he can break his collar
it is too late. Then the three—hero, wife and Rinty—wildly
pursue the child, who is carried by the bird to the summit of
a crag. At last, after a desperate climb, the child is recovered,
and the bird and Rinty, locked in a grip of death, fall to the
foot of the crags.

We are continually asked to show this film, and, as it lasts
an hour and a half, we are most heartily sick of it. But not so
the Tibetans; they gasp and shout encouragement as Rinty
vanquishes the villain. As the hero's wife struggles in vain to
escape and go to the rescue of her child the women weep on
each other's shoulders and themselves shout ineffectual warnings
to the child; finally, when the child is saved, and all ends happily,
they are quite weak with emotion.

It is then necessary to have a Charlie Chaplin to restore their
composure. Of these we have a great stock, mostly of venerable
pre-war vintage. And next to the " Shepada " and shots of

themselves, these are the favourites. And what wonderful films they are! We have " Easy Street ", " The Waiter ", " Shanghaied ", " One o'Clock in the Morning ", " The Crook " —all the old favourites. The irresistible humour of Charlie knocking people over the head with a hammer, of dropping ice-creams down the backs of old ladies' evening-dresses, appeals strongly to the Tibetan mind and never fails to cause a pandemonium of shouts and laughter.

The next item—we have only been going for two hours so far and the night is young—is a film of Tibetan celebrities. The Regent's palanquin leaving Lhasa, the Shap-pes coming to call, the pomp of the Nepalese representative, the Prime Minister and his family at home, and Tsarong himself trying to look stern and then bursting with laughter. Here, again, there are comic interludes; the old Lord Chamberlain, the head of the ecclesiastical party and a total abstainer, rides away from one of our luncheon parties, with his gilt hat at a most rakish angle; Norbhu is blessed by the Regent and the small scarf gets caught up in the charm-box on top of his head, and requires several servants to disentangle it.

A reel of Hendon Air-Pageant, 1929, follows this; another Charlie Chaplin, and then a very popular film of King George V's Jubilee Procession, in which they are amazed at the cleanliness of the streets, and the fact that the horses of the royal coach are not amblers. And so, after four concentrated hours of it, the show stops, and after a final drink our guests mount their ponies and ride home through the clear Tibetan night.

We had a similar cinema party for all the chief officials of Lhasa. Each could bring his women-folk, children and friends. One evening we had an " Old School " party, which was attended by the three Rugbeians, Ringang, Kyipup and Möndö; Jigme, who was at St. Paul's School, Darjeeling; Surkang Se and Derge Se from Ludlow's school at Gyantse. About this time we were shown a letter from Tsarong's sixteen-year-old son, who was at school at Darjeeling, in which he wrote : " Is there any talking picture in Lhasa? I heard there is talking picture in Lhasa and every gentleman doesn't work, but go to see picture every night. I have nothing more to say."

One evening, I think it was when the Duke's family had come to dine, we realized, as we came downstairs, that something unusual was afoot. It transpired that Norbhu had told three or four of the Potala monks that we were having a cinema show that night, and that if they kept the information to themselves they could come. But the walls of the Potala, like other walls, have ears, and about thirty boisterous monks, reinforced by as many soldiers from the neighbouring Norbhu Lingka barracks, had climbed over our wall and "gate-crashed" the room; and while several monks had already taken the chairs reserved for our guests, the rest of the crowd effectively blocked all ways of approach. We made those who were already in the room sit on the floor, while the others were ejected—forcibly where necessary. During the reluctant retreat of a party of monks Morgan was hit on the hand by a stone. After that I have seldom seen monks move faster.

The Regent was very anxious to see our films, but as his sanctity precluded his visiting the Deyki Lingka he asked us to arrange a private view in the throne-room of the monastery in front of his palace. This meant much carrying round of accumulators and other gear, but Nepean and Dagg managed the electrical part with their usual skill; though there was a slight hitch when it was discovered that four of the coolies had stopped at a chang-shop on the way and had got too drunk to complete the journey—luckily this was before the dress rehearsal.

After a Tibetan lunch with the Regent we went across to the monastery roof, where the public-address outfit was blaring forth Scottish military music to an astonished collection of people on surrounding roof-tops. The Regent was delighted and insisted on a three-hours' programme, only letting us go then on condition that we promised to arrange another show later on, which we were able to do in January.

After his return from his visit to Samye in November the Regent became a different man. Whereas before he had been nervous and irresolute and had looked emaciated and ill, now he seemed very much stronger both in mind and body. When he was away from Lhasa he could ride and take a certain amount of exercise, whereas in his Palace this was impossible—though we discovered that he had started playing football with "Simple Simon" and had sent round to Norbhu to ask if we had a spare ball. This alone seemed to justify the Mission! We could never quite fathom the extent of the Regent's influence, or in what direction it was exerted. He always seemed very friendly to us, and declared his intention to visit India some day, and yet there were rumours that he was in communication with China and had even accepted presents and decorations.

The story is told that when he was younger he was due to appear before the Dalai Lama to be examined for a degree corresponding to a Doctorship of Divinity. The Dalai, who knew that the Regent had done no work at all, wrote to him advising him not to sit. But the Regent insisted on coming up, so the Dalai conferred the degree without examination. He became Regent much against his will and continually wanted to be allowed to resign. As some stable figure-head was essential in the critical times which succeeded the death of the Dalai, the Shap-pes persuaded him to stay on, which he would only do on condition that they guaranteed to obey all his orders. Surely this argues a more than ordinary political discernment.

When the Prime Minister heard that we had given a performance in the Regent's house, he demanded one at his home, although we had already given a special cinema party for him at the Deyki Lingka. Another film show was given in the throne-room of Gundeling monastery to the hundred monks who live there, and finally one at the Norbhu Lingka to the bodyguard troops. Had we been able to arrange entertainments at Drepung and Sera I am sure that we should have done a great deal towards establishing even more friendly relations with the monks.

One festivity that must be described was a children's party given at the end of December to celebrate the Political Officer's birthday. Anybody passing the Deyki Lingka that morning might well have imagined either that the Pied Piper had just passed that way or that we were starting a school. By lunch-time about seventy of the sons and daughters of the Lhasa officials had arrived. They came on horseback, either independently, preceded and followed by red-hatted servants, or sharing the saddle with a nurse or groom. The youngest child—Mary Jigme's daughter—was only three, but the majority were in their teens. They wore full-length silk or broadcloth robes, lined with fur, and high-crowned hats with fur-lined ear-flaps. In this becoming dress they resembled gnomes in winter clothing. Mrs. Jigme and Mrs. Ringang came to help with the organization. As soon as the children arrived they were taken upstairs for tea and Christmas cake; it was lucky that a good many were late, as there were more than we had expected and it was difficult to find a seat for everybody in our small room. The Duke's children, true to family tradition, were the last to arrive; they were just in time for tea.

At about one o'clock the cinema show started. The "Shepada" (inevitably), Charlie Chaplin, Aeroplanes, the Grand National, Jubilee Procession, more Charlie Chaplin—it must have been a bewildering experience for children who had never been away from Lhasa, never even read a book (other than the Tibetan Scriptures), much less previously seen a cinema show. After three hours of this they staggered out to the garden for a breath of fresh air in the late evening sunshine.

This was followed by "supper" upstairs. We were much struck to see how charmingly they behaved to each other: if a child was unable to master the difficulties of spoons and forks his neighbour helped him; when one boy spilt his curry into his lap the others laughed with him—not at him—and helped to clear it up. Then came the great event of the day, the Christmas-tree; admittedly a synthetic one made by tying fronds of evergreen on to a carefully pruned poplar. Nevertheless when the children came down to our darkened dining-room, at one end of which the tree glowed like a miracle, lit with electric bulbs of every colour, glistening with tinsel and balls of crystal, and festooned with teddy-bears, humpty-dumpties, scarlet soldiers, and other wonders entirely new to them, they gasped with astonishment and delight.

Then Norbhu, disguised as Father Christmas, but rendered less unfamiliar by the addition of a helmet-shaped monk's hat, made a speech in Tibetan (probably the first time Father Christmas has had to use this tongue) explaining the tree, drew the inevitable comparison between the infant Jesus and the child Dalai Lama, and wished them all a Happy Christmas. After that each child was given a present, and at six o'clock, still looking quite bewildered but clutching in their arms dolls, drums, trumpets, and mechanical toys, they mounted their ponies and rode away for home. We heard afterwards that the chief topic of conversation on the way was whether we would still be in Lhasa next Christmas.

CHAPTER FOURTEEN

CHRISTMAS HOLIDAY INTERLUDE

DURING the early part of December the Government of India decided that in view of the troubles on the North-West Frontier they could no longer spare us two wireless officers. This was unfortunate, as there was more than enough work for two. Not only were Nepean and Dagg transmitting cypher messages direct to the Government of India, but they were carrying out most valuable research in exchanging messages with amateurs in different parts of the world, and working such stations as Jubbalpore and Rawalpindi at scheduled times. In addition to their wireless programmes they had a great deal of electrical work to do in connection with our entertainments. When we had luncheon parties they arranged loud-speakers so that gramophone music could beguile our guests into making the best of English food; and in awkward pauses before and after meals they would arrange for two Tibetans with a gift for comic entertainment to carry on an argument or sing a song in front of the loud-speaker so that it could be relayed to our sitting-room. Much of their time was taken up in working the projector for our numerous cinema shows; if these took place away from our house—at the Regent's monastery or at the Prime Minister's home—hours of preparation were necessary, especially as all the accumulators, the screen, and the projector had always to be carried round by coolies, who usually seemed to get lost or to stop for a gossip on the way. The wireless officers also had to do their share of cypher work, lunching out, sightseeing, and attending functions of one sort or another, so they had as little spare time as the rest of us.

Looking back, it has often struck me how extraordinarily busy we were: not that we were overworked, but we seemed to have absolutely no time to ourselves. And if anybody had a moment to spare from his own job he would always be inveigled into helping with cypher work, mending something, using one of my cameras when several different records were needed of the same thing, or working out Gould's latest " scheme ", for I have never known a man so prolific of ideas or so meticulous of detail as the Political Officer!

So it was that, in spite of Gould's remonstrances, Nepean had to return to India in the middle of December. As I had not slept away from Lhasa since our arrival there, Gould decided that I should be allowed a holiday and would go down with Nepean to the Yamdrok Tso to watch birds, and should wait either at Pede or Nangartse until Major Finch, the new officer in command of the escort at Gyantse, should appear on his way up to Lhasa to spend Christmas with us.

The Tibetans had been tactfully sounded by Norbhu, who reported that they had got so used to our presence that it seemed quite natural that Nepean should be needed by his Corps, and that Finch, the only other European in Tibet (except for the mysterious Kaulback and Tracey, somewhere down in the south-east—if they were still alive, which seemed doubtful), should come up to Lhasa to spend Christmas with us. I will take the description of this journey from my diary:

December 14th, Monday.—How marvellous to be travelling again! I don't think I have ever in my life spent so long in one place, and I have longed to be off, though there has been far too much to do for any hint of boredom. Curious that when one stops work one so often gets attacked by some germ or other. I woke up with a vile cold today. Up at 5 A.M., 14° F., clear, but thin mackerel clouds to the east. These tents, built for comfort and to impress, are not much good for keeping out the cold, especially when one has to wash and shave in them. Packed-up and all ready in time for eggs and bacon at six o'clock. Usual snags before starting: Nepean found that the pony supplied by a local transport contractor had a fearful sore back. The Tibetan in charge satisfied his reputation by beating his muleteer across the shoulders and by giving Nepean a tiny black pony which jogged along at the most comic slow-motion canter I have ever seen: it had no pace between this and a funereal walk, but it always kept its ears forward and never stumbled. My pony, Marpo, rather sleepy today.

Nepean had seven baggage animals; I had two, one carrying a pair of boxes and the other the groom's belongings and my bedding-roll. I have ten days' food with me and a climbing-tent; half a mule-load is taken up with cameras and photographic gear.

Sonham Minghu, an orderly lent to us by Richardson, went

ahead to arrange accommodation. Nurgul, Nepean's Pathan servant, is staying to hurry on the transport, which ought to have got away before us. So we have only Iamtso, my groom, with us. He carries two huge horse-hide saddle-bags, which I had made to carry cameras, lunch and spare clothes. Iamtso was only a grass-cutter at Gangtok; he has made a fairly efficient groom, and now he will have to look after me generally while I am alone at the Yamdrok Tso. Till then, Nurgul, who is most efficient not only as a cook, but at the more difficult task of making Tibetans hurry, will look after us till we part. So we have only four servants—including the muleteer—for two men : a very meagre allowance in this country !

Very cold morning, but not a breath of wind : sun on us now, and the thin cloud has vanished. Curious amethyst-tinted frost on the grass, and iron-hard frozen mud away from the road, very bad for the ponies' feet. How grand to have no ciphers to do and no films to develop ! One must earn a holiday to enjoy it fully. Plenty of traffic on the road, which is blocked in places. Met some sheep, each carrying small loads. Probably salt from the great lakes. Big flocks of yaks, goats and sheep below Drepung waited to be slaughtered.

All the people gaze at Nepean's yellow fur-lined Afghan coat. I wear a long purple corduroy robe, lined with fleece, and with fox-skin cuffs and collar. The long Tibetan sleeves, coming right down over the hands, allow one to hold the reins without gloves. Although Marpo is pulling like the devil, my hands are perfectly warm. We both wear Gilgit boots (made of thick felt coming above the knee), though we have had to get special wide stirrups for them. We also have Tibetan hats with fur-lined flaps coming over the ears and back of the neck. We would be better off still in Tibetan felt boots, for these Gilgit boots are not good when it comes to walking over rough or wet roads. Many bar-headed geese and Brahminy ducks standing on the ice and beside the few pools kept open by the current. Lammergeyers and vultures circle silently above. Many desert-chats about and a few robin-accentors and white-winged redstarts.

Passed Shing-donka, glad of the excuse to walk down the hill to get warm. The sweet smell from the incense-burners atones for the slaughter-house atmosphere here. Yaks and oxen laden with the carcasses of sheep are already leaving for the city, and

N 2

there are piles of entrails, hides, hooves and other offal down by the river. At Trisum bridge, where I stopped to take some colour-films, great chunks of ice were being swept down by the current—made me feel quite home-sick for the Arctic. All the way today met coolies and animals bringing up iron plates and girders for the next span of the bridge.

Soon after this saw immense flocks of twittering snow-finches coming up from the south, flying quite aimlessly; probably just local movements. Several ravens seen to-day, and many choughs with bright crimson beaks, one party of fifteen. Innumerable sparrows, and parties of thirty or forty twites. Occasional rose-finches—what gorgeous birds they are!

At Nethang we missed the main road and found ourselves among a maze of irrigation channels. Iamtso tried to cross one, but his pony never thought of jumping and went in up to its belly. Luckily the camera-bags kept out of the water.

Stopped for lunch by the track where it crosses sand slopes that have been blown up against the bare hills. Watched some Tibetans, laden with great bundles of thorny weeds they had collected in the hills for firewood, sliding down a four-hundred foot sand-chute to the track. Good lunch: half a chicken each and baked potatoes, tea from a thermos. Boiling hot sun now, and we have to take our heavy clothes off. I climbed a hill and made an ascent of a curious pillar of hard-baked mud with lumps of granite embedded in it. I am not sure if it is the remains of an old fort or an outcrop of natural conglomerate.

The track is very difficult here; though the floods have subsided, it is only a narrow path cutting up and down across precarious rock faces. Met many donkeys with loads of glass, sheet-copper and lengths of strip-iron; also yaks carrying skins of butter and bags of tsamba. One has to be very careful meeting these animals suddenly at a corner of the track with a drop of a hundred feet often straight down into the river. There is usually only one driver to every seven or eight animals, and many of them are half out of control. Stampeding past with their bulging loads, they might quite easily push one over the edge. I usually lead Marpo past such hazards, as he is very jumpy and always puts up his ears at yaks. There is usually strong competition for the inner side of the track and the mule's persistent nature usually wins. Except for these places where the track is forced up into the hills by the river, the country is much the same: wide fan-shaped valleys sloping gently up to their apexes with tributary valleys on either side. The lower stretches are stony and barren, but at the top, before the stream has dried up, there is usually a monastery surrounded by stunted trees and terraces of cultivation more than half of which are no longer kept up. The hills are gaunt and rocky low down, but rounded and smooth above, where yaks can occasionally be seen grazing. Down by the main river there is often considerable cultivation where the irrigation has been maintained. In some places part of the river has been dammed up with a wall of stakes and stones to divert the water into well-constructed canals which are dry at this time of the year.

Met several old monks walking along with bundles of holy books tied on to their backs. They look at us with hard arrogant unfriendly faces; other wayfarers regard us with amazement, but they usually smile, especially when I salute them. The monks sometimes don't even reply.

Reached Jangme at three o'clock. Seven and a half hours including lunch, about twenty miles. I like Jangme. A trim village of about a dozen houses built where a high rocky spur comes down to the river. Each house has its own yard, surrounded by outhouses and stables, the flat roofs of which form a balcony accessible from the living-room windows. Here was Sonham Minghu, who showed us to the guest-room in one of the houses. A clean bare room with mud walls and floor, and shuttered windows. Some good frescoes on the walls, the Mongolian Leading Tiger, the Four Friends and a six-armed eleven-headed Chenrezi. The only furniture is some mattress-like cushions on the floor and a couple of Tibetan tables. We didn't expect the baggage for a couple of hours, so we clambered up the spur for a thousand feet or so and came down by a sand-chute.

At the back of the village there are several huge wizened willow trees with sprawling spiral-twisted trunks. Near these are some mud-flats and unfrozen pools. Saw four greenshank here: pale grey heads and necks, and long dark upturned bills; dark wings show in flight. Their liquid fluting note, three or four times repeated, recalls instantly the first time I heard it one night on the Solway marshes. Three or four wood-sandpiper too, much darker and with barred tails, give shrill " pluie " note. Thirty mallard, with the sun lighting up their bottle-green heads. As many teal, and two pairs of goosanders, the males with long drooping black scapulars and pink-flushed breasts. Put up a tiny wren, dark and scolding. At least a couple of hundred bar-headed geese in the fields, and odd Brahminy ducks. Four bottle-shaped swallows' nests between the rafters outside our window.

Nepean put up his camp-bed; I spread my sleeping-bag over the square cushions on the floor. Supper after a day's hard travelling is more a sacrament than a meal. Nurgul produced mulligatawny soup, boiled mutton and vegetables, tinned peas, caramel pudding and welsh rarebit, washed down with a bottle of stout. Spent an hour or two learning Tibetan, though the yak-dung stove smokes so pungently that it is difficult to read.

December 15th, Tuesday.—Hell of a day ! A day that will be remembered among many grim days—unless it be obliterated by innumerable future memories of winter-travel in this bleak land.

Nurgul brought tea at five o'clock, but I had taken some aspirin for my cold and awoke in a clammy sweat at midnight, and was kept awake by a cock *in* the house which had a rasping clarion note. Went out, to see a dawn full of stars—The Great Bear, Capella and many friends—more than friends. Incredible to think I used to steer my sledge on those very stars, and that I used to gaze at them after staggering out of my tent in Lapland or on the Greenland Ice Cap with exactly the same feeling of reverence and delight. A second in their lifetime has elapsed since then : whole ages in mine. Soon the Brahminies and bar-heads started calling sleepily on the pond beside the house, the stars began to pale, and the tinkling bells of pack animals could be heard already leaving the village.

Packed up. Porridge, fried eggs, potato and sausages. All sorts of snags this morning. We hung about while Nurgul packed up the gear, and it wasn't till 7.30 that we got away, just as the sun lit up the hill-tops. A sudden violent burst of song from a wren just as we started; bar-heads, mallard, goosander, Brahminies, and teal on the move. Lammergeyers always soaring above. A big crowd of peasants sitting round drinking tea at the end of the village; I think they are clearing out one of the irrigation canals. I wish I could understand what they said as we passed! The track is exciting here. Many wandering corners under huge overhanging basalt cliffs, and the river rushing past just on our left. Saw many dark-coloured fish here. Buddhas painted on the rocks, and always prayers carved, strings of flags, and piles of holy stones to which each wayfarer adds his contribution to ensure his safety round every sudden corner.

Came out onto the long open plain before Chu-shur. Stony, sandy and barren most of it is, with only the thorny vetch growing. We are still meeting girders going up for the bridge; yaks, mules and donkeys with miscellaneous loads. We kept on the right, on a special track prepared for the recent tour of the Regent. The stones have been removed from the way and have been arranged in lines on each side, leaving an even, sandy surface, fifteen or twenty feet wide. We cantered along most of this. At ten o'clock we saw an important-looking party of horsemen approaching on a parallel track to the left, so we cut across and found, as we expected, that it was Tsarong and his younger wife, also his son and two daughters, and Norbhu's son, who are all returning from school at Darjeeling. Tsarong and his wife have been down to Chu-shur to meet them. The boys wore horn-rimmed glasses and short hair and long silk robes lined with fur. Tsarong, as befits a man of his independence, wore an aged khaki coat and a leather flying-helmet. Anyone else who tried that in Lhasa would be degraded. His wife wore a tall peaked hat, and had her face swathed in scarves with only her eyes showing They had about a dozen servants with them. It was a very embarrassing interview, as the children did not know what to say. The younger Tibetans could speak English, but they were completely tongue-tied, and all my conversation was with Tsarong in Tibetan, luckily he doesn't expect many honorifics! Reached Chu-shur at eleven o'clock.

Many black-necked cranes on the plain and odd flocks of snow-finches, Elwes' horned-larks, rose-finches, etc. Many Tibetan great-tits at Chu-shur. How different it looks now that the floods are down. Found Sonham Minghu here (he said he left Jangme at 3 A.M.) and changed Nepean's stalwart little pony for a too independent-looking mule. Noticed clouds of sand blowing high into the air, along the valley of Tsang-po.

Followed a winding built-up track beside the river and then turned left across shingle banks to the ferry at Chaksam. There is a very attractive smallish monastery on the far side of the river, and a long iron chain running out to an island in mid-stream. This is the remains of a remarkable suspension bridge which is reputed to have been built five hundred years ago by an ancient king of Tibet, whose image is worshipped in the near-by Chaksam monastery. By the time we reached the river we were enveloped in the sand-storm which was roaring down the course of the Tsang-po from west to east. It was absolute hell. We breathed sand and gritted it between our teeth; it filled our eyes so that we could not see, it got into our noses and ears, stung our faces and made life quite intolerable. My camera-bags were filled with sand. The ponies would hardly face it, indeed they were often stopped dead by the sheer force of the wind.

There were two ferry-boats, both on the far side—crude rectangular wooden boxes about twenty feet by eight. The boatmen refused to come over for half an hour or so, as it was too rough. We waited miserably, breathing sand and impatience. The boats are propelled with crude wooden paddles; but the men do not have to row very much: they creep up the steep bank under cover from the wind, making use of a back-water, then they row furiously in the middle until they come into another eddy, which brings them across. It was rather a hazardous business, and most of the time water was being shipped, as the sides of the boats are cut away in the middle so that the animals can get on and off more easily. When we came up against the force of the current and the wind it looked as if we were going to be washed down towards the island. The ferry has one huge steering oar used against an upright beam in the stern. A similar beam at the other end—one can hardly say bows—has a carved horse's head at the summit and a bamboo pole with prayer-flags attached.

No sign of our baggage animals yet. A fine young Tibetan crossed with us; he wore a hat of a complete fox-skin with the tail hanging down behind, and carried slung across his back a Mauser rifle and a beautifully worked silver charm-box with an

image inside. I had a long talk with him and discovered he was
returning to Chung-ye, having been up to Lhasa to conduct some
business concerning a Government estate which had gradually
absorbed his own family property. He told me that before
anyone would take any sort of action it was necessary to visit
Lhasa many times. Letters, apparently, remained unanswered.
He invited us to go and stay with him.

A tricky job getting our ponies off the ferry, as it is half full
of ice. The track then led along at the foot of a rocky hill, with
little hermitages 1000 feet above the river. It seems to be an
exceptionally holy place. There are many chortens here and
painted Buddhas recessed in the rocks and protected by wire-
netting. Whitewash has also been splashed over the rocks.
The storm is dead against us now, and we can make little progress, as the ponies try to turn back. The way leads over miles
of sand-dunes, so that the track is obliterated and the drift so bad
that we almost decided to turn and try again early tomorrow.
At two o'clock, having eaten nothing for eight hours, we stopped
to have some lunch inside a ruined barn; but we ate more sand
than anything else. The wind was most exhausting and our
eyes were very inflamed.

Gradually the path diverged from the river and rose along the
foot of a range of rounded grassy hills on our left. Below was
a level plain of very fertile cultivated land, running down to the
sandy waste which marked the summer flood-limit of the river.
There are some fine-looking isolated farms with swastikas and
other lucky signs whitewashed on the walls. After an hour
we turned up to the left, following a wide fan of flood débris
brought down by a monsoon watercourse. The floods must be
terrific in summer, as the walls of this river-bed are about thirty
feet high and quite vertical. The sides are often a hundred
yards apart. But the bed of the watercourse makes a tolerable
track for us. Passed a village where we ought, if we'd had any
sense, to have stayed the night, but it is ignominious to cut down
one's allotted stage unless absolutely necessary.

The Kamba La is a formidable pass. We had to rise nearly
5000 feet from the Tsang-po. The track zigzagged steeply
upward for miles and miles, and it was rapidly getting dark. I
walked all the way up, as Marpo was tired. Nepean was absolutely dead-beat and only just kept going. Luckily his mule

is very strong and could carry him. We reached the summit of the pass at 5.30, by which time it was dark and very cold. On the way up Sonham Minghu passed us. He had waited behind at Chu-shur to change the baggage animals, and when he reached the ferry they said at first it was unsafe to cross. Sonham, on his own sturdy little Tibetan pony, trotted practically all the way up the hill. I shouldn't have thought it possible, but I suppose the ponies get used to it, as no Tibetan ever walks if it is safe to ride. They have a proverb that if he can't carry you up any hill he's no pony; if you can't walk down you're no man. Heard a snow-cock up in the hills and saw mountain-finches again. There are mouse-hares up here too; I should have thought they would have had the sense to be hibernating.

The descent in the dark was terrifying, as we lost the track and got on to a very precipitous watercourse; we also lost the village of Tremlung until some thoughtful person shone a light for our benefit. At last, at seven o'clock, we found the rest-house. It was terribly cold waiting for our baggage. Our accommodation is a low stable-like room, about twelve feet by thirty, with two pillars supporting an open rafter roof covered with sods. The walls and floor are of rough stones and mud. A door and windows with boarded shutters open on to a balcony which is the roof of the stables. A piece of cloth is hung against the roof to keep the dust from falling on to the cushions and tables. It was bitterly cold, as the wind roared through the room. We borrowed a butter-lamp and a couple of sheep-dung stoves and then drank cup after cup of Tibetan tea. It is the very thing for an occasion like this. Nurgul arrived at ten o'clock quite unperturbed, though the muleteers had wanted to turn back and he had had to use a torch to pick a way over the pass. One pony, with a load of wireless gear, had fallen from the track and turned several somersaults, but seemed none the worse. Supper of Maconochie rations, sardines, cake, Scotch woodcock and tea. Nurgul is a great man! I wish these dung stoves wouldn't smoke so much. They produce pungent fumes which are like moss saturated with chlorine.

It is curious what vicarious pleasure one derives from physical exhaustion and discomfort. It is a strange paradox that the more intolerable a journey is at the time, the more satisfactory does it become in retrospect. Our sensibilities and characters were made to be sharpened against the hard forces of Nature. But how few people nowadays get any chance to test their physical endurance to breaking-point, to feel cold fear gnawing at their hearts, or to have to make decisions that hold life and death in the balance? That is why men flock so easily to war; to test a manhood that is perverted by the present state of civilization.

December 16th, Wednesday. Blew hard all night and still blowing, but no sand drifting. A lovely clear morning; warm reddish tints on the hill-tops opposite; a deep-blue lake with white horses chasing each other across it and on the far side rounded grassy mountain-tops. No trees up here except for some wind-bitten thorn bushes. My pony has gone lame so I rode Iamtso's, while he hired another. Marpo·is running loose; he will have time to recover at Pede.

A short stony descent to the shores of the Yamdrok Tso, then alternate rough-going round spurs, and easy fast-travelling in between. Bitterly cold with a violent wind from the Nangartse end. Down there on the mud-flats sand-devils were being swirled for 1500 feet into the air, but as a rule we are free from them at the Tremlung end. Plenty of fellow-travellers: a party of brigand-like men with dark sunburnt faces and long sheepskin robes; they were all armed with rifles and were followed by even wilder-looking retainers similarly armed. A monk came striding along the road with part of his red robe tied round the top of his head for warmth; he carried a big pack, and on top of it were two tiny dogs fast asleep. A hundred or so yaks laden with planks of wood. Many flocks of sheep and goats in charge of ragged-looking shepherd boys. A couple of post-runners carrying spears on which bells are tied, which jingle as they jog along.

Birds very interesting, quite different from those of the Lhasa valley. Altogether I saw ten male white-winged redstarts and no females, six desert-chats, eight robin-accentors, about five hundred horned-larks, any number of three varieties of snow- and mountain-finches, two kinds of gulls on the lake, many goosanders—a hundred drakes together in one place, odd parties of tufted duck, pochard, mallard and a few teal, several single grebes diving out on the lake. At Pede I saw about thirty red-headed pochard quite close in, near the ruined fort. There are bar-heads feeding along the shallows, and occasional lammer-geyers, buzzards, peregrines, kestrels and harriers. I have seen no choughs, cranes or rose-finches this side of the pass.

At Pede, Sonham had everything ready. This is a place for changing baggage animals, so Nepean got rid of his mule, which has been getting more and more refractory. I shall go on to Nangartse with Nepean and leave Iamtso here with Marpo, who is still very lame.

An extraordinary number of mouse-hares here; I saw a yellow weasel too. Several parties of gazelle up in the hills. This end of the lake is frozen over, but the birds remain beside open pools and at the edge of the ice. Blowing so much now that we could hardly carry on; no wonder the Tibetans finish travelling by midday. We reached Nangartse at 3.30, having had to stop several times to put on more clothes.

As we reached the village nestling at the foot of the fort, some women seized our bridles and led our ponies up the steep cobbled hill to the guest-house just at the back of the fort. It is almost the highest building in Nangartse. We were taken up a steep staircase, through a long dark passage, across a little courtyard open to the sky, and then to a tiny room with a glass window looking right across to the Karo La, and to the plain five hundred feet below. It is a very superior room: there are some religious wall-paintings protected by glass, and embroidered cloths hung against the ceiling to stop things falling on to the silken cushions and carved tables below. Two earthenware jars of smouldering sheep-dung were brought in, and, in spite of the acrid smoke, they made the room quite warm and snug. The baggage arrived at seven o'clock. The wind is whistling and roaring outside our exposed room. The whole building quivers. Had a grand farewell dinner—tomato soup, chicken with fried potatoes and carrots, cherries and custard, prawns, and the odd tot of whisky. Tomorrow Nepean goes on. I shall spend the morning wandering round the lake and then return to Iamtso at Pede to await Finch.

December 17th, Thursday.—Am on my own now. But in this country one cannot get to know the people. In Greenland one could wander off and be perfectly happy with the Eskimos as long as one could speak the language. There one passed as an equal and lived, ate, hunted, and travelled just as they did. We did very well without servants. Here it is fundamentally different. In this feudal country one is a Sahib, and is judged not by one's prowess as a hunter or as a man, but by the number of servants one keeps and the amount one throws one's weight about. Perhaps it would be different with the nomads of the Chang Tang. I think if a man knew the language perfectly, especially if he were a doctor and could really help the people, he might get to know them.

An awe-inspiring view from our window: we look straight down on to the rocks several hundred feet below us, then over some frozen ponds and ploughed fields on either side of the track, along which parties of yaks are already moving, and behind that to the line of the Karo La mountains. Nepean went off at seven, with Sonham and Nurgul. He will take two days to Gyantse. I walked over towards Samding monastery, feeling rather forlorn. There is something peculiarly poignant about partings like this. For several months you see a man all day and every day—your ways divide, and you may never meet again.

There are about three hundred yaks picketed at the foot of the village. Sand is starting to drift already. Many snow- and mountain-finches out on the mud-flats and calandra-larks with their melodious whistle. Literally hundreds of mouse-hares here; they sit up beside their burrows and squeak as you pass. Spent an hour stalking them with a camera. By the lake a skylark was singing a thin song, and a tiny sandpipery bird ran like a ball along the edge of the ice which runs out for about three hundred yards to the open water. Returned to the village and was almost mobbed by the local dogs; luckily the fiercest ones were tied up. I took some photographs of the fort and of the snow-capped mountains beyond the Karo La, then I packed my saddle-bags and set off for Pede.

Although there could be no question of losing the way, a very aged man on an equally aged pony insisted on accompanying me, and we took four hours to reach Pede at an uncomfortable jog-trot which made me very cross and sore. At first the wind was behind us, so it was sunny and quite warm. Saw about twenty pintail today as well as the usual birds, then later I saw a blackbird fly out of some rocks beside the track. Later it got very cold. The wind was so strong that in some places the

water was being blown from the lake up on to the track. I
suppose that is why the lake isn't frozen over here, as it is certainly
cold enough. The water froze stiff on our clothes.

Iamtso says Marpo is still lame, but Finch won't be here for
a day or two. It seems to be a sand crack at the back of the
hoof—the same trouble that several of our ponies have already
had. Pede consists of half a dozen houses on a low spur between
the hills and the lake. The ruined fort looks like a Scottish
castle and also recalls Chillon. I walked along beside the lake.
Some distance out in the water are close packs of several hundred
ducks. Some of these must contain almost a thousand birds.
The majority are red-headed pochards, there are also many
tufted duck and common pochard; they are not all diving ducks;
I can make out mallard, teal and a few gadwall, and, I think, a
widgeon. I saw several parties of about a hundred yaks laden
with wool coming down an exceptionally steep hill just behind
Pede. There is a perfectly good track, but the yaks prefer the
bare hill-side. There seems to be one driver to thirty or forty
animals. Last year the price for wool at Kalimpong was five-
pence per pound; this year it is elevenpence. Normally 12
million pounds go down to India each year, two-thirds going to
Kalimpong. This year many fortunes are being made in the wool
trade.

I have a draughty upstairs room overlooking a courtyard
where noisy mules are picketed. What a remarkable noise
they make when they see their food approaching. Only yak-
hair curtains keep out the wind. While I was shaving off a
three days' beard, some sparrows, who are apparently in the
habit of roosting in some holes in the ceiling, tried to pluck
up their courage to come in and sat chirping on the curtain.
The people here are very interested in me and seem amused
that I can talk to them. I have arranged to go up Yasik Ri
and Pede Ri tomorrow; these are the names the local people
have for the two mountains, about 17,800 feet high, which
stand out from the long range at the back of the lake, whose
surface is 14,000 feet above sea-level. I shall take Iamtso and
a local man to see if I can get any film of gazelle.

December 18th, Friday.—Somewhat disturbed by the muleteers
who started feeding their charges soon after midnight and were
on the road by 1.30 A.M. That's the way to travel at this time

of the year. Iamtso, the local man, and I, set off at seven o'clock, just as the sun rose. We went straight up the steep fell behind the house and almost immediately saw a gazelle. Paler than burrhal and with a more goat-like action. Very white face with little upright black horns, most conspicuous white backside and a black scut. Saw fifteen more higher up. They are exquisitely graceful but very wild. I went on ahead while the other two tried to drive them past me. But there wasn't enough cover and they saw me. We had several more drives but it was very difficult. I got some shots with the six-inch lens. I must have seen about fifty gazelle today. The wind is terrific up here and intolerably cold. One can hardly stand. I sent the other two back after taking some colour film, and went on to the summit alone. From here there is a very good view across to Ningdzingzongka, the 23,000-foot peak to the north of the Karo La. Its north ridge is icy and fluted, but the southern ridge is a fairly easy-looking snow slope, with only the last few hundred feet very steep. I might be allowed to try it on the way back to India.

There is a huge block of snowy mountains down to the southwest. Below me the many-bayed blue lake curls round the feet of brown hills. All the last part of the climb was over loose shale coated in snow and ice. The summit of Pede Ri was built up like a huge fort, with a number of rooms, but all roofless. I wonder who can have done all this: it must have taken months of work. There is snow on the north faces of all the hills. Passes run up nearly every valley over to the Tsang-po, but many of them seem not to be used in winter. I went along the summit ridge for two miles to the top of the other mountain, which is higher and further north. Suddenly I felt very ill, so curled up under a rock and went to sleep. I shouldn't have thought I would have got mountain sickness at about 18,000 after living for several months at 12,000. Perhaps I came up too fast, or hadn't had enough to eat. In the distance to the north and north-east I can see a range of snow-capped mountains—far, far away. The Tsang-po valley can be followed for many miles to the east. Came down a track very slowly, feeling weak and ill. All the streams have overflowed and frozen into great slabs of ice. Saw a dipper on the way down, and several wrens. Got back at four o'clock and drank pints of tea, then practised Tibetan on the family who live here.

I am suffering not only from cracked lips and a sore face owing to the dry cold wind, but have most painful open cracks on the ends and sides of my thumbs and fingers, just as if they had been cut with a razor-blade. I have never experienced this before.

December 19th, Saturday.—Another day alone. Finch might have come today, but will probably arrive tomorrow. Spent the morning trying again to film gazelle. The trouble is that even if you get to exactly the right place they see you the moment they come into the view of the finder and are away in a flash. The best plan is to stalk them from below and " shoot " them leaping away uphill. I got so near to some that I could hear their shrill sneeze-like screams of alarm. I got some quite good " shots " today, but the Tibetans are too impatient and won't give me time to carry out a really good stalk. In the afternoon walked for miles beside the lake. Saw a rough-legged buzzard sitting hunched up on a stone. I also got within twenty yards of a fine drake widgeon who was sheltering in a little bay. A note from Finch, who has already reached Nangartse. He will be along at nine tomorrow. Started *Fire over England*, by A. E. W. Mason, and went on till I had finished it. A thrilling and romantic melodrama in the best Elizabethan style. Practically the first book I've read since leaving India.

December 20th, Sunday.—Packed up by 8 o'clock. Pony still lame. Went round taking a few more photographs, but something is wrong with the ¼-plate camera. Went along the track to meet Finch. Hundreds of yaks laden with wool going down towards Nangartse. I saw one remarkable yak driver wearing a garment of coarse sheepskin slipped off one shoulder, cold though it was. He had a sparse black beard, an expression like John the Baptist, and an untidy pigtail ornamented with an ivory ring, a charm-box and some odd pieces of coral and turquoise. He was turning a prayer-wheel as he rode along on a huge black yak, and slung across his back was an antiquated prong-gun with half a dozen prayer-flags fluttering from the prongs.

I next saw a party of five horsemen approaching, one of whom soon dismounted. I advanced with a very " Doctor Livingstone, I presume? " feeling ! Finch wore a topee and Wellington boots; very English, but he doesn't seem to feel cold. He seems to be just the man for the job—tremendously interested in everything, already a great admirer of the Tibetans and keen to learn the language. He is very excited to be going to Lhasa.

We decided to go as far as Tremlung at this side of the pass today, and to cross the Kamba La to Chu-shur tomorrow, get to Nethang the day after, and reach Lhasa early on the following day. As Marpo is still lame, I rode a hireling which had to be beaten all the time. Finch's Gyantse ponies are very strong and fit. As we rode we discussed everything under the sun, from polo to politics, from Lhasa to the North Pole. We reached Tremlung at two o'clock and after a meal we explored the village. There are many ghost traps over the doors. These, a relic of the old Pön religion, are to avert devils from the inmates of the house. The lower part is the skull of a ram with the horns attached; over this are several flat pieces of wood on which there are paintings rather resembling the court cards in a pack; these are effigies of the people in the house and are meant to divert evil from their originals; above and around these a web of coloured wool is arranged in geometric patterns. The village is extremely dirty: there are piles of dung and offal in most of the courtyards. We watched a woman weaving a narrow strip of coarse woollen cloth on a very primitive but efficient loom. After that we walked up the lake for a mile or two in the opposite direction to Nangartse. Watched twelve gazelle up in the hills. Saw a wall-creeper. Returned by a short-cut over a low pass. Finch has a Tilley heater with him, so we made the room very snug and warm and talked till late. After half a day's acquaintance we know each other far better than one ever gets to know people in ordinary circumstances at home.[1]

December 21st, Monday.—Got away by 6.30 A.M. and walked to the top of the pass before the sun rose. Looking down to the lake I was surprised to see a wooden rowing-boat pulling across from the other side: I didn't know the Tibetans used them. This must be the highest navigable lake in the world: 2000 feet higher than Lake Titicaca.

We sent our ponies on ahead and, leaving the track, followed a long ridge right down to the Tsang-po valley. Stalked three snow-cock and got quite near. They are big grey birds with striped flanks, buff cheeks, orange-red beaks and tails like

[1] Major Finch, I deeply regret to say, died in England as a result of some glandular trouble from which he was suffering at this time.

black-cock. They run away clucking when one gets nearer than twenty yards. The usual vicious gale and dust-storm at Chaksam, and we had to wait for some time before it was safe enough to cross. Reached Chu-shur at midday and stayed in a very beautiful old house belonging to Tsarong. He had told us to come here on our return and to use his wood-stove.

We used the very dark and ancient altar-room which had a big fresco on the wall showing seven generations of one family all living at the same time. It is a Mongolian painting: Bhon-dong Shap-pe has the same fresco in his living-room at Lhasa, so has Tsarong. Along one wall, over some lockers where the family's best clothes are kept, is a rack full of sacred books. There is a photograph of the Tashi Lama cut out of a news-paper, several gilt images hung with scarves, a row of thankas, and a collection of prayer-wheels, travelling charm-boxes, chang pots and tsamba bowls. The people were very friendly and we showed them the photographs in some books about Tibet that Finch had with him. One of the girls is extremely beautiful. But her skin is absolutely filthy and her cheeks are coated with black pigment as a protection against the weather. Her hair is full of dust and pieces of straw, while her coarse homespun is engrained with grease and filth. But she has perfect features and eyes like a gazelle.

I went for a walk up the very fertile valley to the north-west. There is a very complicated irrigation system up here and several watermills for grinding corn. Some fine trees too, and groves of willows, poplars and walnuts. Watched a family of laughing-thrushes and a hoopoe, who seems to be wintering here. Tsarong says hoopoes hibernate and swears he has found them in disused rooms of his house. I shall believe it when I see it.

December 22nd, Tuesday.—A long and fairly uneventful ride past Jangme to Nethang, which we reached in the early after-noon, without much wind. Finch's four servants, some of whom have never been to Lhasa, are very excited at the prospect. At Nethang I went for a walk down by the river and saw flocks of several hundred pintail, nearly all drakes.

At the house where we stayed they were very busy preparing pea- and barley-flour. In a roofed corner of the courtyard there was a large sun-brick stove which was being stoked with dried mustard plants and kept at a roaring heat with the aid of a pair of bellows made from the skin of a goat. A flat pan full of sand was heated up and then handfuls of peas or barley were put in. These became suddenly hot and expanded—just as maize does when it is made into popcorn—the pan being shaken all the time so that nothing was burnt. After that the sand was run off through a sieve and the grain was ready to be ground. The parched peas tasted excellent. This most arduous work was done by the women, who were at it continuously, in spite of the heat, for several hours.

Next day we reached Lhasa without further adventure. The wind seemed to decrease as we went further away from the Tsang-po valley. The sun was shining brightly and we all felt a growing excitement as we approached the scintillating golden shrines on the roof of the Potala.

CHAPTER FIFTEEN

TIBETAN NEW YEAR

THE Tibetan calendar, which has been in use since A.D. 1027, is a peculiar mixture of Chinese and Western (imported through India) origins. Five elements—wood, fire, earth, iron and water—are joined to the twelve beasts of the Chinese zodiac: mouse, ox, tiger, hare, dragon, serpent, horse, sheep, monkey, bird, dog and pig. Each element comes twice, first as male, then as female. The elements are thus " used up " by the tenth year; so the first element, in male then female form, is combined with the eleventh and twelfth animals which are left over. This system gives a cycle of sixty years. Last year (1936) was the Fire-Mouse Year. The New Year (1937, or the eleventh year of the sixteenth Tibetan cycle) is the Fire-Ox Year. Next will be the Earth-Tiger Year.

The Tibetan New Year's Day in 1937 coincided with 12th February of our Calendar. As this is the greatest festival of the Tibetan Year we were extremely lucky to be in Lhasa at this time, for no other living Europeans, except Sir Charles Bell and his doctor, Colonel Kennedy, have witnessed these remarkable celebrations. It was unfortunate that the Mission left Lhasa on

17th February, before the second half of the festivities had taken place; but we were in time to see the great Lama Dance at the Potala, to attend the official New Year reception there, to witness the annual trance of the State Oracle, and to see how the New Year is kept in the Lhasa home. Only Richardson remained in Lhasa to see the latter half of the celebrations during the Monlam, or Great Prayer, when twenty thousand monks are in civil command of the city.

With sound reasoning the Tibetans hold that before they can hope to celebrate an auspicious New Year, all the evil influences that have accumulated in the Old Year must be exorcised and driven from the Holy City. Accordingly, on the twenty-ninth day of the last month of the Old Year a Devil Dance takes place in the great eastern courtyard of the Potala. All Lhasa officials from the Regent downwards must be there.

We had been invited to attend this dance by the Cabinet. From the point of view of photography it was difficult to find out the exact order and times of the various ceremonies; reports were as usual contradictory. At last Jigme, after consulting Tsarong, gave me a beautifully typed programme of events, but was careful to explain that the times given were merely approximate. In some cases they might start as much as four hours late. On this occasion I went especially early to photograph the officials riding up to the northern gateway of the Potala. Jigme and I had examined the track and found a place suitable for photography where the morning sun would shine on the gay dresses of the officials. Jigme said I ought to be there by seven o'clock, but Ringang assured me that no one would appear until eight-thirty or nine. However, I preferred to be on the safe side; so the Doctor and I rode out just as the sun was reddening the top of the holy mountain behind Drepung. The Doctor had volunteered to help, as I wanted records of the procession and dance in every photographic medium. We fixed up the cameras and waited for an hour as the sun slowly transformed the valley beneath us. It was an admirable setting. We could " shoot " the officials just as they turned a corner of the steep zigzag road. In the background was the turquoise pool of the Snake Temple framed by leafless branches.

At first a few old monks and servants straggled up, mounted on mules; then came a group of monk officials, followed by scattered parties of lay officials in geluchay dress. The colours looked unspeakably lovely in the early morning sun: the high monk officials swathed in mulberry-coloured wrappings and with yellow silk showing at the neck and on the crown of their fur-edged hats; a magistrate with basin hat and bright scarlet gown over his silk; and, most resplendent of all, the geluchays, a kaleidoscopic medley of variegated colours. They were all in their best clothes on this day, and I had the impression of watching some gay medieval pageant, some fantastic Hollywood production, or a throng of people in fancy dress. Yuto was wearing a long saffron and green silk robe and wide red-topped fur hat. Tsarong wore a glistening brocade dress with a multi-coloured pattern of scaly dragons. The Shap-pes, who, as befitted their rank, came late, wore brightly patterned robes instead of their yellow silk. They seemed to have even more than the usual crowd of scarlet-hatted outriders, servants and grooms—perhaps because they arrived separately instead of together.

At last there was a great stir down below and we knew that the Regent was coming. For once he was on horseback, and not carried in his palanquin. In front of him rode his usual monk officials, including Simple Simon, grinning from ear to ear and looking colossal on a minute and unfortunate mule. The Regent was dressed in yellow and vermilion silk, and his pony was hung with gay trappings. He wore a large yellow hood, exposing only his face, and dark glasses. I was photographing furiously with one camera after another, but he did not seem to mind. In fact he smiled to us as he passed, as did all the officials except old Lungchungna, who doesn't approve of such new-fangled things as cameras, and one rather apathetic Tegi who had never called on us because he said he could not afford a present. The Ringangs were the last to arrive just as we were moving off at about nine o'clock. Morgan told big Ringang that he ought to carry his pony instead of riding the wretched thing up the hill. This seemed to amuse him vastly. After that we went inside the Potala and down the steps into the eastern court, where the Devil Dance was to be performed.

Here everybody was bustling about getting things ready. They had hung a lovely scarlet, green and gold silk curtain with a huge dragon pattern at the top of the steps. Above some of the windows are large scarlet and yellow pelmets, and over the triple staircase a fringe of many-pointed strips of different-coloured silks gives the impression of a patchwork quilt, except that there is a regular pattern zigzagging through the separate pieces. Right along the northern side of the courtyard an awning with a brightly coloured valance was supported by a series of cords running across to the southern side. The top-centre of this is ornamented in blue appliqué work with a huge scarlet and yellow dragon's head. Beneath it the monk band were collecting their drums and trumpets. There was a very striking stand for the long trumpets, carved in the semblance of two gilded skeletons.

As we did not want to make ourselves too conspicuous, the Doctor and I went up to our balcony immediately above the eastern entrance to the court. We had been offered the one above as being more honourable, but as the lower one is better for photography, Gould decided to leave the upper one to the Chinese, who will think they are one up on us and be duly pleased. I rigged up my cameras (seven of them) while a young monk in a very decorative gold and scarlet braid undercoat brought us Tibetan tea in a great silver-gilt teapot. This was most welcome, as there was a bitter north wind blowing and we were in the shade. It was clouding up by now and threatening snow. We wondered if this would be auspicious.

Down below us the courtyard is gradually filling with a motley crowd of men-at-arms in all kinds of antiquated and dilapidated armour. A few minor officials with ragged pigtails and wearing faded scarlet cloaks over their silk robes are drilling the soldiers— of whom there are several hundred—into some semblance of order. They are in two lines now; some of them are blowing small brass trumpets, while others sing a dirge and stamp to and fro as if the two ranks were enacting a mock battle. Those who are not actually taking part form a great circle round the edge of the court. There seems to be a series of scenes acted by different units. One group wears enormous plumed head-dresses orna- mented with bunches of white fluff, and dances a stately minuet; another has the black tail-feathers of a cock streaming from his hat like an Italian soldier. One scene is acted by solemn spearmen with daggers in their belts. The two ranks close and some argu- ment seems to be carried on, chiefly by the leaders, while they make dignified passes at each other. Their places are soon taken by bowmen who have enormous conical basket-work shields; they wear khaki-coloured uniforms and a halo of rolled cloth round their leather or iron helmets. Their armour consists of metal plates, about two inches long and half an inch in width, threaded loosely together.

The most interesting of these war dances is done by men with incredibly ancient flint-lock guns with rusty barrels encased in wood. The soldiers are drawn up in two lines; after the usual chanting, disputing and goose-stepping, the ranks turn their backs on each other and, holding their weapons at waist level, point them backwards at their opponents. At a word from the scarlet-robed conductor of ceremonies they apply fuses to the breeches of the guns and, after a tremendous explosion, the courtyard is completely filled with smoke. Much to my surprise there were no casualties.

Although they cannot get much practice, these men seem to know the drill extraordinarily well. After their exertions, all the warriors sit down on the courtyard floor and are given tea and tsamba.

Gould and Richardson arrived about this time (ten o'clock), the former wisely wearing his fur-lined Tibetan coat. Meanwhile other spectators were arriving. The gallery on the south, and the flat roof above it, soon filled up with ladies of rank and citizens of Lhasa. We waved to the Tsarong women-folk who were dressed up in all their finery.

Across the top of the banisters above the triple flight of steps there was a silver and gilt trumpet-rest. Down the outer staircase (the central one is normally reserved for the exclusive use of the Dalai Lama) crowds of officials and monks poured; the former sat beneath an awning on the flat roof to our left, while the monks formed a crowd on either side of the foot of the steps. The Regent and the Prime Minister appeared at a sixth-storey window on the left of the great eastern façade of the Potala, while the Shap-pes, Dzasas, Tegis, and other high officials could be seen in one of the long windows directly above the triple staircase. The more senior the official, the worse the view : such is the burden of office.

Suddenly there are three resounding blasts from the great trumpets at the top of the steps, and the fifty or sixty members of the monk band troop down and take their places under the awning. As well as the long bass trumpets there are drums—or rather gongs, shaped like old-fashioned warming-pans supported on their one leg, beaten with curiously curved drumsticks—two sorts of cymbals, and small trumpets with piercing cornet-like notes. Once more the trumpets boom, and a portentous figure with a vermilion gown hung over his long golden robe and wearing a monstrous grinning mask, strides ponderously down the steps and into the court. Hanging from his neck is an enormous rosary. His progress is slow because after every few steps he pauses with one foot raised. This is Hashang, known the world over as " The Laughing Buddha ", the Chinese priest-god of happiness. With him, hand in hand, walk three pairs of atten-dants. The inner pair, whose tiny stature emphasizes Hashang's colossal bulk, are two small Alice-in-Wonderland-like figures with smiling masks, long hair and wide blue-black skirts held tightly in at the waist. The outer couple have pale skeleton masks and red and white costumes. The remaining pair have Brahman-like dresses, recalling the early connection of Lamaism and Hinduism. After turning about and bowing deeply to the Regent, they march to a chair, where Hashang is destined to sit, absolutely motionless, throughout the whole performance, his vast bald head making a foreground for most of my photographs.

The trumpets blow again and two dancers in demon masks run down the steps scattering rice from bowls held by monk attendants. They dance their way down the steps, and, to the insistent music of the band, they start to pirouette round the court. After a few minutes they return up the steps and two more dancers differently attired take their place. The dancing is much the same all the time. With arms outstretched to make the most of their long and highly ornamented sleeves, the dancers balance on one foot, turn slowly, hop once or twice, and turn again. The measure is simple but effective, combining stylized posturing with acrobatic pirouet-ting. Considerable control of balance is required, as they often turn round several times on one leg before putting down the other foot. Some of the masks are horned to represent bulls or stags; others have exaggeratedly hideous faces, scarlet, gold or green, with staring eyes and grinning fangs. Yet they look grotesquely realistic, being skilfully made of wood or papier mâché, while the back of the mask is hidden by a piece of cloth which hangs down behind. The dresses themselves are very long and full enough to flow as the dancer swings and turns. In the front hangs an apron of gorgeous embroidery, and the wide pointed sleeves are cut so as almost to reach the ground. Every imaginable colour is there, with black, red, and yellow predominating.

After nine pairs of these dancers have come and gone, the crowd, which has been comparatively silent until now, suddenly starts to whistle. This is the traditional reception for the skeleton dancers, four of whom now appear scattering white ashes as they hop down the steps. These are ghoulish figures with grinning skeleton heads, large ears, and long bony fingers and claws. Instead of flowing robes they wear close-fitting red garments on which the bones stand out in white, and they dance with considerable agility to a rapid pulsating measure. In the middle of the courtyard there is now a square carpet with the crude effigy of a head at one end, and arms and legs at the corners. Round this " corpse " the figures dance, mopping and mowing and clattering their thin bony fingers.

Meanwhile another actor has made his entry. This is the Ancient Man. Wearing an astonishingly life-like mask, with a tonsured head and long grey beard, he leans on his stick and totters round the court. The crowd shouts with joy as he sinks pathetically to the ground and feebly raises himself, only to fall again and again. Now he is given a large bowl of dried fruits and sweets. At a given signal the crowd rushes him and scrambles for the dainties, in spite of attendants who belabour them with whips. At last a tiger-skin rug is put on the carpet where the Ancient Man carries on his antics. He walks slowly towards it, then gives it a tremendous blow with his stick; after that he rolls over and over with it in mortal struggle until at last he prevails. Now he is suddenly rejuvenated, and, casting aside the slain tiger, he leaps to his feet and dances round the court like a young man. This scene is an innovation (surely a very rare thing in Tibet) of the late Dalai Tama. While he was in China he dreamed this scene, and on his return to Lhasa he included it in the performance.

While the Ancient Man is playing the fool, the skeleton dancers scamper away and the trumpets proclaim the chief actor of the day. This is the Black Hat magician who is to lead the remainder of the ceremony. Although, as a rule, when we asked for any interpretation of the dances the answers we received were vague and contradictory, in the case of the Black Hat dance there is a well-known historical interpretation.

At the end of the ninth century Lang-dar-ma, an adherent of

the Pön religion, having murdered his brother, became king of Tibet, and within a few years had almost exterminated Tibetan Buddhism. Then a certain lama whose monastery had been destroyed determined to put an end to this reign of tyranny. Wearing black robes and a tall black hat, both of which were lined with white, and riding a white horse which he had carefully covered with soot, he attracted the attention of the king by his peculiar dance. Lang-dar-ma sent for this man and made him dance before him. The black-hatted lama, in the course of his fascinating dance, circled nearer and nearer to the king, and eventually shot him with a bow and arrow which he had concealed in his robes. In the ensuing confusion the lama reversed his hat and robe, and splashed through a river on his horse, which, as the soot was washed off, rapidly became white. The search for a black-robed assassin was therefore futile, and the lama escaped in safety.

A most impressive figure is the Black Hat dancer as, with slow dignity, he descends the steps. He wears an immense hat with a wide black-edged brim; a pyramid of gilded woodwork, carved like flames, surmounts some miniature skulls and leads up to a rosette of peacock feathers. From the back of this hat, hanging over the brim and stretching half-way to the ground, is a wide strip of gold cloth. His flowing brocade robes are ornamented with the dorje thunderbolt and with skulls set in a scarlet and yellow border. Over this he wears an apron of beads carved from human bones. His movements are fluent and graceful beyond those of former dancers as he pirouettes slowly round the court with outstretched arms, holding in one hand a dorje dagger with a blue cloth that flaps as he dances, and in the other a small imitation of a human skull, complete with flowing hair. He is weaving spells as he goes, and the crowd are silent once more.

The sun has gone in, and a violent north wind is threatening to tear away the pelmets above the windows. One corner of the great awning has broken from its noorings and flaps furiously as some men try to secure it. There are snow-squalls in the hills and it is bitterly cold.

Soon a procession of monks appears with yellow hats and long pleated cloaks. Between their shoulders a strip of scarlet-fringed brocade hangs from a diamond-shaped gold and turquoise ornament. They bear golden censers and sticks of incense. Many of them blow shrill trumpets. They lead into the courtyard about twenty more Black Hat dancers, dressed like their leader, but less resplendently. Slowly they dance round until they are arranged in a circle about the chief magician, who continues to weave his spells in the centre. Then all the masked dancers who had appeared earlier return and form an inner circle.

The court is now almost full of figures dancing slowly round. The band has become more animated and the continued pounding rhythm has an almost hypnotic effect. Every now and then there is a burst of music much resembling that of bagpipes, and always the clanging of cymbals drowned at intervals by the ponderous booming of the long trumpets.

Just beyond the mock corpse—which has had to be weighted down to prevent it blowing away—a table has been put, covered with a silk cloth, and beside the " corpse " a square tiger-skin rug edged with blue. On the table are various religious insignia, a bell, a dorje, axes, swords, daggers, a chain, and bowls and drums made from human skulls. Behind the table stand several lamas with gold libation jugs and a large golden dish. The chief magician now goes through a complicated ceremony, taking each of these insignia in turn and, after dancing round, brandishes them over the corpse. Finally water and blood are poured from skulls over the corpse, which has now been chained; and the Black Hats, who have been dancing for several hours continuously, are at last allowed to rest.

The wind is now howling round the court, and many of the spectators have gone home. Clouds are sweeping overhead. It seems that the very elements have been invoked in this potent ceremony of driving away the devils.

All at once the rhythm of the band increases to an insistent " Tum, tum, te-tum. Tum, tum, te-tum ", and a tiny figure, dressed in silver and with a huge stag's-head mask, jigs down the steps. This goblin-like creature dances at great speed with his arms held straight out in front of him. He rushes round with flying robes, kicking first one leg then the other high in the air. At last he squats over the corpse, still with his arms stretched out in front. He twitches up and down in time with the music and every now and then jumps right round, landing on his haunches again : he is certainly something of an acrobat.

O

All this time, in one corner of the court, a fire of thorns has been heating a huge cauldron of rancid mustard-oil. The chief magician, with dignified and portentous movements, approaches this and pours a skullful of spirit into it. There is a tremendous flash and the oil blazes up. The stand is pulled from beneath the cauldron, and the burning oil pours over the floor. A paper with effigies of all the devils is consumed in the flames.

This is the end of the dance. All at once, as if the devils that have accumulated in the Old Year are indeed destroyed, the sky is miraculously cleared, the wind drops, and the evening sun shines through once more. The dancers—how weary they must be!—slowly ascend the steps. The band straggles away. The officials are no longer seen at the upper windows. Hashang, with his line of supporters, walks slowly back across the court, his scarlet robe blazing in the evening sunlight. Once more the stage is filled with the motley army—a medley of plumed hats, venerable muskets and shields. Copper trumpets, blown by small warriors, sound from either end of the court, and a procession of monks headed by acolytes with censers streams down the steps. Once they are in the court two enormous thankas are hung in front of the silk curtain.

This is the final act of the ceremony, when a *torma*, or image made of dough and invested with devils, is carried down the Potala steps and burnt beside the obelisk at the foot.

The procession, several hundred strong, is most impressive. It is headed by monks carrying tall cylindrical banners surmounted by tridents; then follow a great number of monks with crested yellow hats and pleated cloaks. About thirty of them carry on their shoulders golden drums, which they beat with the long curving drumsticks. Others have cymbals, bells or trumpets. After these come men in silk robes of a chequered pattern we have not hitherto seen, and with scarlet fur-edged hats. As the procession leaves the court the soldiers give wild war-cries, trumpets are blown, and guns fired into the air. Right down the long zigzag staircase and through the southern gate they stream, then, crossing the road, they stop just beside the stone column on which past history is recorded. Here, after more music and a wild fusillade of shots, the torma is solemnly burnt in a great fire of thorns and mustard-straw.

The people disperse silently to their homes. The sun sets

incarnadine behind the mountains. The devils are finally and effectually driven away from the Holy City.

On 12th February the New Year was officially celebrated in the Potala by a religious ceremony which had to be attended by all officials, wearing robes reserved for this special occasion.

The Tibetan Government paid us a great compliment by inviting us on this day; for the Chinese, Nepalese and Bhutanese representatives came for the second and less intimate ceremony of the following day.

On the first day of the New Year everyone is awakened before it is light and begins the year with a bowl of chang, which must be drained even by small children. Then all officials go at dawn to the Cathedral, where they visit the more important shrines, and then on to the Potala.

The chief of the New Year ceremonies is celebrated in the Dalai Lama's throne-room, a large pillared hall lit only by skylights in the roof. At the northern end of the hall is the high throne of the Dalai Lama, covered in silken cloth and cushions. On the right are much lower thrones for the Regent and the Prime Minister. Next to them, separated by a few yards, are the abbots of Ganden, Drepung and Sera, " The Three Pillars of the State ", muffled against the cold in yellow cloaks with broad edgings of red brocade. Opposite the Dalai Lama's throne are the Duke, Shap-pes, Dzasas and Tegis (the fourth-rank officials). Some of them wear robes with an edging of silver-fox fur on the skirt and cuffs, and with a short cape, similarly bordered, falling over their shoulders; others wear dresses of heavy flowered brocade. All wear wide flat fur hats with scarlet tops. We sit on low cushions on the fourth side of this square while the fifth-rank and junior officials sit behind in their many-hued geluchay dresses. Suddenly the shrill note of cornets is heard and lights flicker in the dark passage. An attendant unrolls a strip of white silk carpet from the door to the foot of the throne. Robes and other possessions of the late Dalai Lama are arranged on the throne to represent his presence. (Tucked into the robes is an object which looks suspiciously like an aluminium hot-water bottle.) When all has been arranged with loving care by the Lord Chamberlain and other monk officials, the lights and trumpeting come nearer, and the Regent enters the hall clad in yellow robes and wearing a mitre-shaped yellow hat. He takes off this cap, prostrates himself three times before the throne, then offers a scarf. The Prime Minister and other officials follow in order of precedence and present scarves to the throne and then to the Regent and the Prime Minister. We also present our scarves, and then the Lord Chamberlain goes round the assembly with an enquiry from the Regent as to the health of all the officers. Tea is then served in a heavy gold dragon-patterned teapot for the Dalai Lama's presence, and in silver for the rest of the company. Each of the officials produces his own wooden teacup from his robe.

The Dalai Lama's tea is first tasted by a monk official, as a precaution against poison. The monk officials go round filling up the teacups, swirling the pot round and round to make sure that it is well mixed.

Two abbots, one from Drepung and the other from Sera, stand on one side of the throne and begin a religious debate, making their points with much pounding of the palm and occasional shrill cries. The smaller one, who is more frail, seems to be completely browbeaten by the other, who speaks and shouts with overbearing vehemence. There are two monks sitting on cushions in the middle of the hall. Upon asking what their function is, we are told they are recording history; but the history of this ceremony must long since have become a matter of mere repetition, and they are not even provided with pens and paper.

A band strikes up, and thirteen curious figures in blue and red flowered robes and flat tam-o'-shanter hats file into the hall. These are the Dalai Lama's dancing boys, a lay troupe whose services are a form of taxation. Each carries a small battle-axe in his hands. The troupe have suffered neglect since the Dalai died (or perhaps it is inauspicious to repair their clothes), for their boots are out at heel and their robes torn and faded. Keeping in line, they perform a number of formal dances, sometimes posturing with hips protruded sideways and striking stylized attitudes, at other times displaying considerable acrobatic skill. The dance is quite short, and is succeeded by a further instalment of the debate and more tea. Each official is then presented with a large bone covered with meat, but this is more in the nature of a symbol and —to our great relief—is not meant to be eaten.

The dancers return, and then messengers come in with letters and presents for the Dalai Lama, and tables loaded with food of all kinds are set out in the middle of the hall. There are great piles of bread and maize-cakes, plates of dried fruits and sweets, joints of beef and mutton, and whole dried carcasses of sheep and yaks, complete with head and horns. There seems to be enough food for an army.

Soon some of the offerings are laid before the Dalai Lama's throne and others are handed round to the officials; after this the Potala servants are allowed to scramble for the rest. There is a rush and the vast pile is covered with struggling figures, who drag away the carcasses and fill their robes with what they can lay hands on. Tall monk attendants belabour the fighting mass with whips and sticks, a precaution against any but the poor taking part, and to prevent anyone getting more than his share; but the victims wear plenty of thick clothes and do not seem to mind the beating.

When the floor is again clear the debate goes on and is followed by a third and final dance. Then one of the abbots recites a long prayer before the throne, ending with a high-pitched cry.

The ceremony is at an end. The Regent and the Prime Minister withdraw in procession as they came, and after them all the officials leave the hall and go up on to the Potala roof for the final part of the ceremony.

This is the real Tibetan New Year's Day, and is celebrated by the Lhasa people in no uncertain way. For days past they have been baking cakes and biscuits and brewing enormous quantities of chang. In front of the family altar is arranged a wooden box containing barley-flour, butter ornaments painted and picked out with gold leaf, bowls of chang, pots of green barley-shoots and other traditional offerings.

Many calls are paid on this day, and as soon as the visitor arrives he is offered the box of barley-flour in which stands a piece of wood ornamented with coloured butter designs and a few shoots of a red-stalked spiraea that grows in the hills. The guest takes a pinch of the flour between the thumb and third finger of the right hand and throws it skywards as a libation to the gods.

The streets of Lhasa are crowded with people in their best clothes, skipping, kicking up the shuttlecock, letting off cheap Chinese fireworks and gambling. A vast quantity of chang is drunk, and the people stagger about arm-in-arm singing songs or dancing.

As soon as we got home from the Potala, Tsarong came to

present a scarf of greeting and a small gift to each of us. He was wearing a remarkable brocade dress of such heavy silk that it would practically stand up even if he were not in it. The general colour was pale saffron, and it had a large pattern of dragons and flowers. We discovered it had cost him two thousand rupees (£150).

During the course of the day several other officials came to pay their respects to the Political Officer, but no one stayed long for there were many other visits to be made.

The traditional greeting is, " *Tashi dela phun-sum tso, tendu dewa thop-pa sho* " ! which means " May you enjoy the three blessings (health, wealth, and good repute), and may your days be filled with peace and happiness."

Several officials told me of a very special ceremonial dress that is stored in the Potala and is worn for this one ceremony of the New Year by thirteen young officials chosen by the Dalai Lama or Regent. They said it would not upset anybody if I went up at about eight o'clock while the officials were dressing-up, to photograph them. I was rather reluctant to " butt in " where I had not officially been invited, but Norbhu seemed to think it was all right, so up I went. Yuto and Kyipup were among the thirteen, and they promised to look after me.

The dress, which is supposed to be part of the actual wardrobe of the ancient kings of Tibet, was even beyond my expectations. Over somewhat tattered silk robes, each wore two long necklaces, one of amber with beads as big as tangerines, and the other of coral. In the centre was a golden breast-plate six inches in diameter set with concentric rings of turquoises. From each side of the head two ornaments were suspended; one, a bar of gold eighteen inches long studded with a row of ancient Tibetan turquoises, was so heavy that it had to be supported in the hand; the other, also of gold and turquoises, was in the shape of a flattened pear, and possibly represented a conch-shell. Two of the thirteen were selected for special ceremonial duties; they wore high-crowned scarlet hats adorned with peacock feathers, while the others wore a smaller silken head-dress. Having photographed these dresses in colour, I slipped away before any of the others arrived.

The ceremony on this day was much the same as the one we

witnessed on the day before; but whereas the other had been the priestly celebration of the New Year, this was particularly for the laymen. The abbots were not present; the debate was conducted by Doctors of Divinity; the dancers carried swords instead of battle-axes, and there was a short Devil Dance. After the ceremony all the officials went up on to the roof of the Potala, where there was much blowing of cornets and of the long deep-toned trumpets.

Then followed a ceremony that all Lhasa turned out to see. In the old days a yak-hair rope was stretched from the roof of the Potala to a stone edict pillar at the foot of the southern staircase, hundreds of feet below. Then several men, protected by leather saddles, slid down the rope at terrific speed. To provide these men was a form of taxation levied on certain villages. The men usually arrived at the bottom in a half-dead condition, and on one occasion a performer slipped beneath the rope in his descent and was nearly killed. So the Dalai Lama stopped this performance on the grounds of cruelty, and substituted another acrobatic feat, which I was lucky enough to witness and photograph from the flat roof of the " War Office " building overlooking the edict pillar.

Here a tall pole, say fifty feet high, swathed in yak-hair cloth to prevent it splitting, was put up on the flat paved platform at the foot of the wide Potala staircase, and was held in position by yak-hair shrouds. Meanwhile crowds of people were settling themselves down to wait on the steps—which are here about eight yards wide—and on the flat-topped balustrade alongside. On the roofs of the neighbouring houses there were many chang parties in progress, and everybody seemed to be laughing and happy. Many ladies of fashion appeared in all their finery of seed-pearl and coral head-dresses, purple silk robes, and turquoise charm-boxes.

The majority wore the triangular Lhasa head-dress, but there were several of the tall-hooped Gyantse fashion. On this day I saw one—the only one I ever saw in Lhasa—of a design which was fashionable (judging by old photographs) some years ago. It consisted of the usual framework studded with turquoise and coral, but it was coiled close to the head like a tiara. It seemed to me to be much more practicable than either of the head-dresses which are at present fashionable.

On the roof next to mine several tents had been put up. I could see a group of buxom nuns in small yellow conical hats exchanging pleasantries with some blue-uniformed Nepalese soldiers who, like most people on this day, had been drinking plenty of chang.

Sitting on the ample steps of the Potala were the poorer people: a party of tousle-headed Khampa shepherds wearing coarse sheep-skin robes; some monks with close-cropped hair and voluminous claret-coloured dresses; some beggar-women spinning prayer-wheels, and in front of the crowd a small boy with a mask over his shoulder shrilly asking for alms.

At last, after most of us have been there for several hours, the orchestra on the Potala roof works itself up to a furious crescendo, and the officials are seen to be descending. There is a sudden stir up above, and a couple of men come rushing down the steps dragging by its legs the carcass of a yak with its sharp-horned head swinging from side to side and effectively clearing a way through the crowd for the officials, who came down the steps in small groups. On this day alone of the year even the highest officials must wear geluchay dress, and I can pick out Tsarong with his white cockle-hat, and the Shap-pes similarly dressed. To-day many of the servants, and quite junior officials, wear silk dresses and scarlet-topped hats. From above, a ribbon of gay colours appears to descend through the middle of the sombrely clad crowd like a rainbow in a stormy sky. Some of the officials, having seen this performance many times before, ride away through the crowd that has by now filled the roadways below.

All at once there is a hush, and a man looking—and probably feeling—singularly like a sacrifice, is swung astride a rope pre-paratory to being hauled to the top of the pole. While he is only just above the heads of the crowd he starts to chant, and drinks a cup of tea which is handed up to him. His head is bound with a white cloth. On the summit of the pole is a small platform on which there is just room to stand. Above this projects a short rod of iron. To begin with, the man, chanting all the time, stands for a moment on the platform; but a strong wind makes this too precarious, and he is obviously not too confident. After ·all, the pole was only put up a few hours ago, and he cannot have had much opportunity for rehearsals. He takes his boots off and throws them down into the crowd. Several times he stands up with his arms outstretched, but only for a brief moment. Then, tying a bobbin-shaped piece of wood on to his stomach, he fits this over the top of the metal rod and, with arms and legs outstretched, starts to spin round and round. After he has repeated this several times he is allowed to return to terra firma, where he bows down three times towards the Potala, offering thanks that his ordeal is safely over. Many of the crowd throw coins into his hat as they disperse to their homes.

On the following day, 14th February, all the officials, including the Regent and Prime Minister, had to go to the monastery of the State Oracle. We had not been invited to attend this, but Tsarong thought it would be a good chance for me to get some photographs, and offered to take me with him and to look after me.

That morning it snowed for the first time since the early autumn, and the procession was two hours late in starting. But by then, ten o'clock, blue sky appeared through the snow-clouds. There was an inch of snow everywhere and the sun was just breaking through. The Regent's palanquin was well ahead by now, so we had to hurry. The mountains, already glistening white in the sunshine, glowed through the lifting snow-clouds with the remarkable luminosity of icebergs in moonlight which has not yet touched the surrounding waves.

Hundreds and hundreds of monks from Drepung were streaming along the track on their way to the city, where twenty thousand would be assembled that night to take over control of Lhasa during the Great Prayer. Never have I seen a more evil-looking crowd. They refused to get out of the way of Tsarong's pony, and one who was squatting down right in the middle of the track just stayed there while Tsarong had to turn aside. Hardly a single friendly face or smile of salutation did I see. Many of the monks had blackened their faces; Jigme said that this denotes special bravery. When I asked how a monk proved his bravery, he answered, " By fighting with his fellows ".

Not till we reached the turning leading to Drepung and Nechung did we catch up with the procession. Nearly every official in Lhasa seemed to be there. About twenty of them were actually waiting on the Regent, while the others went on in front. Including servants, there must have been about four hundred riders. I rode with Surkang-Se and Yuto—nobody seemed at all surprised to see me. Leaving our ponies under the big trees which surrounded Nechung, we followed the narrow passage to the main entrance of the court. Tsarong found a place for me just beside the entrance but beneath the cloister roof, so I was fairly inconspicuous and the light was excellent. I collected a small table to stand on so that I could take photographs above the heads of the crowd who half filled the court. Eight drummers of the band were sitting on the floor in front of the steps which led to an ante-room in front of the main hall of the monastery. Here seats for the officials had been prepared. On each side of the steps was a white porcelain Chinese lion picked out in green and blue. A rather crude frieze consisting of different-coloured rectangles of cloth was hung right round the court. All the pillars were swathed in red cloth and were decorated with a ring of warlike emblems. There were suits of armour, old muzzle-loading guns, helmets, swords and copper trumpets.

Almost immediately the Regent, Prime Minister, Shap-pes and a crowd of monk and lay officials walked across the courtyard and took up their positions on the raised balcony in strict order of precedence. Tea was brought round, and the dance started.

This Nechung Devil Dance was quite different from that at the Potala. The whole dance was finished in less than an hour, and though the Black Hats were there, most of the dresses were new to me. One party of eight or so monk-like figures, two of whom were tall, but the rest children, wore checkered red and yellow cloaks over their lamas' robes, and wide-brimmed lacquered hats. Another group wore skeleton masks and white costumes ornamented only with two big squares of green, red, yellow, and blue. One act was performed by men dressed entirely in black, and in another, costumes similar to those worn by the Lhasa mummers appeared. There was also a procession of the multi-coloured cylindrical banners held high on poles. After the dance more tea was served, and the Oracle, dressed splendidly in cloth of gold and wearing an enormous jewelled and feathered head-dress, appeared from the door just behind me and walked, unobserved by the crowd, to a side door leading to the main shrine of the monastery, which lay just beyond where the officials were drinking tea.

Now that the droning of the long trumpets had stopped there was comparative silence, except for the crowing of two gorgeously coloured cocks that had wandered on to the dance-floor. Looking round, I was struck by the extraordinarily macabre tone of the decoration. Grinning skulls leered malignantly from the tops of the pillars, and all the back wall and roof of the cloister were covered with paintings of the many Buddhist hells. Here a demoniacal figure with grinning fangs crushed a poor diminutive mortal beneath his tongue, in his hand he held a skull from which the eyes, but recently gouged out, were still suspended. All the varied tortures of the tantalized spirits were graphically depicted. Never have I seen paintings executed with so gruesome a fantasy.

There seemed to be a pause in the proceedings, but from the inside of the main monastery hall could be heard the incessant and monotonous beating of drums and the rhythmic clanging of cymbals where the Oracle was being possessed by the Spirit of Nechung.

All at once there was a stir at the top of the steps: the officials near the inner doorway stood up; somebody upset a table and the cups tinkled on to the stone floor. The Oracle, shaking all over and very red in the face, emerged from the inner room. His outstretched arms were supported by two monks; others were in close attendance.

It was difficult to see exactly what happened, as the Oracle was surrounded by officials in the confined and shadowy space at the top of the steps. I was disappointed that he did not descend into the courtyard. At one moment he became violent: I saw the officials press back out of his way—for on several occasions the Oracles have injured people when possessed—and I could see the attendant monks clinging with difficulty to his outstretched arms. But the spasm passed, and all was still again except for the tremulous agitation of the plumes in his tall head-dress and the movement of a monk who was straightening out the Oracle's robes. For some time he seemed to be whispering to the Regent, who could be seen leaning forward on his throne. Then he swayed gently to and fro until he suddenly disappeared as he collapsed into the arms of his attendants.

The Regent did not disclose what was said to him, and the message to the general public was unintelligible; but in any case it is only understood by his attendant monks, who interpret it as they think fit. But I gather his utterances resemble those of

the Delphic Oracle in being conveniently equivocal. After the
Oracle had been assisted back to the inner hall the officials dispersed,
and I hurried ahead to photograph the returning procession. I
had hoped to take it in the beautiful and unusual setting of snow,
but by now it had all melted. I noted that the monk officials
surrounding the Regent were wearing tall fur hats of a type I had
not seen before. It was like a busby in shape, wider at the top
than at the bottom, and surmounted by a jewelled emblem. I
rode back with Möndö, who seemed much amused by the whole
proceeding. It must be difficult for an old Rugbeian to live up
to the standard of credulity demanded by the Lamaist faith.
Tsarong had said that the snow was most auspicious, and as Yuto
had stated that it was extremely inauspicious, I asked Möndö what
he thought, "Well," he replied, " I don't think it makes any
difference ".

In the afternoon there was an archery competition on the plain
beside the mansion of Lhalu. Tsarong had asked us to lunch with
him in the Lhalu house and then to watch the sport.

Young Lhalu was in attendance on the Regent, who was con-
ducting some ceremony at the Potala, but his wife (if she is his
wife; someone told me she was his adopted mother) acted as
hostess. Lhalu is the son of the ill-fated Lungsha who lies in the
Potala dungeons; but in Tibet they do not visit the sins of the
fathers upon the children, and, having changed his name, he was
taken into the family of Lhalu, which at that time had suffered a
succession of misfortunes and was left without an heir. The lady
of Lhalu was of middle age and extremely stout. She wore the
most wonderful jewellery, and was more made-up than any
Tibetan woman I had seen. Being the daughter of one Kung and
the widow of another, she is one of the first ladies of Lhasa.

We had lunch in a completely bare room with whitewashed
walls, the only articles of furniture being a large table and chairs.
It was little consolation to discover that this was " the English
room ".

Our hostess was wonderfully good company. She and
Tsarong, who were old friends, exchanged lively repartee throughout the meal. The lunch was excellent, but our indefatigable
hostess made us eat far more than we wanted, and absolutely
forced us to drink quantities of excellent but most potent chang.
Tsarong, who had not been let off quite so lightly as ourselves,

remarked as, somewhat unsteadily, we left the house, " That fat Mrs.; very difficult! " and roared with laughter.

The archery contests were rather spoilt by the fact that the sun had gone in and a bitterly cold wind was blowing. The " grand-stand " consisted of a flat-roofed building shaped like a square with one side missing. The Shap-pes, who were judging the competition, sat under cover at the back; we were given a place on the roof, unfortunately in the direct line of smoke from a thorn fire below us where an immense urn of tea was being boiled.

At the open side of the building the competitors, most of them servants representing various officials, were stringing their bows preparatory to shooting in the long-distance competition. In front of the archers swastikas and other lucky signs had been drawn in white on the ground.

The mark was a flag some two hundred yards distant, but many of the competitors shot almost another hundred yards beyond it. It was noticeable that at nearly every shot the bowstring broke. In Bhutan the strings are made of cord woven from the skin of stinging-nettles; these do not break. In Tibet they use grass or reeds. The bows were made of wild yak-horn or simply of bamboo.

Yuto Depön, in an interval, measured the lengths of the shots (this was appropriate, seeing that depön literally means " lord of the arrow ").

Later on, whistling-arrows were shot at a small ring suspended in front of a curtain. Some of the officers themselves competed, among them an old City Magistrate who is a famous archer; he, in fact, won the competition. The whistling noise is made by a flat-ended square of wood which takes the place of the point of the arrow. It is so pierced that a deep vibrant hum is caused as the arrow cleaves the air.

In the evening we all went to Tsarong's house to see how the New Year is celebrated in the home. Tsarong was very anxious that we should see this, and had made special arrangements so that I could take photographs by artificial light.

In front of his private altar were the traditional boxes of tsamba and grain, jugs of chang, bowls of dried and fresh fruit, plates of sugar and other sweetmeats, and rams' skulls filled with barley-dough and adorned with patterns of coloured butter and gold

leaf. There were also intricate ornaments—made by the monks
—of barley-dough and picked out in the same way, and the bowls
of sprouting barley which were to be seen in every house.

On one side of the room was a high throne for Tsarong, and
next to it on the left, another, slightly lower, for his wife, and
others, lower still, for the three children. Seats for the guests
of the house were arranged on another side of the room. In
front of each seat were carved Tibetan tables, also graded in height,
on each of which was placed a chang-bowl, a circular wooden
bowl with its lid held up on a square column of barley-dough, and
a fluted silver basin for scraps. Tsarong wore his heavy brocade
robe and fur hat, while the women, as well as their accustomed
finery, wore round their shoulders sashes of many-coloured silk
similar to the scarf worn in geluchay dress.

A servant then brought round the box of tsamba and grain, and
silver bowls of chang; of these a little had to be taken between the
thumb and third finger and thrown into the air. Tea, and bowls
of a root not unlike truffles cooked in butter, and rice were put in
front of each person. These are auspicious food, of which each
person has to eat a little. After this a woman-servant held up a
bowl of chang in front of Tsarong; and the other servants, of
whom there were about twenty, lined up behind her and danced
and sang a song of good wishes. The steward then poured out
chang from the silver bowl for Tsarong. Three separate draughts
had to be drunk; the cup being filled again after each draught.
When Tsarong had done this, the steward respectfully hung a
white silk scarf round his neck. He then gave chang to each
member of the family in the same way and hung scarves round their
necks. Then the servants came up with their bowls, and Tsarong
now gave chang to them. The servants then brought trays of
food as an offering and laid them before each member of the
family; finally they took off their hats, bowed, and put out their
tongues. The presents were removed and the ceremony was over.
It was all very simple, and the atmosphere, although dignified, was
friendly, and emphasized the patriarchal nature of the family. It
would be hard to find a people who can keep up their tradition
with greater dignity and less self-consciousness than the Tibetans.

By now, the fourth day of the New Year, the *Monlam*, or
" Great Prayer ", had started, some thirty thousand monks having
come into the city on 14th February. The object of this festival

is to shorten the time which must elapse before the reign of the Coming Buddha of " Conquering Love ".

The Great Prayer was instituted by Tsong-kapa at the beginning of the fifteenth century, and was added to by the fifth Dalai Lama a hundred and fifty years later.

The monks are quartered on the people, and for three weeks two Provosts of Drepung rule the city, assisted by a number of monk " police " armed with whips. Before the provosts are carried the square metal maces which we had seen at Drepung and Sera. In former times the monks used to abuse their power by paying off old grudges against the lay officials and by extorting large sums of money in fines. But the late Dalai Lama very much lessened this abuse.

When we were riding out one evening to pay a farewell call, we met one of these provosts riding in state through the streets, preceded by his mace-bearers and a group of monks who were inspecting the houses. During the Great Prayer the monks insist on a high standard of cleanliness in the streets, and we found that clean valances had been hung over windows and doors, and that the street in front of each house had been swept clean and ornamented with auspicious designs traced in white ash.

Every day services are held in the great assembly-room of the Cathedral, which is capable of holding 20,000 monks. When we went to bid farewell to the Cabinet in a small room leading off the Cathedral roof, we looked down and saw there thousands of red-robed monks swaying backwards and forwards in prayer, and producing a noise like the murmur of a distant storm.

On the fifteenth day of the first month there is a festival of lights similar to that described to commemorate the death of Tsong-kapa.

After the reign of the monks, several days are devoted to the New Year games, over which two young officials are chosen to preside.

First there is a procession of cavalry dressed and armed like the mounted soldier of the ancient Tibetan kings. Then there are horse-races; the ponies are always riderless, but they are directed by relays of mounted grooms. Each official is bound to send in a certain number of entries, according to his rank. These are followed by foot-races and wrestling contests, and by shooting at targets with guns and bows from the back of a galloping horse.

And in addition to all this, there are religious ceremonies.   One day huge images of butter and tsamba are fashioned by the lamas. An image of the Coming Buddha is carried round the city in solemn procession.   The Nechung Oracle visits Lhasa and foretells the prosperity of the coming year.

And so, the declining reign of Gautama Buddha is hurried towards its close, and that of " Conquering Love " is brought nearer.

CONCLUSION

ALTHOUGH, during our stay in Lhasa, there were frequent rumours that the Tashi Lama had actually set out for his monastery at Tashi-lhünpo, it became clear by the end of January that the return of His Serenity was as remote as ever.   Except for the matter of the Chinese escort, the Tibetan Government had conceded almost everything that the Tashi Lama had requested; but still he found excuses to remain the precarious guest of China.

It was heard in Lhasa that among the hundreds of camel-loads of his advance baggage was found a consignment of bombs; this did little to convince the Government of the Tashi Lama's friendly intentions.

We were forced to realize either that he was so much indebted to China that he was no longer a free agent, or that the officials of his entourage, wedded to Chinese wives, and in the generous pay of the Nanking Government, were so reluctant to hazard an uncertain welcome in Tibet that they had convinced the Tashi Lama of the futility and dangers of his homecoming without the protection of an escort.

Except that we had been unable to settle this matter, we seemed to have achieved our objects.   The maintenance of the Mission was expensive, and Gould had other work to do in Sikkim and Bhutan.   A Lhasa official likened the presence of the Mission to the shade of a great tree in the plains of India.   Though we had been passive rather than active in our contacts with the people, yet we were on extraordinarily friendly terms with all classes of Tibetan society.   Their great need for advice on political questions, the multifarious efforts of the Doctor, the entertainment provided by the cinema projector and the wireless loud-speaker had all done their share in breaking down what few barriers there are between the Tibetans and ourselves—for here there is nothing of the rigid caste system of the Hindus, the purdah of Mohammedan women, or any taboos on food or drink. Many of the officials had formed the habit of " dropping in " to the Deyki Lingka for tea or supper; and we had formed lasting friendships with many of the younger Tibetans.

They had grown used to the presence of the Mission. It had seemed quite natural to them that Major Finch, left alone at Gyantse, should have come up to Lhasa to spend Christmas with us. And when the main body of the Mission left for India, Richardson was left behind to suggest an element of permanency, a reminder that we had not forgotten their problems and difficulties.

Shortly before we left Lhasa the Shap-pes came to have lunch with us. When they arrived they handed to Norbhu a small scroll, together with a scarf of greeting. This was the permission for the 1938 Everest Expedition, which Gould had asked them for a few weeks previously. As Mount Everest is extremely holy to the Tibetans, they are always very reluctant to grant this permission. They were now careful to point out that they were getting rather tired of the matter, and hoped that we would make a great effort to avoid the necessity of asking for it again.

As the time of our departure drew near the officials came to say good-bye and to bring us presents. As the Government of India had paid for those we had given to them on our first visits, these presents were not our property, though in most cases we were allowed to buy them back from the Government of India. Several ponies were presented, various skins—stone-marten, fox, snow-leopard and lynx—Tibetan carpets and quantities of locally woven cloth, ceremonial robes, ornate saddlery, inlaid swords, cloisonné work, china bowls, a few thankas and innumerable silver or copper teapots, pen-cases, chang-bowls and prayer-wheels.

On 14th February we went to pay our official farewell call on the Regent and Prime Minister at the Potala. They received us in the small upper room in which we had first paid our respects to them. As it was a formal visit it was brief; and they both thanked the Political Officer for being able to stay for so long, and for all the help he had given them.

On 17th February, accompanied for a short distance by a guard of honour and a small group of officials, we bade farewell to the Holy City and set off for India.

At the beginning of December, 1937, the news reached Europe that His Serenity the Tashi Lama—that saintly and tragic figure— had died at Jyekundo.

MAPS

*Trade Route from Gangtok to Lhasa, as followed
by the Lhasa Mission 1936–7*

TIBET